PERGAMON INTERNATIONAL LIBRARY
of Science, Technology, Engineering and Social Studies

*The 1000-volume original paperback library in aid of education,
industrial training and the enjoyment of leisure*

Publisher: Robert Maxwell, M.C.

PROGRAM EVALUATION IN SOCIAL RESEARCH

THE PERGAMON TEXTBOOK
INSPECTION COPY SERVICE

An inspection copy of any book published in the Pergamon International Library
will gladly be sent to academic staff without obligation for their consideration for
course adoption or recommendation. Copies may be retained for a period of 60 days
from receipt and returned if not suitable. When a particular title is adopted or
recommended for adoption for class use and the recommendation results in a sale
of 12 or more copies, the inspection copy may be retained with our compliments.
The Publishers will be pleased to receive suggestions for revised editions and new
titles to be published in this important International Library.

Pergamon Titles of Related Interest

PROGRAM EVALUATION IN SOCIAL RESEARCH

Jonathan A. Morell

Department of Mental Health Sciences
The Hahnemann Medical College
and Hospital

Pergamon Press

New York   Oxford   Toronto   Sydney   Frankfurt   Paris

Pergamon Press Offices:

U.S.A. Pergamon Press Inc., Maxwell House, Fairview Park, Elmsford, New York 10523, U.S.A.

U.K. Pergamon Press Ltd., Headington Hill Hall, Oxford OX3 0BW, England

CANADA Pergamon of Canada, Ltd., 150 Consumers Road, Willowdale, Ontario M2J, 1P9, Canada

AUSTRALIA Pergamon Press (Aust) Pty. Ltd., P O Box 544, Potts Point, NSW 2011, Australia

FRANCE Pergamon Press SARL, 24 rue des Ecoles, 75240 Paris, Cedex 05, France

FEDERAL REPUBLIC OF GERMANY Pergamon Press GmbH, 6242 Kronberg/Taunus, Pferdstrasse 1, Federal Republic of Germany

Library of Congress Catloging in Publication Data

Morell, Jonathan Alan, 1946-
  Program evaluation in social research.

  (Pergamon general psychology series)
  Bibliography: p.
  Includes index.
  1. Evaluation research (Social action programs)
2. Social science research. I. Title. II. Series.
H62.M644 1979 300'.7'2 79-11949
ISBN 0-08-023360-0
ISBN 0-08-023359-7 pbk.

Printed in the United States of America

This book is dedicated to the memory of

GAIL LEVINE

A golden friend I had

CONTENTS

TABLES

PREFACE

This book presents a plan for developing evaluation into a new form of applied social research which will be methodologically sound, relevant to the problems of society, and built on a technological (as opposed to a scientific) model. It is a plan which I believe can be achieved, will have general utility and will insure the place of evaluation in the world of social research. Many efforts have already been made in that direction. This book is an effort to assess where those efforts have brought us, to specify the options which are open, and to suggest directions which should be chosen. I firmly believe that the model presented here will have wide utility; but above all, this book is a personal statement of what evaluation means to me.

I have tried to make that statement clear, coherent, and consistent. In that effort, I know that I have failed. As I developed this book, I found strains that I could not separate one from the other, and elements which, despite my best efforts, defied clear categorization or explanation. Further, my beliefs and attitudes about many aspects of evaluation were often ambivalent, and try as I might, that ambivalence could not be eliminated from my consciousness. Thus much of that ambivalence is incorporated in the text, with the result that at times some parts of the work may seem contradictory to others. Still, writing this book has helped me immensely in understanding what evaluation is, what it might be, and how it should be performed. I hope that it will help others as well.

The work was a developmental process. When I started to write, I was sure that the entire structure and the main points of the work were firmly ensconced in my mind. How wrong I was. How different this book is from the one I thought I was going to write. The book is an attempt to conceptualize evaluation as something special—as something different—from other aspects of social research. In order to develop that conceptualization, I had to bring to bear many diverse fields. Research methodology. Epistemology. Sociology. Psychology. Ethics. And many more. The number of pieces needed to construct the model were considerably greater than what I had originally anticipated, and I found myself in constant debate with myself and with others concerning what was important, how elements fit together, and what lessons could be drawn from other fields about evaluation. Each time a new element or dimension was drawn into consideration, I had to consider its influence on the entire line of reasoning in the book. Each new element involved a consideration of what went before, and what was to come. Small wonder that the final product was different from what I had originally intended. The sections on the ethics of evaluation, the professionalization of evaluation and the differences between science and technology were unforeseen when I first conceptualized the book, and all these areas had profound influence on my thinking about what evaluation is and what it might become.

I have tried to organize the book in a way that clearly presents the various themes and foci that exist in evaluation. In order to do this, I had to draw distinctions in a sharper light than is actually the case. Many distinctions and categories were developed for the sake of explanation and better understanding. I hope the exaggerations which were made for the sake of explanation will be useful, and that the distortions introduced by the exaggerations will be forgiven. I also hope that the redundancy which is sometimes apparent will be forgiven. I have tried to cut the repetition to a minimum, but by making some forced categorizations, I found it necessary on occasion to repeat myself.

The book could have been organized in an infinite variety of ways, and I had no lack of suggestions as to how it should be done. Each method of organization and presentation made some arguments easier to follow, and some more difficult. By juxtaposing certain elements, I had to separate others, and the choice was largely a matter of preference, style, and a sense of what I thought were the most important aspects of the work. Many disagreed with those choices, and argued that other elements should have been emphasized or that a different organization should have been followed. As an example, I could have taken a particular aspect of methodology, and shown how it operated across each type of evaluation. In so doing, major section headings would have dealt with methodology, and minor headings with each of the three types of evaluation. I chose not to do this, as I wanted to make it clear that there are three distinct types of evaluation and that although they share some methodological difficulties, the emphasis of methodological concern does in fact differ for each. I am grateful to those who advanced different opinions about the book's organization as those suggestions helped me to understand what I really wanted to do with the book.

I believe that program evaluation is merely the latest fad in social research, and that as with all popular ideas, it will fade from prominence. But I also believe that as a distinct form of social research, evaluation has something enduring to offer, and that in one guise or another, it is likely to be important for some time. More accurately, I believe that we can make evaluation into a pursuit which will have enduring interest and value, but that it is entirely possible to develop the field in ways which will insure its quick oblivion. Evaluation is a unique type of social research which is *applied, relevant* and *technological*. If these attributes are developed and exploited, evaluation will become an important strategy for helping to solve social problems. If these attributes are not developed, evaluation will be swallowed up by the trends to come, reabsorbed by its parent disciplines, and fade from existence as a distinct field or discipline. This would be a shame, as evaluation does in fact have something to contribute to our search for a better life for all.

This is a short book. Deliberately so. I tried not to repeat information which was well developed by others. Rather, I settled for as cogent a summary as I could write about those already developed ideas, and added as complete a reference list as I could. I did this for several reasons. First, others can explain various concepts far better than I. Second, the book draws on so many areas that a complete treatment of even a few of them would have made this book unwieldy. Third, I wanted this book to be about *evaluation*, and not about survey research, quasi-experimental designs, the dynamics of organizational change, or any one of the myriad concepts and traditions which bear on the conduct of program evaluation. Finally, I prefer to read short books. As a consequence of making this book short, it will not do as a self-contained text or handbook on the field of program evaluation. Readers will have to draw on numerous other works when they actually attempt to do an evaluation. This is not necessarily a loss, as the need for multiple sources is probably a necessity in any case. I do hope that the book will help people understand how evaluation is different from its historical antecedents, and how to bring specialized knowledge from many areas to bear on the problem of intelligently evaluating social programs.

This book is influenced by my interests and background, and readers are entitled to know what those influences are. In thinking about what I have written, I have been able to identify nine relatively distinct intellectual elements which have gone into the making of this book. First, I was trained within a psychology department as a social psychologist. Hence the psychological nature of examples used in this book. Second, I am involved in evaluation training, both as Associate Director of the Evaluation Training Program at Hahnemann, and through my work with the Training Committee of the Evaluation Research Society. Third, I have always been intrigued with the types of explanations which can be derived from sociological levels of analysis. Fourth, I feel strongly that I could not understand methodology or research unless I grasped a basic philosophical sense of what it means to discover and to know. Hence my interest in the philosophy of science. Fifth, I believe that a special responsibility is implied in accepting the role of a social researcher. That responsibility derives from the power of the researcher's special expertise, and from the societal implications of conducting social research. Sixth, my experience as editor of *Evaluation and Program Planning* has given me an opportunity to know what is going on in the field of evaluation, to understand the trends which are developing, and to form opinions about the implications of those trends. Those opinions, however, are formed by the type of articles which are submitted to *Evaluation and Program Planning* and may not be representative of all aspects of evaluation. Seventh, I have conducted a lot of evaluation and research in the areas of mental health, drug abuse, and education. My experiences in those efforts have profoundly shaped my sense of what can be done and what should be done. Eighth, I have always had a passion for categorizing events and trying to see the implications of the interactions among a wide variety of diverse ideas. Hence the emphasis in this book is on fitting a wide diversity on concepts into neat categories. I hope my zealousness in that regard has not been overbearing. Finally, my most basic interest is in the methodology of social research. I hope this book adequately conveys my strong belief that if evaluation does not have methodological credibility, it has nothing. I recite these details in order to convey a sense of what this book is about, what it is trying to do, and what biases the reader may expect. I have been assured by many critics of earlier drafts that the book has wide utility, but it is most certainly biased, and for that I make no apologies.

ACKNOWLEDGMENTS

First and foremost, to Donald T. Campbell, who provided me with a model of the scientist-scholar, and who by providing that model, gave me a sense of how diverse concepts can be forged into a framework for understanding the use, abuse, and potential of social research. His book, *Experimental and Quasi-Experimental Designs for Research* helped to bring about a paradigm shift in social research, and much of Don's later work helped to develop the quasi-experimental research perspective into a true evaluation research. During my years at Northwestern University I had a chance to be close to the avant-garde of that development, and I found the experience to be tremendously exciting. I do not know if I shall ever be so close to that type of activity again, and I am immensely grateful for having had a chance to experience the excitement of that type of intellectual activity.

Many thanks also go to the entire faculty of the Psychology Department at Northwestern University, and to my fellow graduate students at the time I was there. Intense intellectual climates can only be sustained by groups, and each person in his or her own way contributed to that climate in general, and to my particular understanding of psychology and social research.

Barbara Edelman, my friend and colleague, was an immense help. She read what I wrote, understood what I meant, told me what I said, and suggested what I should change. That was no easy task, and the book is much improved for her efforts. She believed that what I said was worthwhile and in a project of this magnitude, that kind of support is crucial. But she did not always think that I was right, and that kind of criticism is also crucial. I thank her both for her support and for her criticism.

I am also indebted to Lois-ellin Datta, whose wise and perceptive comments on Chapter 5 brought about considerable improvement in the final draft. She also provided sound criticism and basic support. I owe her a deep debt of gratitude.

Nanie Flaherty and I have spent many hours talking about evaluation, developing *Evaluation and Program Planning*, co-authoring papers, and speculating about the future. The intellectual stimulation provided by our collaboration has been a major factor in my professional development, and I am profoundly grateful for the opportunity of working with her.

Carol Black, Marsha Richardson and Janet Segvick labored long and hard over the typing of more versions of this book than I care to contemplate. This work would not have been completed without their labor, and I thank them for their efforts.

George Spivack provided a work environment which allowed me time to think and time to write. As Director of the Research and Evaluation Service at the Hahnemann Community Mental Health and Mental Retardation Center, he could have done otherwise, and I thank him for his support and his indulgence. Writing this book needed a good deal of both, and both he supplied in ample amounts.

Over the last four years, my students in the Evaluation Training Program at Hahnemann have asked me a lot of questions, some easy and many not so easy. Those questions, and my attempts to teach evaluation, were instrumental in forming my sense of what evaluation is and what it should be. Many thanks to all of them for all of the questions.

For many helpful comments and suggestions, I would like to acknowledge Gerald Britan, Karen Chernitsky, Jeff Dielman and Steve Pellegrini.

The index could not have been completed without the hard and diligent efforts of Mary Zukiewicz.

My parents taught me to love thinking and to value critical analysis. As far back as I can remember, I always enjoyed toying with ideas, and as far back as I can remember, my parents encouraged that play. Many thanks for that.

Finally, I would like to thank my wife Marge. Writing drained considerable time and effort from our life together, and I thank her for her patience, indulgence, and love. This book will be born about the same time as our first child, and neither of us is sure which labor was more difficult. We do know that the book had the longer gestation period. Up until a short time ago I thought that my next book would be a text on social research, but other things are more important. I am now compiling notes for "Autobiography of My Serene Years Spent with My Wife and Young Child." For a while anyway, the textbook will have to wait.

I wrote this book in order to provide a set of organizing principles for the planning of evaluation. I hope that the plan I have developed will help others to understand evaluation as much as it has helped me.

1
Evaluation As Applied, Relevant Social Research

BASIC PERSPECTIVES

Program evaluation can become a form of social research distinctly different from its intellectual predecessors, and with a unique capability to direct solutions to social problems. The purpose of this book is to lay out a blueprint for that development and to discuss its consequences for the conduct of social research and for society at large.

The development of evaluation is a historical process composed of .many traditions in the fields of research, management, planning, and information utilization. These traditions can combine in innumerable ways to yield many possible futures for evaluation. Although many courses of development may result in a useful and practical concept of program evaluation, one among them is particularly likely to result in a powerful system for guiding the development of social programs. That course necessitates a particular integration and synthesis of evaluation's parent traditions, and that integration will not take place unless it is specifically nurtured and purposefully developed.

A basic premise throughout the book is that whatever else evaluation may be, it must concern itself with outcome, i.e., with the influence of a social program on its clients and/or its societal context. With this premise in mind, I will attempt to show how evaluation can be made into a method of generating practical and powerful suggestions for planning successful social programs.

ORGANIZATION OF THE BOOK

A Multidimensional Concept of Outcome Evaluation

As a first step in the process it is necessary to organize the concept of "outcome evaluation" into meaningful categories which can be used for the intelligent planning of appropriate evaluation activities. Although outcome evaluation has often (and correctly) been differentiated from other types of evaluation, the structure of outcome evaluation itself has not been adequately explored. Efforts have been made to develop, categorize and assess research designs which can be of use to evaluators (Cook and Campbell 1976; Hatry, Winnie and Fisk 1973; Isaac and Michael 1974). The concept of outcome evaluation, however, transcends the boundaries of research design. Consequently, any attempt to understand the value of outcome evaluation solely in terms of a methodological critique is bound to yield incomplete and often misleading information. Thus a major effort in this book will be to develop a multidimensional typology of outcome evaluation which can serve as a comprehensive approach to planning evaluation studies.

The proposed evaluation typology will be organized around three basic questions. First, what are the types of evaluation that are carried out at present, and what are the relative merits of each type? Second, how can the validity of each type be optimized? Third, how can the usefulness of each type be optimized?

Three categories of evaluation type and four categories of evaluation usefulness will be presented. Evaluation type will be discussed in terms of "client-type comparison" studies, "follow-up" studies and "modality tests." Evaluation usefulness will be dealt with in terms of an evaluation plan's ability to help establish realistic expectations, to improve service over the short term, to help with long-range planning, and to be of value in the political arena. Although the concepts of type, validity and usefulness are related, there is a surprisingly large amount of independence among them. Each type of evaluation may be carried out in a more or less valid manner. Although one type of evaluation may be better than another on some scale of validity, it is also true that within the limitations of each method, validity can vary a great deal. This perspective is particularly important because the demands of particular situations may suggest the use of one or another type of evaluation. By considering evaluation type and evaluation validity separately, one is not forced into insisting on an inappropriate evaluation plan merely to satisfy the demands of adequate validity. The analysis to be presented in this book will try to convince the reader that the concepts of "type of evaluation" and "validity of evaluation" are reasonably independent of each other. At least, that they are independent enough so that it makes sense to deal with each as separate considerations in any attempt to assess the value of an evaluation plan.

Similarly, the validity and the usefulness of an evaluation must be considered as separate entities. The literature on research utilization makes it quite clear that a host of factors other than validity or scientific value are involved in the determination of which evaluation studies will be important. A few of the more important factors are the relevance of the information, the source of the information, compatibility between suggested change and organizational structure, difficulty of implementation, and the makeup of an organization's staff (National Institute of Mental Health 1973, vols. 1 and 2). In fact one if hard put to find mention of issues concerning scientific validity in discussions of crucial factors in the utilization of research or evaluation data. Consequently, if an evaluation is to have maximum impact, factors related to utilization must be considered in the design stage, and these factors must be dealt with in their own right rather than as adjuncts to the matter of research validity.

A common problem with the development and implementation of evaluation is a feeling on the part of service delivery, management, or planning personnel that the evaluation in which they must participate is irrelevant. Such opinions may well be correct. They arise when evaluators draw up plans which fail to consider adequately issues of usefulness. One reason for such failure might be an undue concern with validity or type of evaluation, and an attendant failure to realize that evaluation usefulness does not automatically derive from an appropriate or valid evaluation study. Usefulness is a complex issue which must be dealt with in its own right. An important consequence of considering one element to the exclusion of others is a frustrating and futile attempt to jam a square peg into a round hole—an inappropriate evaluation design into a particular evaluation setting. The system to be proposed is designed to minimize such problems.

A separate chapter will be devoted to each of the three dimensions of outcome evaluation—type, validity, and usefulness. A case will be made to the effect that each dimension exists as a continuum, and the nature of each dimension will be clarified. These three sections will also present methods of optimizing the value of evaluation along the appropriate dimensions. The purpose of these chapters will be to provide a useful framework for understanding the notion of worthwhile outcome evaluation, and to present a method by which the potential value of any given evaluation plan can be determined. The intention is to convey a sense of a three-dimensional "evaluation space" within which any potential evaluation plan can be located. Once located within that space, the plan's value can readily be assessed by seeing how it stands relative to axes of type, validity, and usefulness. This three dimensional typology represents the first part of the blueprint for developing a powerful conception of evaluation.

The Technological Nature of Program Evaluation

Superimposed upon the three-dimensional structure of outcome evaluation is the matter of the technological as opposed to the scientific nature of evaluation research. Much time and effort is wasted as a result of attempts to use evaluation to add to the body of social science knowledge, or to transpose directly scientific methods and theories into the technological endeavor that is evaluation. This problem is particularly serious because the scientific enterprise is not optimally suited to the task of effecting the types of changes that are desired by those who fund human service programs. Scientific models are not likely to produce information that is directly applicable to the improvement of service programs. The relationship between social science and the technology of improving human service programs is at best convoluted, diffuse, and indirect. Although there are important and beneficial interactions between these areas of endeavor, those benefits cannot be fully appreciated until the relationship between science and technology is understood and the limits of each are defined. Thus a section of the book will be devoted to the relationship between social science and the technology of human service. The analysis will indicate that the most useful designs in the three-dimensional "evaluation space" are those which are technological rather than scientific in character, but which fully exploit relevant elements of social science. Thus a thorough understanding of the technological model of evaluation compliments the "type-validity-usefulness" model, and together they provide a highly effective guide to the choice of optimally valuable evaluation plans.

The Evaluation Implementation Problem

While "evaluation space" and technological models may be sufficient for the design of powerful evaluation studies, they are inadequate as guides to the implementation of those studies. Since evaluation must actually be implemented before it can help solve social problems, the third step in developing powerful evaluation is an analysis of the implementation problem. It is extremely difficult to carry out evaluation in ongoing social programs, and many evaluators find themselves trapped by forces which they do not understand and cannot control. Since the quality of an evaluation plan is no guarantee of its use, it is important to focus specific attention on the problems of implementation. Those problems are part of a general historical and sociological dynamic which effects the relationship between social science and social service, and the analysis will proceed within that general framework. It will show why problems exist, why those problems are difficult to solve, and how solutions might be effected.

The Professionalization of Evaluation

Developing powerful new evaluation paradigms will almost certainly have consequences for the professional structure of social research. Some of those consequences are likely to be counterproductive both for evaluation and for society at large, and we must be ready to counteract difficulties which may arise. The purpose of this section will be to anticipate problems, to understand why they are likely to occur, and to explore what can be done about them.

The Field of Evaluation: Content and Responsibilities

The book will close with a summary of what evaluation will be like if the actions suggested here are taken. The picture will be quite different from evaluation as we now know it, and the purpose of the closing chapter will be to present as clear a sense as possible of that picture. The chapter will also include a discussion of the ethical responsibilities of evaluators, as that is an issue which must be confronted if evaluators deliberately attempt to become an important element in the design of social programs. This book is designed to increase the power and credibility of evaluation and of evaluators. To the extent that the plan succeeds, evaluators must bear increased responsibility for the social consequences of their actions.

ON THE USE OF ARTIFICIAL DISTINCTIONS

Crucial to the analysis about to be presented is the contention that the numerous categories and distinctions which make up the type-validity-usefulness typology are indeed different from one another, and, therefore, should be treated separately. Such an assertion can be justified by three arguments. First, the same concepts cannot be invoked to explain each dimension. Quite the contrary. Concepts which are useful in understanding one dimension are of little or no use in understanding the others. Second, the proposed system has considerable usefulness in helping to understand evaluation, and that usefulness supports the validity of the categorizations that will be made. Finally, it will be clear that the proposed distinctions often turn up as dominant and identifiable themes in a large number of evaluation studies. In short, the divisions reflect real differences in the world of evaluation.

It will also be obvious to the reader that many of the categorizations and distinctions in the analysis are somewhat forced. All boundaries have ambiguities. No boundary will act as a perfect differentiator. This is certainly the case here, where the proposed distinctions yield a relatively large number of ambiguous cases. The system, however, is intended merely as a useful tool and not as a theoretical construct whose validity must be demonstrated in order to corroborate a theoretical proposition. Thus the validity of the distinctions lies only in their usefulness as a guide to understanding, and that usefulness, I hope, will be amply demonstrated.

2

Evaluation Types

INTRODUCTION

A survey of the literature on the evaluation of effectiveness in social service leaves one with the distinct impression that such studies can be classified according to three distinct themes: client comparison; follow-up; and modality test.[1] Client-type comparison evaluations are concerned with the relative effect of a program on various subpopulations of its members, between the characteristics of those who receive treatment versus those who do not, or occasionally, between people who manifest a particular problem with people who do not exhibit such problems. In all such cases the focus of interest is on sociopsychological factors which differentiate one group of people from another. Follow-up evaluations are those whose main efforts are directed at surveying people who have left the immediate locus of a treatment which they have received.[2] The object of follow-up evaluation is to see how people fare once the immediate effects of the program or treatment have been removed. The third type of evaluation is most appropriately termed "modality test" evaluation. The object of such work is to estimate the relative effects of some method (or methods) of bringing about an identifiable desired change.

The "comparison-follow-up-modality" typology assumes a very liberal view of the concept of "outcome" or "impact" evaluation. One could quite justifi-

6

ably argue that modality tests are the only legitimate form of outcome evaluation since they are the most direct tests of program effectiveness. Although such a claim might be legitimate, it also has the effect of forcing an extremely restricted view of outcome evaluation, and of excluding from consideration a good deal of information that is extremely important for understanding issues of program effectiveness and impact. Justifications for taking a more liberal view of evaluation include five considerations. First, an extremely important aspect of research is to describe events accurately rather than to test specific hypotheses (Forcese and Richer 1973, chap. 6). It seems clear that many important questions concerning impact and effectiveness fall into the descriptive research category. These might include questions about the lasting power of a treatment, the characteristics of populations or situations in which a treatment can or cannot operate, and the discovery and description of unintended consequences of action. As will be seen, modality test evaluation may not be the method of choice in answering such questions.

Second, the basic value of a program or treatment is often accepted (rightly or wrongly) as given, and the questions which remain involve details concerning long-range effects, the relative effect of a program on various populations, issues of selecting the most promising prospects for treatment, and the like.[3] These questions are logical extensions of the basic question: Is the program effective? Thus it is appropriate to consider these matters when the phenomenon of impact or effectiveness is considered.

Third, an important purpose of outcome evaluation is to help form theories concerning the operation and effectiveness of social programs. Although evaluation which follows the experimental prescription may well be the most useful tool for such an endeavor, it is by no means the only tool. The development of theory is far removed from a one-to-one correspondence with experimental results, and factors such as plausibility and reasonability play an important role in theory development (Harré 1970; Kaplan 1964; Popper 1965). Those concepts emerge from an intimate understanding of the program or treatment under study, and one must give serious consideration to any research technique which may help increase such understanding. In this regard, follow-up and client comparison evaluation most certainly have great potential to be of assistance.

Fourth, program evaluation must be concerned not only with effectiveness but also with efficiency. Although efficiency is not a part of the scientific enterprise, it is a cornerstone of the technological endeavor. (See Chapter 5 for more on this topic.) Efficiency is certainly an important concern for the social services, and consequently, evaluation must operate on a technological model if it is to be of use. Client comparison and follow-up are most definitely able to contribute to the development of efficient social service and, hence, are legitimate elements in the evaluator's repertoire.

A final consideration deals with yet another aspect of the technological approach to problem solving. According to Wiesner (1970, p. 85):

> Technologists apply science when they can, and in fact achieve their most elegant solutions when an adequate theoretical base exists for their work, but normally are not halted by the lack of a theoretical base. They fill gaps by drawing on experience, intuition, judgment and experimentally obtained information.

In other words, technological problems are solved by the use of far more than the application of science, and, in fact, the use of a wide variety of information is necessary for the accomplishment of such tasks. Viewed from this perspective, information derived from client comparison or follow-up evaluation can most certainly be of considerable use to planners and evaluators.

The "client comparison-follow-up-modality test" distinctions do not exist in isolation. Almost all evaluation studies contain at least some elements of more than one category of evaluation. We are really dealing with issues of theme and emphasis rather than with discrete, mutually exclusive categories. A major assumption in this book is that it is important to take these dominant themes into account if appropriate evaluations are to be carried out. Although one category of evaluation may be inherently superior to another in terms of the quality of information it generates, some questions are far more appropriate to the tools and techniques of one method than another. Thus, any critique of evaluation research must include an analysis of how *each individual* type of evaluation can be improved.

THE "EVALUATION-TYPE" CONTINUUM

The basis for treating "evaluation type" as a continuum rests on the extent to which each type of evaluation can provide information of direct relevance for improving the program under study. Modality test evaluation clearly focuses on the specific actions of the program or treatment in question. Follow-up evaluation deals with program effects, but only in a rather diffuse or diluted way, since follow-up evaluation measures the complex interaction between treatment and the normal life situation of individuals. Client-type comparison certainly has the potential to yield interesting and important information concerning a treatment, but its primary focus is on the people who receive a treatment rather than on the treatment itself. Thus, the three basic types of evaluation can be ordered in terms of their direct relevance to inferences concerning treatment effects.

CLIENT-COMPARISON EVALUATION

Uses and Advantages of Client-Comparison Evaluation

One of the most common objectives of this method is to identify those individuals or groups who are most likely to be helped by a program or treatment.

Such knowledge might be of considerable use in decisions concerning program changes for the sake of improving service. If, for example, a drug rehabilitation program is most successful with older male clients, a careful scrutiny of the treatments that are offered to young persons and older females is in order. A second example might be the case of a halfway house which found that its most successful residents were those who entered with particularly high levels of motivation and a positive self-image. Such a finding might not be surprising, but it does suggest that it would be wise to assess these characteristics for all incoming residents, and to direct initial efforts at increasing levels of motivation and self-image. Although such information may not afford a logically sound causal inference, it does relate to the decision-making process of administrators and clinicians. That process utilizes some unknown combination of science, intuition, experience and luck; and the role of evaluation is to input quality information into as many elements of that process as possible.

A second reason for the use of client-comparison evaluation involves the study of differences between populations which are eligible for a particular treatment and those which are not. The differences between child-abusing and non-child-abusing parents is one example. Other examples include: studies of differences between alcoholics and nonalcoholics, runaway children and those who stay at home, people who respond to traffic law compliance programs and those who do not, and the like. In all these cases, particular programs might be aimed at one group but not at the others. Although this type of work is relatively closely allied with pure research, it also has clear implications which relate to matters of evaluation. Evaluation of this type may well discover unknown characteristics of a potential clientele which would make effective service delivery especially difficult. In such cases, evaluation would allow decision makers to develop solutions before a program is actually put into operation.

A third (and perhaps most important) use of client-comparison knowledge is as a screening device for potential recipients of a treatment. The funding of any social program presents questions of where and how resources can best be invested, and a program may wish to spend its time and energy on those individuals who have the greatest chance of deriving benefit from what is offered. Unfortunately, screening programs take place far less frequently than one might wish. Unwillingness to implement screening may be based on ethical, philosophical, political or practical considerations. Valid empirical data is needed if the importance of these objections is to be put in its proper context. Consider the following illustrative examples.

1) One would be hard pressed to turn children away from a compensatory education program merely because the children were unlikely to derive particularly great benefit from the program.

2) The social work profession has as one of its "overriding priorities" the elimination of poverty and racism.[4] These concerns derive from a moral imperative which makes it very difficult for social workers in human service programs to deny treatment which is aimed at the reduction of poverty or racism,

even if the probability of success of the program is low. This is not meant to imply that a social work program would not attempt to invest its resources where they will do the most good. It does mean that once a program is functioning and there are no immediately available alternatives, it would be extremely difficult to abandon the efforts on the grounds that there is a low probability of helping clients who are recipients of the program's efforts.

3) The concept of community mental health was developed out of a philosophical position regarding the need for self-help, the need for community involvement, and conceptions regarding the etiology and cause of social and psychological problems (Macht 1976). These concepts were institutionalized into the Community Mental Health Act of 1975 (Public Law 94-63) in terms of mandates to provide people and communities with particular mental health services. A private practitioner in the field of mental health has the right to turn down a prospective client on the grounds that the practitioner does not have the ability to help the client. Further, the practitioner may do this even if he or she cannot provide a referral to another source who can provide the necessary service. Although mental health professionals undoubtedly do their best to provide treatment or to provide an adequate referral, they may on occasion be unable to do so, and in such cases they are justified in not making an attempt to be of service. This is not the case for a practitioner in a community mental health center. In such situations the denial of treatment is made more difficult as a result of funding mandates, the philosophical underpinnings of the system, and the need for maintaining good relations with the community. Thus, the ability to screen may not be of vital importance if the function of the screening is to discriminate between those who can and cannot be helped by the services of the community mental health center.

4) Finally, an organization's credibility often depends to a large extent on keeping full enrollment, and any factor which would exclude clients who might otherwise be eligible is not regarded favorably, even if the factor served to exclude inappropriate clients from a treatment.

All of these examples merely serve to illustrate the well-known fact that organizations are not singularly and totally devoted to maximum efficiency in the use of resources to meet a well-defined goal. (An excellent analysis of this issue can be found in Etzioni 1969.) Although an organization's behavior may be influenced by numerous and often conflicting legitimate factors, it is still true that rational planning is an extremely important element of human service programming, and that part of the evaluator's responsibilities is to help with that planning.[5] Further, legitimate arguments against excluding people from treatment must be measured against a realistic assessment of whether people can be helped. The appropriate allocation of clients to particular human services is a vital element in program planning, and client-comparison evaluation can make an important contribution to that endeavor.

Not all screening procedures are designed to determine who will be treated by a particular organization. Screening can also be used to determine the allocation of clients to a diversity of services which a single agency might provide. Here too, client comparison may be the evaluation method of choice, as it can provide guidance as to how an organization's resources might be used most efficiently.

A major advantage of client-comparison evaluation is that it allows evaluators to investigate which types of changes are largest with particular types of clients. The changes sought by human and social service programs are usually complex and multidimensional. Ex-offender programs, for example, may attempt to change a person's criminal behavior, friendship patterns, self-image, social values, aspirations for success, attitudes about work and school, and ability to solve personal and family problems. It is quite reasonable to expect a program or treatment to have a greatly varied impact on these facets of change, and it is also likely that different types of people will have a unique rate of change for each aspect of rehabilitation. Thus, a program's pattern of success and failure may well be different with different types of clients, and such effects can only be discerned if evaluators are able to detect meaningful distinctions between various types of clients.

Client comparison evaluation can also be used to suggest links between treatment and observed change. It can do this by documenting progress for particular categories of treatment recipients. If such documentation exists, and if one can discover valid recipient categories, then one can begin to answer the question: For whom is the program beneficial?

Perhaps the most common arena for studies of this type lies in the field of psychotherapy, where powerful efforts have been exerted at differentiating those who do and do not benefit from various forms of psychotherapy. Meltzoff and Kornreich (1970, chap. 10), for example, present a thorough review of ten patient classification factors which might relate to success in psychotherapy. (The factors discussed are: age, IQ, education, sex, marital status, social class, motivation, environmental factors such as conditions and settings, therapy readiness, and expectancy.) All the studies cited in the review are attempts to in some way determine which categories of patients have the best prognosis for improvement in psychotherapy.

Another example of contexts where this type of evaluation is often found is the area of education, where the characteristics of students are often matched with the efficacy of various methods of instruction.

The diverse fields of psychotherapy and education serve to convey a sense of the varied contexts in which client-comparison evaluation is carried out, and where specific client-comparison research is needed to answer questions which are of direct relevance to service providers. These examples indicate that client comparison evaluation may often be the method of choice to obtain specific types of information which are needed for the rational planning of social services.

Disadvantages of Client-Comparison Evaluation

The major disadvantage of client-comparison evaluation is its relatively low potential to contribute to the "theory" element of program planning. Client-comparison evaluation may indeed be useful in generating accurate information (experiment), or in contributing to experience, intuition, and judgment, but these alone are not enough to insure adequate planning. A coherent model based on causal explanation is needed to integrate information and to help predict events. Any evaluation that cannot help to form or elaborate such a model is, of necessity, incomplete.

There are two reasons why client-comparison evaluation cannot be expected to contribute much toward theories relating to program planning. First, if client-comparison evaluation is to be helpful, one must be able to differentiate reliably one population from another. Although it may seem as if such a differentiation is easy, experience indicates otherwise. The application of client-comparison information to program planning is very likely to necessitate the measurement of some element of personality or of internal psychological states in the recipients of a treatment. This is certainly true in services dealing with psychotherapy, education, corrections, drug abuse, and other psychologically oriented programs. But it may be true of numerous other areas as well. Income maintenance studies may be interested in need achievement. Housing programs may want to know about tolerance for crowded living conditions. Police-citizen cooperation projects may need data on people's attitudes toward law enforcement. The list is endless. In addition to assessing psychological factors, effective client-comparison evaluation is also likely to necessitate relating knowledge of internal states to the prediction of behavior. Unfortunately, the difficulty of accurately measuring psychological states is surpassed by the difficulty of relating those states to behavior. An excellent case in point is found in the area of drug abuse rehabilitation, where studies of the "drug abusing personality" abound. Careful reviews of the literature have indicated that one cannot in any consistent manner isolate a core of personality characteristics that differentiate drug abusers from non-drug abusers (Platt and Labate 1976).

The difficulty of isolating populations on the basis of personality characteristics is also supported by theoretical research in the psychology of personality. Mischel (1973) offers powerful arguments against the notion that consistencies in people's behavior can be predicted from a knowledge of "personality traits" which form a stable element of an individual's makeup. As an alternative, Mischel offers a set of variables which relate to the manner in which an individual perceives the potential chances for (and value of) success in any given decision-making situation. Precise methods of testing these variables in a wide variety of situations have not, however, as yet been developed. Bem and Allen (1974) take a somewhat more sanguine attitude concerning the possibility of studying "cross-situational consistencies in behavior." They believe that traditional personality variables may indeed be useful for such tasks, but their analysis makes it quite clear that the prediction of behavior from a knowledge of personality characteristics is an extremely difficult and complex task.

At best, a large number of psychological variables must be measured very carefully before any sort of behavior—psychological state relationship can be determined. At worst, a large amount of basic research remains to be done concerning the measurement and identification of appropriate variables before a knowledge of psychological states will be useful in human service program planning. The prognosis for client comparison research *qua* evaluation is made even bleaker because human service organizations have considerably more to do than turn themselves into the types of psychological and psychometric laboratories which would be able to carry out the necessary research in a meaningful way. The percentage of organizational resources that would be needed to extract useful data would be so large relative to the probability of a marked advantage to service, that the effort simply could not be justified.

Another example of the limitations of client-comparison evaluation for planning can be found in research on social area analysis. Briefly, social area analysis is an attempt to match the demographic characteristics of a geographic area with various social, psychological and health-related problems that are particularly prevalent in that area (Struening 1975).

Another example of client-comparison evaluation can be found in which the "clients" are whole organizations. One such case are the routine efforts of the National Institute of Mental Health to compare Community Mental Health Centers on a large number of characteristics. Such comparisons are also common in many State level reporting systems which attempt to keep track of the activities of various human service organizations. Quality Assurance systems in hospitals can be put to similar purposes. In short, any attempt to oversee the efforts of a great many service delivery organizations is likely to lead to "client comparison" evaluation in which "clients" are made up of whole organizations.

Although both social area analysis and large scale organizational monitoring have excellent potential to help in practical planning, they have relatively little potential to contribute to the "theory" aspect of program development.[6] This is because these approaches must rely on data which may be only gross indicators of a state of affairs, which were not fine tuned for specific research purposes, and which may not have been carefully checked for errors. Such data does not lend itself to the precise differentiations which may be necessary for discovering cause and effect relationships among planning, service, and constructive change.

The second major difficulty with client comparison evaluation is that even if populations could be differentiated reliably, the variables that lead to differentiation may not be of use in planning better treatment. The fact of differences among populations does not necessarily imply that different treatments are needed. Many reliable differentiators might be quite useless as guides to how individuals should best be treated. A knowledge of differentiator variables must be overlayed with a knowledge of which factors are truly crucial for bringing about a desired change. There are precious few client-comparison evaluations that are able to provide information of this nature.

It is quite likely that those who specialize in studying the relationship between client characteristics and behavior will come up with information that will be of use to program planners. It is also true that such work has a theoretical value which is quite independent of any program evaluation uses to which it might be put. As evaluation, however, pure client-comparison work is extremely difficult to justify given the amount of work involved, the potential payoff for program planning, and the amount of service organizations' resources that must be committed to such efforts.

A final problem with the value of client-comparison evaluation for program planning is the inability of many programs to make use of the information when it does become available. The full use of such information necessitates careful screening, which implies more work for program staff as well as the possibility of failing to meet enrollment quotas. In addition, the use of such information might well entail more individual tailoring of programs than many service organizations are willing or able to provide.

In sum, client-comparison evaluation can be most valuable only when the population at risk can be reliably identified on the basis of variables which play an operative role in the change process. As we have seen, it is not likely that such variables can indeed be identified. Additional complications arise because a large number of client-comparison evaluations (implicitly) assume a simple relation between psychological states and behavior. They further assume that the relationship between behavior and psychological states can be of use in the treatment process. Although such a relation might exist, it is certainly not simple or easy to incorporate into the treatment process. Finally, even if all necessary conditions are met, social service organizations may not be able nor willing to incorporate evaluation findings into their daily operations.

FOLLOW-UP EVALUATION

Uses and Advantages of Follow-up Evaluation

A basic premise of any treatment in the human service field is that some beneficial effects of a treatment will stay with clients for some reasonable length of time after the treatment has ended. The question, of course, is how much stays with a client and for how long a period of time. The phenomenon of "attenuation with time" is an all too well known factor in social service and rehabilitation work. If one is to have an accurate picture of the value of a program, it is important to develop an accurate estimate of the rate of the attenuation phenomenon. If enough of a beneficial effect lasts for a long enough period of time, a program or treatment would be considered worthwhile. It is also true that there are critical levels over which the effects of a treatment might increase or remain stable over long periods of time, rather than decrease. Although the human service field has all too few examples of this effect, the possibility of its occurrence cannot be ignored. In both of these cases, accurate follow-up is the only way to obtain information on changes of program effects as a function of time.

A second use for follow-up evaluation is to determine whether a particular treatment had any unintended consequences, beneficial or otherwise. It is not unreasonable to assume that human service programs impact their clients' lives in numerous ways, many of which cannot be predicted prior to the implementation of the program. As examples, one need only consider such classic cases as the effects of institutionalization (Goffman 1961), the education that people receive when they are incarcerated, or the effects of our educational system on factors other than the mastering of curriculum (Kozol 1967). These examples may seem obvious now, but they were discovered and explained only as a result of careful and creative research and analysis. It is best to assume that any form of social action will have unintended consequences, that the magnitude of those consequences may fluctuate over time, and that a knowledge of such phenomena might well play a crucial role in determining a program's value. Thus, we arrive at a second important use of follow-up evaluation—the study of unintended consequences. Without follow-up, one could obtain, at best, a partial and restricted view of the development and occurrence of such consequences.

Almost no social or human service effort will ever be an unqualified success. Judgments concerning the value of such programs are of necessity, relative. Thus, it is important to obtain an estimate of the "total" effect of a treatment, i.e., the amount of change brought about by a treatment over a reasonably long time period, and the pattern of fluctuation of treatment effects as a function of time.[7] Any judgment concerning the value of a program must take four elements into account: the time and resources that go into a treatment; the amount of positive and negative changes brought about by the treatment; the fluctuations of those changes over time; and the value of the changes that are brought about. The final consideration is not within the realm of the evaluator but is, rather, a matter of public policy and political debate. The first issue may or may not be an issue for the evaluator, depending on whether one takes a cost-benefit approach to the field of evaluation. The second and third considerations—amount of change and fluctuations over time—are unquestionably prime concerns for evaluators. Clearly, questions concerning the fluctuation of effects cannot be investigated without a follow-up approach to evaluation. A classic example can be found in the realm of education, where a basic question involves the effects of education on the life-long abilities and experiences of those who go through our educational system (Hyman, Wright, and Reed 1975). The educational system is an extremely complex treatment; its effects are assumed by all concerned to be pervasive and long-term. Thus, a long-term perspective is needed if meaningful evaluation is to be done in this area.

A third use of follow-up evaluation is related to a need for understanding the dynamics by which program effects change over time. Such information can have direct bearing on program planning, and it can only be collected in a follow-up context. An excellent example can be found in the area of early intervention. In a comprehensive review of the literature, Bronfenbrenner (1975) has concluded that the benefits produced by such programs are disappointing. The disappointment is even greater because many early intervention programs do show short-term positive effects. Over a few years, however, those gains attenuate. Long-term research has yielded some insight into this attenuation problem, and thus may help to design better programs. For instance, it seems that early parental involvement (during the first year of life) serves to decrease the attenuation problem. This is a finding with strong implications for program planning which would have been invisible without a long-range evaluation strategy.

There are many occasions in human and social service when the question of what happens to clients after they leave a treatment is the only matter of real interest to those who are involved in program planning. Client-comparison evaluation may not be important because an organization may have little or no substantive control over the types of clients it accepts. Further, even if an organization did have a choice in client selection, it might be extremely difficult to justify turning people away because of their sex, age, or the outcome of a psychological test. In short, entry into a human service program is often governed by convention, political necessity, program work force considerations, and other factors which have little to do with whether a client can actually be helped. Once a program is established, it is difficult to choose a clientele so that those who receive service will have the highest likelihood of being aided by the service being rendered.

Similarly, modality test evaluation may not be a priority for a variety of reasons. Convention may have institutionalized a particular type of treatment and the continuance of that treatment may be insured by factors such as bureaucratic momentum, vested interests, public expectations, and the like. As examples, it is not likely that modality test evaluation will have much direct bearing on the continuance of programs such as drug abuse rehabilitation, halfway houses of various types, child abuse hotline services, residential treatment, poison control hotlines, or any one of numerous other social services. In cases such as these, the very basic question, "Should the modality exist, and can it be replaced with more effective approaches?," is not of immediate concern to the evaluator. This is not to say that questions of this type are not important. On the contrary, they are unquestionably the most important issues that can be addressed by evaluators. But political reality may preclude the use of any evaluation results which touch on such basic questions, and less basic questions may remain which are important, and whose answers will improve the quality of service.

If a program has relatively little control over the people it must accept, if it does not have the potential to do sophisticated screening, and if the existence of the modality is a foregone conclusion, follow-up evaluation remains the only approach that might yield useful information to a program's staff and to decision makers. At the very least, this type of evaluation can help to give service providers a sense of what is realistically possible in their work context. Much effort in many fields of social service is undoubtedly wasted in the pursuit of unobtainable objectives. Follow-up evaluation provides a way to determine what is feasible in terms of the life space of one's clients, and consequently, to strive for the obtainable.

A final (and secondary) advantage of follow-up evaluation is that it does not tend to involve the researcher in the day-to-day business of the program that is being evaluated. Whenever evaluators and service providers come into daily working contact, a friction develops that is notorious for its ubiquity and for its resistance to repeated efforts at reduction. The political determinants of social service spending, the defensiveness of bureaucratic entities, the pressing daily concerns of administrators and service providers—all these are incompatible with the delicacy of research designs, the demands of researchers for staff time, and the potential negative judgments that so often accompany the results of evaluation. Follow-up studies have the unique advantage of removing the evaluation work from immediate and extensive contact with the service delivery system. Although this advantage of follow-up evaluation is secondary to its use for measuring the totality of treatment effects, the separation of service and evaluation is by no means a trivial matter, as follow-up evaluation may often turn out to be the only type of evaluation that can be carried out in an adequate and methodologically defensible manner.

Disadvantages of Follow-up Evaluation

Although follow-up evaluation is a valuable tool in determining the process of transition and interaction between a treatment and a client's life-style, the method is silent on the process by which a person is initially affected by the treatment in question. One can, of course, ask ex-clients to report on the elements of a program which affected them most, and such "critical incident" and self-report studies are not uncommon. (The methodology of critical incident research can be found in Flanagan 1954.) Unfortunately it would be a mistake to assume that people's memories accurately record the subtle and complex process of change that was brought about by a particular treatment. Further, it would be a mistake to assume that people attend to and remember those elements of a program which were most instrumental in their process of change. To make matters worse, whatever small hope exists for using follow-up information to learn about the relation between treatment and client change fades rapidly as the length of the follow-up increases. The root of the problem is that follow-up evaluation in its purest form devotes the bulk of its efforts and resources to the development of follow-up measures and to the considerable effort that is needed to collect information from people after they have left a program or an agency. The problem is complicated by the effects of time on the initial treatment. Whatever effect originally existed will most likely become increasingly small and difficult to detect as time goes by. Even if the treatment did result in lasting changes, those changes are likely to become increasingly more subtle and complex as they become ever more intertwined with the multitudinous factors that constantly impinge upon a person's life.

A second difficulty with follow-up evaluation is the cost and difficulty of identifying, locating and collecting data from past recipients of treatment. People move, drop out, or lose interest. Intrusions into one's personal life are often resented. Geographical dispersion often necessitates a large staff, a lot of traveling and a good deal of money. One always has to balance the value of one's data with its ability to offer constructive feedback to a program or to provide policy makers with guidance and direction. In this regard, one must consider the reasons why it might be advantageous to direct evaluation efforts away from a follow-up emphasis. First, as the length of time of follow-up increases, the evaluation becomes less and less linked to the actual efforts of the original treatment, until such work eventually resembles research on the life-styles of a particular population. Second, one could argue that legitimate evaluation must include at least some study of the elements of a treatment that were most important in bringing about constructive change. If there is any validity at all in this point of view, follow-up evaluation cannot be justified as the primary aspect of an evaluation study. It may certainly be valuable as an adjunct to modality tests, but it may not be justifiable as a project in its own right.

Finally, there is always the chance that biased samples due to difficulties in locating people or obtaining responses may present considerable difficulties in data analysis. In essence, one might be stuck in the position of not really knowing whether a sample differs from the original group of recipients in substantive or important ways. Adequate data collection during the course of treatment might help an evaluator make such a determination. Unfortunately, such data is very often lacking. Although there are effective methods of increasing response rates, practical considerations often preclude the use of those techniques. (These issues will be elaborated upon when the validity of follow-up evaluation is discussed.)

In sum, overemphasis on the follow-up aspect of evaluation must be avoided because of the difficulty of separating program effects from changes due to life-style, and because of difficulties in following people over a long period of time. Each of these problems has several dimensions which add up to a low probability that follow-up evaluation *in and of itself* will be able to provide administrators with enough program-relevant information to make the evaluation effort worthwhile.

MODALITY TEST EVALUATION

Uses and Advantages of Modality Test Evaluation

Of the three types of evaluation discussed in this chapter, the modality test approach is the only one that is directly concerned with precise assessment of treatment effectiveness. The defining characteristic of modality test evaluation is the conceptualization of human service programs (or distinct aspects of programs) as independent, or predictor variables in an evaluation study. The actual methodology may be experimental, quasi-experimental, correlational or even qualitative. Whatever its form, modality test evaluations are based on the assumption that a particular treatment (or some part of it) will result in well-defined, detectable changes in clients. This assumption is not necessarily a part of follow-up evaluation, where the time component can blur precise treatment effects. Likewise it is not necessarily an inherent part of client-comparison evaluation, whose focus is on who is being helped in which areas, and not on how or why people are being helped. In contrast, the major focus of modality test evaluation is precisely the matter of how people are being helped, and the nature of the relation between treatment and change.

One might claim that modality tests are the only legitimate form of program evaluation, and that within the modality test category, experimental methodologies are most desirable. It would not be hard to find strong arguments in favor of such a point of view. In essence this is the "social experimentation" perspective on evaluation which has been ably defended by many writers. (See, for example, Riecken and Boruch 1974.) A perusal of outcome evaluation work clearly indicates that the social experimentation point of view is not universally accepted, even in cases where modality tests are conducted. Just as client-comparison and follow-up studies can be defended vis-à-vis modality tests, so can one defend nonexperimental modality test evaluation. Nonexperimental work may not be as rigorous as the experimental variety, but it may be more appropriate for a particular problem, setting, or level of analysis. This book is predicated on the assumption that the varieties of outcome evaluation as currently practiced are worthwhile undertakings, that each is particularly well suited to answer different types of important questions, and that ways must be found to make each type of evaluation as valid and as useful as possible.

Information obtained from modality test evaluation relates directly to program effectiveness. Judgments on program success do not have to be inferred indirectly from data that was obtained with other purposes in mind. To the extent that one is interested in information concerning how a program can improve its effectiveness, modality test information is unquestionably superior to that yielded by any other form of evaluation. The superiority stems from the fact that the overall research plan is a direct attempt to relate program activity to program impact. Hence a major proportion of evaluation efforts are aimed at determining effectiveness. These efforts include the use of relevant theory, the construction of appropriate research designs, the choice of data and data collection methods, the use of assistants, the application of appropriate methods of statistical analysis, and the like. By comparison, client-type and follow-up evaluation invest the bulk of their efforts toward other ends, to the inevitable detriment of discovering the precise impact of the treatment under study.

As an example of how evaluation efforts may differ according to evaluation type, consider two different strategies for the evaluation of a child abuse prevention program—a modality test and a client-comparison approach. Appropriate theory in the former case might center on determining variables which would identify child-abusing parents. Efforts to find useful theory in the modality test situation may go in an entirely different direction. They may, for instance, center on theories of family interaction, and the relation between types of interaction and techniques for bringing about behavior change. Efforts at research design will also differ radically for the two evaluation strategies. Design efforts in the client-comparison study might center on the proper use of social area analysis, psychometric testing, field interview techniques, and the like. The modality test evaluator is likely to be most concerned with a different set of design problems—the allocation of subjects to conditions, determining appropriate comparison groups, and conceptualizing multiple measures of program success. Similarly, there will be differences in data analysis strategies. The client-comparison evaluator will likely be concerned with checking the reliability and validity of a large variety of tests and measures. Another major concern would be the appropriate use of factor analytic techniques to determine basic differences between abusing and non-abusing clients. The modality test evaluator will be most concerned with finding the most appropriate and powerful methods of detecting program effects. This might include concerns about covariance analysis, estimating the power of various tests, and the like. In short, the modality test and client-comparison evaluators will spend their time reading different material, contemplating different design and analysis methods, and conceptualizing different problems. The entire thrust and direction of the two efforts will differ. Can an evaluator do it all? No. Not all evaluation questions will have equal importance. Resources are limited. Expertise is limited. Time and organizational constraints limit the complexity of evaluation designs. Choices must be made, and dominant themes must be chosen.

Another advantage of the modality test approach is its ability to yield information on the magnitude of changes that are brought about by a treatment. Such information is considerably different from the identification of changes and the linking of those changes to program activity. The evaluator must be able to perform analyses that go beyond the measurement of statistical significance. He or she must be able to relate empirically derived estimates of the magnitude of effects to two other complex concepts.[8] First, the evaluator must compare the observed amount of change with the theoretically ideal change that might be expected in contexts similar to the one under study. It is by no means unreasonable to assume that the stated goals of a program might be impossible to meet and that a program's worth must be determined by matching the obtained change with a theoretical estimate of what can realistically be expected. The second concept is a sense of the difference between "statistical significance" and "practical significance." The fact that a particular change did not occur by chance is not a guarantee that the change is important enough to incorporate into program planning. These two concepts can be enormously powerful guides to the improvement of social service, as they can provide otherwise unobtainable assessments of what a program is doing relative to what it might be doing, and relative to what is important. Hence the importance of modality test evaluation, as it is only within the context of "cause and effect" information that knowledge of the size and importance of effects can be meaningfully understood.

A third advantage of modality test evaluation is that it can be combined with process evaluation information in a manner that makes for profound understanding of an organization or treatment process. Process evaluation is, in essence, the study of the inner workings and dynamics of an organization as they relate to the functioning and accomplishments of the organization. Although process evaluation is primarily designed to give decision makers immediate feedback on how to proceed on a day-to-day basis, it is also extremely valuable in providing contextual information that is necessary to interpret the results of outcome evaluation. A well-done process evaluation will tell one what program actions "really" were, how various parties to a treatment perceived the situation, and whether or not unforeseen events might have impacted upon any results which were observed. Such information is vital for any attempt at establishing a link between a program's actions and the consequences of those actions.

Cook and Campbell (1976) cite several excellent examples of instances where an intimate knowledge of program dynamics are vital for valid evaluation. For instance, they cite the possibility of "treatment contamination." This is a situation in which people in a program who are receiving different treatments are in a position to observe the various treatments which are being administered, and are able to communicate freely about them. It is not unreasonable to assume that under such conditions, there is a cross-over of treatments from one group to another. An even more flagrant difficulty is cited by Patton (1978). Patton brings an example of a program which was evaluated even though it was never implemented. It seems that a parenting education program for welfare recipients was so bogged down by political problems that the program never became operative. The evaluators were unaware of these problems, and carefully carried out their pre- and post-tests. Needless to say, little change was detected. These kinds of difficulties—whether flagrant or subtle—can only be detected by an understanding of the day-to-day operations of a program, and knowledge of such problems is crucial to the evaluation of an innovation.

A well-developed process-outcome relationship is also valuable for those who are primarily interested in the process, or organizational dynamic aspects of evaluation. This is so because the internal dynamics of an organization cannot be fully understood without a clear sense of what the organization is accomplishing, and how those accomplishments affect organizational operation. Presumably an organization's impact (negative and positive) on its clients has some influence on morale, preceptions of mission, relation to outside agencies, and the like. These influences may be overt or subtle, important or trivial, constant or changeable. Whatever their nature, it is not likely that program effects will be obvious to the naked eye. Specialized detection methods are necessary, and those methods lie within the province of modality test evaluation.

A final advantage to modality test evaluation is that it is most amenable to designs that will yield causal inferences on program-outcome relationships. Fairly strong methodological requirements must be met before a study can yield causal inference and not all modality test evaluations will meet those requirements (in fact, the majority probably do not). But if one does wish to obtain causal information, modality test evaluation is the method of choice. Causal inference is most likely to derive from the deliberate manipulation of specific variables, and it is very difficult to exercise such control over the personal characteristics of clients or over the life experiences that befall people after they leave a program. One can, however, control the type of treatment that a person receives while he or she is a member of a specific human service program, and it is precisely that control which facilitates causal inference.

Disadvantages of Modality Test Evaluation

The principle problems with modality test evaluation are practical rather than conceptual. The method is powerful and has excellent potential to yield useful high-quality information. Unfortunately, this type of evaluation is likely to require interference by evaluators in the daily affairs of the program that is being studied. Service personnel often have to collect special data, fill out extra forms, and in various ways change their normal working routine. A great deal has been written about the strains that exist between researchers and clinicians, and nowhere is it more likely for these strains to develop than in the conduct of a well-designed modality test evaluation. (Aronson and Sherwood 1967; Rodman and Kolodny 1964; Twain 1975; Zusman and Bissonette 1973.) The problem is exacerbated because the most powerful evaluation designs are also the most vulnerable to harm through small changes in procedure.

As an example, consider a modality test study which requires the random allocation of subjects to conditions, the delivery of well-defined specified treatments to particular groups, a carefully detailed testing schedule, and the collection of a great deal of special data. Such a design is likely to yield unambiguous information on the value of the treatment which is being tested. Any change in the design will increase the ambiguity of results, as it will open those results to competing alternate explanations. But as the design presently stands, it usurps some of the program's traditional autonomy. It restricts the type of people who are treated. It determines treatment plans for those who are treated. It imposes a timetable of activities on treatment delivery personnel. It mandates extra work for the purposes of data collection. Over and above these tangible changes, the evaluation also imposes a value judgment about the importance of research and of various aspects of research design.

Thus, an attempt at causal modality test evaluation sets up conditions in which program personnel are very likely to resent the intrusion of the evaluator while the evaluator will be forced to resist changes in evaluation design which would make life easier for harassed service personnel and administrators. These problems need not always arise and methods do exist to circumvent or to ameliorate them. (See Chapter 3 for more on this topic.) Further, modality test evaluations can be designed which are likely to be highly useful to all parties involved. Unfortunately, it remains a fact that the potential for serious friction between evaluators and service personnel is considerably heightened when modality test evaluation is attempted.

Thus, the age-old problem of having to pay the highest price for the highest quality has reasserted itself. Modality test evaluation offers a direct test of the type and amount of change that is brought about by particular aspects of a treatment program. It is also a labor-intensive effort which must (in all likelihood) be carried out in close cooperation with the staff of a service organization. Such cooperation can be extremely difficult since it might well entail a change in the standard operating procedure of the agency, extra work for personnel, and an increase in evaluation apprehension. The problem is made even more difficult because, by its nature, small changes in the design of a modality test evaluation can lead to large increases in the ambiguity of results. The sensitivity of modality test evaluation designs to small changes, together with the problems of implementing such designs, unquestionably constitutes the most serious disadvantage of the modality test approach.

CHAPTER SUMMARY

We have concluded consideration of the first of the three dimensions that constitute the ''space'' within which the boundaries of good evaluation can be determined, and within which the relative merits of various evaluation plans can be compared. The dimension we have dealt with was termed evaluation type. The lowest end of the continuum is held by client-type comparison evaluation, the mid-point is occupied by follow-up evaluation and the highest end of the continuum is considered to be modality test evaluation. These categories of evaluation are derived from an inspection of the type of evaluation that is actually carried out by social scientists. The continuum on which these approaches has been placed is based upon the direct relevance of evaluation information to understanding the consequences of program actions. Although each approach has unique advantages that are not shared by the others, the relevance continuum does serve as a meaningful and useful framework for differentiating between approaches to evaluation. The justification for using this criterion rests with the assumption that the major purpose of evaluation is to provide feedback on the implications and effects of a program's activities. The present chapter has been an attempt to explain the uses, advantages and disadvantages of each method. We will now turn our attention to the second dimension of ''evaluation space''—the validity of evaluation designs.

NOTES

[1]Although the ubiquity of these categories cannot in any sense be proven, it is worthwhile to note the variety of fields in which these categories appear as distinct and identifiable themes. As examples, consider the following representative articles. A review of evaluation in drug abuse rehabilitation by Morell (1977a) reveals evaluation papers with titles such as:

Personality Correlates of Success in a Maintenance Program (Levine, Levin, Sloan, and Chappel 1972);
A Follow-up Study of Narcotic Addicts in the NARA Program (Langenauer and Bowden 1971);
Phoenix House: Changes in Psychopathological Signs of Resident Drug Addicts (De Leon, Skodol, and Rosenthal 1973).

Boruch (1974) has produced a bibliography entitled "Illustrative Randomized Field Experiments for Program Planning and Evaluation." In that review one finds the following titles (among others):

Personality Evaluation of Correctional Institution Inmates Awaiting Plastic Surgery and a Control Group of Inmates (Holt and Marchionne 1967);
Minimal Intervention at Age Two and Three, and Subsequent Intellective Changes (Palmer 1972);
Effects of Short-term Psychiatric Treatment on Boys in Two California Youth Authority Institutions (Guttman 1963);
Social and Psychological Factors in the Treatment of Chronic Alcoholism (Kissin and Su 1970);
Student Personality Characters and Optimal College Learning Conditions: An Extensive Search for Trait by Treatment Interaction Effects (Goldberg 1973);
An Analysis of the Effectiveness of Different (Mailed Questionnaire) Follow-up Techniques (Astin and Panos 1969).

Other reviews of literature in the human and social service fields yield evaluation study titles with similarly characteristic titles, i.e., titles that are indicative of the types of evaluation that are proposed in the current typology.

Admittedly the examples chosen here are a highly selective group which were picked precisely because they do reflect themes in evaluation which are indicative of the "client-comparison-follow-up-modality" system. The point, however, was not to prove the all-inclusive validity of the system, but to demonstrate that these themes do indeed emerge in a wide variety of evaluation contexts.

[2]"Treatment" is not necessarily used here in the sense of a therapeutic endeavor in one of the health fields. Although many social service efforts are health- or mental health-related, this is by no means always the case. In this book "treatment" will be used more in its research sense, to mean any specific effort to bring about a particular desired change.

[3]It is most unfortunate that the basic effectiveness of many programs is assumed to exist merely because effectiveness cannot be tested and some form of service must be provided. Evaluation questions must be posed in the correct logical order and the suggestions advanced in this book must not be taken as a justification for assuming to be correct that which is in fact unknown.

[4]The source for this statement comes from the newspaper of the National Association of Social Workers 1977. There is a call for manuscripts by the Association's Book Committee (p. 8). In that call the following statement is made:

Manuscripts must meet one or more of the NASW priorities set by the Delegate Assembly and the criteria established by the Publications Committee and approved by the Board of Directors:

NASW Priorities

Elimination of racism ⎤
Elimination of poverty ⎦ —overriding priorities

1. Delivery of social services
2. Income maintenance
3. Man- and womanpower
4. Adult and juvenile justice systems
5. Woman and social welfare.

[5]As examples of the importance of this theme to the evaluation endeavor, consider the following statements by various people who have helped to set the groundwork for evaluation as we know it today.

In his seminal work on the nature of evaluation research, Suchman (1967, p. 2) makes the following comment:

All social institutions, whether medical, educational, religious, economic, or political, are required to provide "proof" of their legitimacy and effectiveness in order to justify society's continued support. Both the demand for and the type of acceptable "proof" will depend largely upon the nature of the relationship between the social institution and the public. In general, a balance will be struck between faith and fact, reflecting the degree of man's respect for authority and tradition within the particular system versus his skepticism and desire for tangible "proofs of work."

As part of their advocacy of a decision-theoretical approach to evaluation, Edwards, Guttentag, and Snapper (1975, p. 140) state:

Evaluations, we believe, exist (or perhaps only should exist) to facilitate intelligent decision-making.

As part of the ground work for understanding the experimenting society, Campbell (1971, p. 1) makes the following claim:

The experimenting society will be one which will vigorously try proposed solutions to recurrent problems, which will make hard-headed and multidimensional evaluations of the outcomes, and which will move on to try other alternatives when evaluation shows one reform to have been ineffective or harmful.

[6]The purpose of these remarks is *not* to negate the value of social area analysis as a tool in human service planning. The method most certainly has excellent potential to be of use in this regard. Further, theories relating demographic characteristics to social problems do exist. But it remains a fact that social area analysis must contend with all the ambiguity and unreliability that is inherent in the analysis of large bodies of complex uncontrolled data.

[7]Actually "time" per se is not a factor of major interest because "time" is not a causal variable. We are really interested in events that occur during a particular time frame which influence the magnitude of treatment effects. Classifying events as a function of time is merely a convenient method of conceptualizing the problem for descriptive purposes, and is most useful in cases where the factors which directly influence a treatment are unknown.

[8]For those interested in statistical methods of measuring the magnitude of effects in research, the following sources are recommended as an excellent beginning: Cohen 1969; Gaebelein, Soderquist, and Powers 1976; McNemar 1969. Cohen's book is an excellent work on the statistical power of tests which are commonly used in the behavioral sciences. In addition to discussions of the magnitude of effects, it contains a wealth of information on power analysis which should be of immense benefit to anyone who is seriously interested in employing powerful statistical tests in evaluation. Gaebelein, Soderquist, and Powers represent the latest in a long series of articles in *Psychological Bulletin* concerning appropriate methods of measuring the magnitude of effects in analysis of variance designs. McNemar's discussion of correlation includes an excellent introduction to the general issue of estimating the amount of variance that is accounted for in correlational designs.

3
Validity of Evaluation

Evaluation must be carried out only when there is some assurance that findings will attain a reasonable degree of validity. Consider the following example of an evaluation plan which should be modified as a result of issues related to validity. Pressing evaluation priorities dictate the performance of a modality test evaluation within a human service agency, but very high resistance to the evaluation can be expected from service providers who work in the agency which is to be evaluated. To make the situation of the evaluator even more difficult, let us assume that the resistance is justified on the basis of the amount of extra work which service providers would have to supply and the detrimental effect of evaluation on organizational procedure. In such a case, resistance might well result in incomplete data collection and in the sloppy execution of the evaluation design. Those same service providers who object to an intrusive modality test evaluation might be keenly interested in what happens to clients after they leave the program. This interest might spring from serious professional and clinical interest in obtaining follow-up information on people who are treated. As a result of their concern, service providers might be willing to prime their clients to expect follow-up contact and to act as liaison between ex-clients and the evaluation team. In such an admittedly contrived (but not too far fetched) case, the evaluator might do well to perform a valid follow-up evaluation rather than a modality test whose validity would be threatened from innumerable sources.[1]

THE VALIDITY CONTINUUM

If validity is too low, evaluation is a waste of time, effort, and resources. Opinions to the contrary are delusion. In order for this point of view to be meaningful two conditions have to be met. First, it must make sense to consider a "continuum of validity" as a legitimate consideration in the planning of research. It is not obvious that one should do so. After all, a researcher is duty bound to make his or her research as valid as possible, and nobody would deliberately perform an invalid piece of research. Second, there must be a way to determine a minimum standard of validity. These are important considerations because if it is not legitimate to choose a less valid study deliberately over a more valid study, the three-dimensional model of "evaluation space" (type-validity-usefulness) loses one of its elements. If there is no intelligent guide for choosing a minimum standard, the utility of the validity dimension is greatly diminished. These matters will be discussed in turn.

There are two sources of support for the concept of a validity continuum: First, the practice of research as it is actually carried out; and second, the concept of social science methodology as it has been developed by those who have specialized in such matters.

A careful reading of the "discussion" sections of numerous research reports reveals the concern of many workers with speculations on: "What would have been if. . . ." Many of these speculations deal with methods by which validity could have been improved if various changes had been made in research design. Although many of these changes are based on the discovery of problems which emerged as a result of data analysis, a substantial proportion of the speculation deals with the effects of problems that *were known to exist* when the research was started. It is clear that the researcher could have solved at least some of those problems but chose not to because of constraints on factors such as time, work force, money, or the research context. If we assume that these choices were made as a result of considered judgment rather than out of ignorance, it becomes clear that many factors other than validity come into play in the determination of a research project. If we give researchers the benefit of the doubt and assume that their actions result from considered and knowledgeable judgment, we must also assume that researchers have a concept of validity as a variable quantity. Further, we must assume that researchers have a sense of what constitutes minimally acceptable levels of validity, and the ability to appropriately trade validity for other benefits to a research design. Thus in the de facto world of social research, validity is treated as a variable quantity.

The writings of social science methodologists make it clear that researchers' attitudes concerning the variable character of validity is justified. The concept of validity as a complex and multidimensional concept has been solidly established. Not only do we recognize internal validity as a separate concept from external validity, but we also recognize each of these categories as being composed of numerous subdimensions (Campbell and Stanley 1966; Cook and Campbell

1976). It is clear from these writings that the various types of validity are not always logically dependent on each other, and consequently special efforts may be put into assuring one form of validity at the expense of others. Further, research studies themselves are often multidimensional, and special efforts are often expended to increase the validity of one part of a study at the expense of other elements of the same study.

The Campbell and Stanley (1966) notion of "plausible rival hypothesis" also supports the concept of validity as a variable quantity. In essence, their approach assumes that the purpose of research is to make statements concerning a particular phenomenon or state of affairs. A rival hypothesis is an explanation other than the one drawn by a researcher from obtained data. If it is reasonable to assume that the rival hypothesis is as likely to be correct as the one advanced by the researcher, and if the data collected cannot differentiate between the two hypotheses, the validity of the study becomes suspect. The entire "quasi-experimental design" typology advanced by Campbell and Stanley is an attempt to identify sources of such hypotheses for various types of research designs, and to identify which types of rival hypotheses are admitted or ruled out by particular designs. Since the number and type of likely competing explanations differ for each design they propose, one must assume that the "amount" of validity associated with each design also varies.

The variability of validity also emerges from statistical considerations of test validity. In this context validity can be defined by the correlation coefficient between two entities. As Edwards (1974, p. 203) puts it: "The correlation between scores on text X and some independent criterion that it is hoped the scores will predict, is called a *validity coefficient.*" Although one might not be able to transpose completely concepts of test validity to matters concerning the validity of research design, there is an important relation between the two. As the validity of tests used in a research study increases or decreases so too does the overall validity of the research design which incorporates those tests. After all, a research study can be no better than the quality of the data which it collects.

Thus, the methodological overseers of research practice clearly recognize that validity is not an all or nothing concept and that one can indeed make decisions which will increase or decrease the validity of research. In fact, the ability to make such decisions forms the basis for much of their work, and very likely provides the motivation to grapple with problems of research design in the first place.

ESTABLISHING MINIMUM ACCEPTABLE LEVELS OF VALIDITY

What is the minimum level of validity that should be expected from a credible research or evaluation study? Unfortunately there is no quantitative answer to this question, as there has yet to be developed a standard metric to measure "amount" of validity. Further, even if such a metric were to be developed, it is doubtful if social scientists could reach agreement concerning the application of that metric. The concept of validity of a research study is qualitative, and so it is destined to remain for the foreseeable future. Thus we are confronted with a well-developed qualitative concept of validity, an ethic which exhorts us to make our research as valid as possible, and very little hope that the concept of "validity" will be quantified in a meaningful and useful manner. Within these constraints we must find some way to determine the minimum acceptable level of validity that should be built into an evaluation study. The need to develop methods of validity determination springs from the assumption that if information is too untrustworthy, it should not be used as a basis for program planning. The idea that "some information is better than no information" ceases to operate when the quality of the information becomes too low. The remainder of this section will be devoted to specifying guidelines by which each individual evaluator can make an informed choice concerning minimum acceptable levels of validity. The reader is cautioned not to expect any radical new methods of measuring validity, as I cannot do what I have already claimed to be almost impossible. The analysis will consist of a prescription for the organized application of well-known general principles which operate in the conduct of social science. Once the guidelines are established, the discussion will turn to specific methods of increasing the validity of each of the three types of outcome evaluation. The object of the discussion will be to help evaluators insure the credibility of their work by recognizing when the validity of a study may be too low, and by proposing techniques by which the validity of evaluation will be kept as far above the minimum level as is possible.

Establishing Minimum Standards of Validity: Step 1—Identifying Sources of Threats to Validity

As a first step, the evaluator must determine the threats to validity that are likely to emerge from a given evaluation study. As a minimum, such an analysis must include an estimate of the validity of the measuring instruments which will be employed, combined with an analysis of validity problems that are a function of the evaluation design. Although the Campbell and Stanley (1966) quasi-experimental design typology is probably most useful for such purposes, almost any careful consideration of likely plausible rival hypotheses will suffice. (The later version of this typology by Cook and Campbell [1976] is particularly valuable for evaluators, as it deals with threats to validity which are likely to arise due to the nature of work in field settings.)

An analysis of validity as a function of the logic of a research design is, however, only the first step in the process. Perhaps the most serious validity problems in evaluation emerge not from flaws in the original design, but as a consequence of unforeseen problems in the implementation of evaluation designs. Although such problems occur in any research project (alas, Murphy's law is always with us), they are particularly serious in the conduct of evaluation. The validity of evaluation studies is threatened not only by the vicissitudes of research in applied settings, but also by problems due to evaluation apprehension, the political atmosphere in which evaluation is conducted, and frictions between researchers and service agency personnel. What is the likelihood that one will be forced to make major changes in the evaluation plan after it is implemented and functioning? Is there a strong possibility that an atmosphere of goodwill and cooperation which is vital for data collection will change as the evaluation progresses? Is an evaluator's authority over evaluation work likely to change while the work is in progress? Is the nature of the treatment or organization which is being studied likely to be altered while the evaluation is being conducted? Is the evaluation design likely to lose its integrity? All of these questions and many more play a part in determining the probable validity of a finished evaluation product.

Another important guide to evaluation planning is the fate of other evaluations which were conducted in similar settings. Because it is impossible to foresee all problems that might arise, it may be helpful to look at problems that actually occurred in like circumstances. Such information will allow the evaluator to judge which difficulties should be expected, and whether or not effective steps can be taken to eliminate or ameliorate those problems.

Invalidity in an evaluation study can emanate from three sources: First, validity problems which are associated with the measuring instruments that are used; second, the amount of validity that is a function of the manner in which information is collected, i.e., the research design; third, validity problems which are associated with changes in the evaluation plan that may occur after the plan is implemented. Although these sources of invalidity exist in all social research, the third is particularly likely to occur in the case of evaluation. Assessing the magnitude of these problems must come about from an intimate understanding of the context in which the evaluation will take place, and through a study of problems that are known to have occurred in similar contexts. Although one would be hard pressed to tell an evaluator precisely how to weigh all these factors, it is safe to say that on some level and in some way, they must all be considered. Further, the more explicit and direct the consideration of each factor, the greater the likelihood that the evaluator will be able to make an intelligent judgment concerning the potential validity of a proposed evaluation plan.

Establishing Minimum Standards of Validity: Step 2—Personal Values

Evaluators must clarify their personal values concerning the use and importance of evaluation. Beliefs about these matters can be conceptualized as belonging to four categories, each of which must be inspected in order to derive a sense of how valid one believes that evaluation studies must be. First is the evaluator's sense of a "job well done." At what point does the validity of a study decrease to the point where the evaluator loses a sense of having turned out a product of acceptable quality?

Next, one must consider the possible uses to which the evaluation results will be put, and the quality of information that the evaluator wishes to present for such use. Evaluation cannot be an impartial test of a program's worth because the design of an evaluation cannot be separated from basic philosophical approaches to the goals and potential usefulness of a program (Weiss 1975). The measures that are included in a study, the sources from which information is collected, concepts of what is or is not a desirable outcome, comparisons that one chooses to make, areas that one tends to investigate or leave alone—all these and numerous other factors are founded on value-based decisions, and all have an influence on what an evaluation study will reveal about a program or a treatment.[2] These issues are particularly crucial in evaluation because evaluation is usually concerned with the study of public programs which are funded by public funds and which are designed to solve widespread social problems. Further, the very definition of a social problem is a function of a sociopolitical process. Consequently social programs are likely to have advocates and detractors, and the evaluator must expect his or her work to be used by one or another camp to support a particular point of view.[3] The evaluator must make a personal decision concerning the quality of information that he or she is willing to input into that sociopolitical decision-making process. The problem is particularly serious because the validity of evaluation studies may very well *not* be a major factor in whether or how evaluation information will be used. Evaluators are in a situation where the information they present might have profound consequences, but where the quality of that information may not play a major role in determining those consequences. (Some excellent examples of such situations can be found in Adams 1975, chap. 3.) Since it is likely that evaluation information may be used without consideration of the validity of the evaluation, evaluators must make a fundamental decision as to the quality of information which they wish to present. Once evaluation begins it may be difficult to stop, and once an evaluation report is written it is almost impossible to control the use of that report.

The third set of values concerning evaluation relates to the evaluator's beliefs about the public's right to have accurate information concerning the behavior of programs which are funded through the public purse. Few would deny that such a right exists, but there is probably wide variation in how seriously evaluators consider themselves instruments in the "right to know" process. Presumably one's sense of obligation to produce valid evaluation information will vary with one's self-perception as an expert who is uniquely qualified to inform the public on matters about which the public has a right to be informed.

Finally, evaluators must decide upon their obligations to their employers. It is quite likely that those who employ evaluators are not in a position to judge accurately the validity of information that will be produced. The primary expertise of those who hire evaluators lies in the areas of administration, planning, and specific areas of social or human service. Such people are not likely to be expert judges of the quality of evaluation designs. Although an evaluator's employers may be (and hopefully are) intelligent and informed consumers of evaluation information, it is reasonable to assume that the evaluator's expertise in evaluation surpasses that of those who purchase evaluation services. As a result of the evaluator's specialized knowledge, it becomes a matter of professional ethics to assure the quality of evaluation services.

Although validity is certainly an important determinant of the quality of evaluation services, there are other factors which must also be considered. Timeliness and relevance are two of those factors. A need to support a predetermined position or argument is another. Developing an empirical rationale for a decision that has already been made is still a third. Unfortunately these legitimate needs of planners and administrators may be counterproductive to the conduct of a highly valid evaluation study. What are an evaluator's obligations to an employer when such factors are operative? How do such factors impinge on an evaluator's professional ethics concerning the production of valid information? How does the vector sum of these forces help determine an evaluator's sense of minimum acceptable levels of validity for evaluation work? (A more extensive analysis of the ethical responsibilities of evaluators can be found in Windle and Neigher [1978], and in the responses which accompany that article.)

In sum, an evaluator's personal values play an important part in the determination of minimum acceptable levels of validity for evaluation studies. The system proposed here identifies four areas in which these values might be found. First is the evaluator's sense of satisfaction from the performance of high-quality evaluation. Second, the evaluator must consider the uses to which evaluation information might be put and the quality of information that one wishes to make a part of that utilization process. Third, an evaluator must decide whether he or she is producing information that the public has a right to have and the validity of information that is destined for public consumption. Fourth, the obligations of an evaluator to his or her employer must be inspected. Administrators and planners might have many different uses for evaluation, not all of which are conducive to the conduct of valid evaluation studies. The evaluator's ethical obligation to meet those needs must be balanced with ethical considerations concerning validity.

Establishing Minimum Standards of Validity: Step 3—The Professional Climate of Opinion

The final factor in determining the minimum acceptable level of validity for an evaluation study is the collective judgment of others who are working in the same field—the community to whom an evaluator looks for approval as a professional. That professional community is certainly not unanimous in opinions concerning the importance of validity in evaluation, nor does it have a consensus concerning the possible factors that should shape evaluation studies. On the other hand, there are levels of validity which would clearly be rejected by substantial and/or influential elements of the evaluation community. The extent to which evaluators are bound by such standards is shaped by several factors: the amount of consensus which exists on the issue within the evaluation community; the importance of that community for the evaluator's self-esteem; and the importance of that community for the evaluator's professional credibility.

Although an evaluator looking for guidance on standards for validity will not be able to find clear instructions, it might well be worthwhile to inspect implicit standards which emanate from debates within the evaluation community. Such an inspection would involve looking at evaluation studies that are praised and/or damned because of their validity, and attempting to discern any common elements of design or analysis that differentiate one group from another. As an example, consider the debate over the validity of covariance as a technique for equating nonrandomly allocated control groups (Cook and Reichardt 1976). Most methodologists and statisticians have grave reservations about the use of this technique. All agree that if the technique is used, extreme caution should be observed in drawing inferences from data. Results cannot be taken strictly at face value and one or more corrective procedures to the statistical analysis should be taken. Surely there is a lesson to be learned in this debate concerning standards for validity in the use of covariance analysis for evaluation. It is a standard that can be only roughly defined, but it does exist and it does provide relatively clear guidance in the matter of using covariance as a method of equating nonequivalent control groups.

Establishing Minimum Standards of Validity: Summary

We have dealt with three factors that shape an evaluator's sense of minimal acceptable levels of validity for evaluation studies. These factors are experience with previous work that is similar to a proposed evaluation study, personal values relating to the use and conduct of evaluation, and the standards that are set by members of the evaluation community. These factors were proposed in an effort to demonstrate that workable guidelines do exist to aid in the determination of minimum standards of validity. We will now turn to a consideration of specific methods of increasing the validity of each of the three different types of evaluation studies. The purpose of the discussion will be to allow evaluators to elevate the validity of evaluation as high as possible over those minimum standards.

VALIDITY ISSUES IN CLIENT-COMPARISON EVALUATION

The most basic question that can be asked about client-comparison evaluation is whether or not it is meaningful to search for characteristics that will validly differentiate successful from unsuccessful recipients of a treatment. The answer to this question must deal separately with psychological and demographic variables.

Psychological Variables as Elements in Program Evaluation

Psychological variables can be useful in evaluation only if those variables can be used not only to differentiate but also to predict success in treatment. Unfortunately the literature on this topic represents a quagmire of conflicting research evidence and varying theories (Bem and Allen 1974; Hogan, DeSoto, and Solano 1977; Kelman and Liska 1975; Mischel 1977). The resolution seems to be that psychological variables do have some use in predicting behavior, but it is very difficult to know how much of a part they play and how they interact with other variables that affect behavior.

Although some psychological variables may be excellent predictors of behavior, only a small subset of those variables are likely to be applicable or useful for a given human or social service program. It is one thing to identify psychological differences between successful and unsuccessful recipients of a treatment. It is quite something else to identify differences that will be useful in predicting client success and which are also meaningful within the context of their application. Each problem is difficult in and of itself. Taken together they make it extremely difficult for an evaluator to perform meaningful client-comparison evaluation through the exclusive use of psychological information.

Assuming that potentially useful variables have been identified, the evaluator then faces the task of accurate measurement. Here, too, problems abound. The general matter of reliability and validity in psychological testing is always a serious problem. In addition, the evaluator must contend with errors that develop as a function of the setting in which the test is administered, the method of administration, and the attitudes of treatment recipients to being tested. These factors are likely to vary a great deal in different social or human service settings. They are also likely to differ considerably from the ideal context of administration as set out by the developers of a test.

A related problem is that most psychological tests are developed and validated for specific well-defined populations. There is an unfortunate tendency not to observe these restrictions during the press of evaluation business. If a variable needs to be measured, convenient tests may be pressed into service without proper consideration of the validity of the test for the population in which it will be employed.

In many cases problems such as those outlined above are not particularly serious. Many tests have been widely used for a long time in a wide variety of contexts. In such cases, the effects of various testing contexts on a wide variety of populations may be known, or at least reliably guessed. Further, many tests have a well-developed theoretical backing which might give an investigator an excellent perspective to judge the probable applicability of a test in a particular context. IQ tests are an excellent example. They have been extensively researched in a wide variety of forms, and much data has been collected on their applicability to numerous different populations. Tests of field dependence and cognitive style are also examples of measures which have an extensive theoretical backing and wide use with many diverse populations. Unfortunately, a very large number of personality, attitude and cognitive measures are not embedded in knowledge of this kind.

Another problem with using psychological variables as elements in evaluation is the large and diverse body of research evidence which indicates that psychological variables per se are not crucial operative factors in determining behavior. Rather, it is the *interaction* of environmental and psychological factors that are important. One source of this evidence comes from the work of social learning theorists (Mischel 1973). This school claims that the weight of research evidence is against the trait theory of personality, and that it does not make sense to expect human beings to exhibit behavioral consistency across varying situations. The argument is that a person's behavior is determined by his or her needs, combined with his or her perceptions of such factors as the importance of a task, the probability of success, and other similar factors. A second line of evidence comes from those theorists who believe that behavior can be understood only if a study is made of the interaction between personal characteristics and externally imposed events (Cronbach 1975). The weight of evidence indicates that the nature of these interactions is quite complex and, consequently, information on psychological variables cannot provide a simple or easy guide to understanding behavior.

If the above reasoning has any validity, it makes the task of the evaluator engaged in client comparison evaluation extremely complex. The evaluator must not only make sure that psychological tests are valid for the population in question and administered properly, but he or she must also try to collect data in such a way that interactions between psychological variables and other sets of variables are made clear.

The Demographic Variable Solution

The simplest solution to the problem of using psychological variables in evaluation is to abandon or underplay their use and to limit investigations to demographic or environmental information. There is a lot of appeal to this plan. Demographic and environmental information is relatively easy to collect and validate. It does not involve the laborious process of finding, preparing and administering psychological tests. It is relatively inexpensive. It has a high potential to be of use to social programs because the information can easily fit into client screening plans or the administrative decision-making process.

An important drawback to the exclusion of psychological information is a resultant gap in knowledge that is analogous to the question of how "sociological fact" is translated into individual action. To the extent that one is interested in practical evaluation and planning, however, the existence of such gaps might be only a minor concern.

Another objection to abandoning psychological variables is that by so doing, one may deprive service providers of important and interesting information. Service providers often deal with people's psychological functioning, and information about psychological differences between successful and unsuccessful clients may be of great use. To the extent that providing such information is a legitimate evaluation function, psychological information cannot be excluded from evaluation plans.

Finally, one must consider the fact that numerous social action and social service programs are designed to deal primarily with psychological factors in their clientele. In such cases it is difficult (if not impossible) to justify the exclusion of psychological variables in evaluation. Clearly, a meaningful strategy of incorporating psychological factors into evaluation must be developed.

As a first step, only those psychological variables that can reasonably be expected to yield useful information should be employed. Evaluators must avoid the temptation to use psychological tests that merely happen to be available, or happen to be easy to employ, or happen to be of special personal interest to the evaluator. Previous research and the informed opinions of service providers, administrators and other experts must be sought before a psychological factor is introduced as an element in evaluation. The evaluator must make sure that proposed tests have been validated on the population with which the test will be used, or be prepared to perform the necessary validation studies. It is also important to make sure that the personnel and resources exist to administer tests in the appropriate manner.

If an evaluation design calls for the collection of psychological information on the same individuals more than once, problems of test reactivity must be carefully thought out and planned. Do such problems exist? If so, is the sample large enough to divide randomly into several groups so that all people will not receive all tests at each testing period? Is there a possibility of developing a design that will allow the evaluator to estimate the magnitude and direction of reactivity effects?

Over and above the choice of appropriate psychological tests and variables, the evaluator must consider the choice of environmental and demographic information which will help make psychological data meaningful. As an example, Clum (1975) has conducted an extensive review of intrapsychic and environmental factors as they relate to prognosis in mental health. Among his conclusions are that (p. 113): "The patient's environment also relates to outcome of illness and may account for some relationships between intrapsychic variables and prognosis." A case in point is his finding about the environmental factor of being married. In considering this issue, Clum concluded that (p. 427): "Social isolation conceived of solely as a personality trait is insufficient to account for its relationship to prognosis." Thus, the evaluator must make provisions to collect environmental data which will help to explain any psychological factors which are of interest. Does a study have such provisions? Does the evaluator have a clear sense of why such information is important and how it will be used to understand psychological factors? These are the types of questions which must be answered during the planning stages of an evaluation study.

Specification of Criteria for Success

If one is going to differentiate the characteristics of successful and unsuccessful recipients of a treatment, one must first define the concepts of "success" and "failure." As an example of how complex such problems can become, consider the following examples. How does one classify a criminal who maintains his or her criminal life-style but as a result of a treatment now has a better family life, a more positive self-image, and less anxiety? How should one classify a drug addict who, as a result of a rehabilitation program, has reduced drug intake by 20 percent, or has switched to the use of less dangerous drugs, but has not substantially changed friendship patterns, basic values, criminal activity, or employment status? What about the classification of an alcoholic who started treatment with a poor prognosis but, as a result of treatment, has not gotten worse? What does one do about the classification of people in a school dropout prevention program who stay in school longer than would normally be expected but eventually drop out anyway?

A standard solution to this problem in a good deal of client comparison evaluation is to define a single success criterion and to divide people into two or three basic categories. Unfortunately, the criteria that are used are often simplistic or not based on a comprehensive understanding of how success and failure are conceptualized by experts in a given field. In many areas of human service a good deal of thought has been given to the problem of defining success. The treatment staff of any given program, treatment, or social service organization is likely to have given this problem much thought. Considerable research might have been conducted using a variety of success measures. Thus the first step of the evaluator is to use the expertise of others to develop meaningful definitions of success and failure for a particular context. If those definitions are not meaningful, the results of client comparison evaluation cannot be meaningful.

It is not likely that an evaluator will be able to find strong agreement among experts on questions concerning definitions of success and failure, since definitions are always value-laden and not precise. Even so, those who have wrestled with the problem are more likely to have meaningful answers than those who seek a quick and simple definition for the sake of convenience. In any given human service area, success is undoubtedly a complex process which is most accurately described as a continuum or a multidimensional process. Client-comparison evaluation that fails to take such complexities into account is bound to produce inadequate, distorted or simplistic descriptions or differences between those who benefit from a treatment and those who do not.

There seems to be an implicit assumption in much client-comparison evaluation that small client changes in an appropriate direction portend even greater changes in that direction. If this assumption is true, it makes sense to search for defining characteristics of those who exhibit small desirable changes. Unfortunately this is an untested assumption which, although reasonable, is by no means necessarily correct. Thus evaluations which attempt to differentiate between clients who exhibit small changes may produce conclusions based on random variations or on systematic differences which do not relate to client progress.

The Importance of No-Treatment Comparisons

If client-comparison research is to be useful as evaluation, it must produce valid answers not only to the question: "What type of people change for the better?" but also to the question: "What type of people change for the better *as a result of the treatment?*" Many problems that may be amenable to treatment also exhibit spontaneous recovery. Evaluators must be interested not only in who recovers, but in who needs the help of a particular treatment in order to recover.

If an evaluation is planned in time, a proper comparison group might be established. Even if randomized groups cannot be constituted, other appropriate comparison groups might still be formed. These might include people on a waiting list, early dropouts, or people who inquired about a treatment but never made formal attempts to enter. Although all comparison groups of this sort suffer from the standard (and very serious) problems of nonrandomized control groups, it is also true that multiple comparisons with imperfect controls can yield extremely useful information (Cook and Reichardt 1976). As an example consider a client-comparison evaluation with three separate subgroups: those who went through an entire treatment, early dropouts, and people on a waiting list. Suppose that evaluation showed that a higher proportion of successes were found among the group that completed treatment; that the characteristics of successes who stayed in treatment differed from the characteristics of successes among the dropouts; and that the characteristics of successes among waiting-list people were similar to the pattern for successful dropouts. These results indicate not only that treatment was effective, but also that the dynamics of change for program participants is probably different from the "natural" rehabilitation process.

Of course it is most unlikely that an actual evaluation will be as clear-cut as the example given above. This contrived example is brought only to demonstrate how imperfect comparison groups can be useful in the conduct of client-comparison evaluation. If such groups are not available, the evaluator must be content with comparing the characteristics of those who succeeded and failed in a treatment with what is generally known about spontaneous recovery from similar problems.

The Use of Information in Post Hoc Client-Comparison Evaluation

A major reason for the use of client-comparison evaluation is that the need for evaluation arises after a program has been in operation for some time. In such cases it is often impossible to collect the pretreatment baseline data that is necessary for modality test evaluation. Consequently, evaluation becomes an investigation of differences between successful and unsuccessful clients. Unfortunately pretreatment information is also necessary for client-comparison studies. Any time evaluation plans are laid after a program has started, the evaluator runs the risk of having to rely on pretreatment data that is of low quality for the purposes of comparing clients. Important information may be missing, existing data may be only partially relevant to evaluation, or proper control on data quality may not be exercised. One must assume that there is at best only a very rough correspondence between the data needs of evaluators, service providers and administrators. Although no evaluation will be maximally successful in the absence of proper pretreatment information, one might be able to salvage a reasonably good client-comparison evaluation from such situations. Although a salvage job can always be attempted with any type of evaluation, such attempts have the greatest likelihood of paying off in the case of client-comparison situations. The greater one's interest in making a causal statement about a program or treatment, the lower the chances that deficiencies of poor design can be corrected after the fact. Of all three types of evaluation, the client-comparison method is furthest from attempts at causal inference.

The basic problem is that without pretreatment information it is impossible to know whether or not successful and unsuccessful clients started treatment with the same prognosis. Without such information, it is impossible to use evaluation information to set up a meaningful screening program or to make decisions concerning treatment plans or organizational functioning. One solution is the use of post hoc comparison in order to constitute some type of meaningful comparison group. In other words, the original status of a group is reconstructed after a period of time has passed. Although this tactic cannot be disregarded, it must be used only with extreme caution due to the possibility of bias which stems from regression artifacts (Campbell and Erlebacher 1970). Bias of this type may result from any treatment-control comparison in which the groups being compared start out at different mean levels. Due to factors which arise from the selection of individuals for treatment, the reconstruction of pretreatment comparison groups is especially prone to regression-artifact problems.

A second solution is to carry out, along with the evaluation of primary interest, several concurrent studies. Such studies might include pretest and post-test information on programs that are similar to the program of primary interest, or they may simply consist of several simultaneous evaluations of similar organizations, all of which are of the post-test only variety. Although these procedures cannot yield formal control groups, they can be used to help clarify and analyze data from the primary evaluation. First, concurrent evaluation will help provide contextual information concerning the program under study. Second, it can supply nonequivalent comparison groups, and such groups can be extremely useful in data analysis. The use of contextual information and nonequivalent comparisons allow the evaluator to develop a sense of which conclusions are reasonable and plausible; to discover situational factors which might influence data interpretation; and to learn about the stability of one's findings for a particular time and place. They also supply the evaluator with increased opportunity to check on the plausibility of alternate rival hypotheses.

This prescription boils down to exerting all efforts at fortifying an inherently weak design and uncertain information with as much related data as possible. The greater the amount of supporting data, the higher the probability that the evaluator may be able to make a meaningful statement about the question of primary interest.

Another important advantage to the tactic of conducting concurrent evaluations is that it is *not* based on statistical techniques which purport to correct for weaknesses in design. As Cook and Reichardt (1976) indicate, the use of such methods is the center of a heated debate which involves relatively complex statistical concepts. For many people, the use of statistical corrections for design problems involves a degree of faith in one or another group of experts. Such debates should be carried on and statistical correction should be used in as powerful and intelligent a manner as possible. But it is comforting to know that evaluations can also be carried out in which arguments concerning findings and conclusions are based on concepts that are readily understandable to any who take the trouble to read carefully and analyze the evaluator's report.

A third solution to the problems posed by post hoc client-comparison evaluation is to collect data that will provide a measure of where program members stood prior to treatment. In certain cases this may be possible. It is likely that people have reasonably accurate memories concerning issues such as work, school, family problems, and the like. Further, much of this information can be validated from key informants or from existing records. Unfortunately, it is difficult to find valid data concerning past psychological states, and this places a severe restriction on post hoc evaluation.

No matter how post hoc client-comparison evaluation is carried out, such work should make as full use as possible of available data. More important, the reporting of such evaluation should contain conclusions that are written as clearly as possible and the problems of validity must be comprehensively discussed. If these conditions are met, informed readers will be able to reach their own judgments concerning the worth of the evaluation. The value of an evaluation (or any research for that matter) is ultimately determined by the opinions of people who did not actually carry out the investigation. Thus the investigation must be presented in a manner that will allow others to form intelligent judgments. Although such advice is worthwhile for all research and evaluation, it is particularly important for those elements of evaluation that fall near the lower ends of the validity continuum, and post hoc client-comparison most certainly fulfills this condition.

Summary: Increasing the Validity of Client-Comparison Evaluation

Client-comparison evaluation is not merely an easy evaluation strategy that can be "grabbed at" whenever a quick and easy evaluation must be conducted. Psychological variables must be carefully chosen with ample thought given to their conceptual importance, practical meaningfulness, and potential to be collected validly and reliably. Measures of social, behavioral and environmental factors should be corroborated from various sources and must provide a meaningful context within which psychological information can be understood. Proper pretreatment and comparison group information must be collected. Definitions of success and failure must be conceptualized so as to be useful and meaningful, both on theoretical and practical levels. Further, those definitions must be acceptable to the consumers of the evaluation. None of these conditions are easy to meet. Client-comparison evaluation should be employed only if it is the most appropriate method to answer a particular question.

Client-comparison evaluation is a very popular evaluation tactic, but one is hard pressed to find methodological discussions that are specifically aimed at increasing the validity of such work. This section has been an attempt to draw from the diverse literature on social research methodology and to pull together those elements that are most crucial to proper conduct of client comparison evaluation. It has attempted to point out the most serious difficulties, and to point the way to a resolution of those difficulties.

VALIDITY ISSUES IN FOLLOW-UP EVALUATION[4]

Follow-up evaluation can be divided into two categories: Studies which necessitate locating clients after they have left treatment, and studies which are designed and implemented while clients are still receiving treatment. Although many of the strategies for preplanned evaluation must also be applied to the *post hoc* case, the latter is especially problematical, and requires special planning.

Post Hoc Follow-up Evaluation

Factors Which Bias Post Hoc Follow-up Evaluation. The first and most important rule concerning post hoc follow-up evaluation is to avoid it unless there is absolutely no other choice. The reason for this caution is that a difficult bias may arise due to the phenomenon of differential response. People who are located and who provide data may be very different from people who are not located, or who are located and who refuse to cooperate. Empirical evidence indicates that this difficulty is not merely hypothetical. In a large-scale survey dealing with education, occupation and earnings, Sewell and Hauser (1975) cite evidence to the effect that dropout dynamics did not affect correlations among variables, but that it did affect the representativeness of the sample. Thus for purposes of parameter estimation, dropouts were a problem. For purposes of studying relations among variables, however, the dropout problem could be ignored. Unfortunately, Sewell and Hauser (1975) also indicated that this result should not be generalized. They cite other survey studies, some of which confirmed their finding, and some of which did not. In sum, the operation of dropout dynamics may or may not bias research findings. Bias is a distinct possibility, and it is impossible to know a priori how or if that bias is operating. The problem must be specifically studied each time follow-up research is conducted.

Although differential response is an issue in all follow-up research, it is particularly troublesome in the post hoc case. This is because the greater the time lag between receiving treatment and follow-up contact, the greater (or at least the more complex) the bias due to selective location of treatment recipients. (The same problem holds for bias due to selective cooperation from those who are located.) Those who cannot be located a short time after treatment may very well be different from those who remain visible for longer periods, but who eventually become invisible. Further, it is not unreasonable to assume that as time goes on, only the most successful treatment recipients will be found. The more socially functional people become, the greater the likelihood that they will put down the kinds of roots (work, school, family, etc.) that will allow them to be located. One might also speculate that the opposite is true. It may be the least successful who are easiest to locate. Such people may not be able to function socially, and hence, are likely to be found in police or various institutional records, or simply may not move very far from their initial location. Whatever the case may be, evaluators can be fairly sure that biases of this sort do operate, and that as time between treatment and initial contact increases, so does the difficulty of discerning the magnitude and direction of that bias. To complicate matters, post hoc evaluation does not allow collection of pretest data which may serve to explain differences between responders and nonresponders.

Another problem in post hoc follow-up evaluation is that respondents are likely to be interviewed only once rather than at several different times. Consequently, the evaluator has no consistency check on respondents' data, little knowledge of the "decay function" of the treatment's effects, little knowledge of the types of people that become invisible at varying lengths of time after treatment, and less chance to check on bias due to selective location of respondents or selective cooperation from treatment recipients.

A final serious problem is that post hoc follow-up evaluation necessitates asking people to remember what happened to them during a reasonably long time period. People's memories are fallible and obtaining validation from secondary sources may be an extremely expensive and time-consuming process, assuming of course that it could be done at all. To complicate matters, post hoc follow-up evaluation often samples people from a variety of post-treatment time periods, which means that some people have to remember further back than others. This only adds more bias to the list already discussed.

The problem of dropouts, or missing respondents, is not unique to follow-up evaluation and it is a very serious matter whenever it occurs (Baekeland and Lundwall 1975). In post hoc follow-up evaluation, however, a large proportion of the evaluator's resources must be put into the difficult task of locating and interviewing past treatment recipients. Little time or money may be left for the task of collecting supporting data from individual treatment records or from other sources. Consequently, there is likely to be no information that can be used to help understand the data obtained during follow-up, or to place such data in a meaningful perspective. In the absence of data, neither statistical nor intuitive corrections can be applied, and one can only guess at whether missing information is systematically related to how people fared when they were in treatment.

Minimizing Bias in Post Hoc Follow-up Evaluation. Several strategies can be employed to make results from this type of evaluation more valid. In general, the plan must be to minimize the bias that does exist, to estimate the size of the bias that remains, and to determine the characteristics of the population for whom results are most accurate.

As a first step, one might start by limiting a follow-up study to a relatively small well-defined subset of the entire population of interest. Although this would limit generalizability, it would also greatly increase the validity of conclusions drawn from the study. The higher the percentage of nonrespondents in a sample, the greater the probability that data obtained from that sample cannot be trusted. By limiting the population of interest, greater efforts can be put into locating and interviewing one hundred percent of those who were chosen.

There is yet another advantage to limiting participation to as homogeneous a subsample of the population as is practical. The more homogeneous the sample, the lower the chances that within-group variation will wash out otherwise observable patterns. Limiting sample variability may also make dropout bias more consistent. It is certainly reasonable to assume that different populations exhibit somewhat different "dropout dynamics." Thus the greater the heterogeneity of the sample, the more varied the "dropout dynamics" that will be operating to bias the evaluation data.

An intimate understanding of an evaluation situation coupled with a carefully drawn sample, appropriate data, and careful analysis *might* combine to explain how or why a particular group of people cannot be located or interviewed. At least a qualitative guess could be made under these circumstances, and such a guess might go a long way in helping to understand the meaning of evaluation results. If a follow-up study involves many different groups of people who are dropping out for many different reasons, even a qualitative guess is close to impossible.

The foregoing tactics involve a kind of trade of external validity for internal validity. Valid information on a narrow segment of program participants is obtained at the expense of the ability to generalize to wide segments of treatment recipients. The representativeness of a sample is decreased in order to increase the probability of drawing meaningful and accurate conclusions about a highly select group of people. This advice is given because very serious threats to validity exist in post hoc follow-up evaluation. Evaluators run a risk of collecting data that is almost impossible to interpret in a meaningful manner, and good data on a limited population is preferable to poor data on a large population.

Once a sample is drawn, participation may be increased by payment to respondents for their efforts. In a sense, respondents in an evaluation study act in the role of expert consultants without whose knowledge a scientific investigation could not be carried out. They possess unique information and as with all experts, a dollar value can be placed on their knowledge and on their time. The tactic of paying respondents for information is not without its drawbacks. It will not solve the problem of people who simply cannot be located. Further, people who refuse to cooperate until they know they will be paid may bring a very special set of respondents and responses into the data. The percentage of participants may increase, but the bias problem may be made even more complex. Luckily one can perform an analysis that might determine whether or not such biases exist. Data should be analyzed separately for those who agreed to participate before they knew that payment was involved and for the group that did not agree to participate until after they found out about the payment. If the analyses do not yield contradictory information, it is probably safe to lump all data together in order to obtain accurate estimates of program effects.

Quality Control of Data. In a sense, data can be regarded as serving a dual purpose. First, it is needed to answer a question or questions of major interest. Second, it can be used as a quality control on itself. The second use of data involves checks on reliability and validity, the use of particular analyses to look for the occurrence of bias, the performance of secondary analyses which serve to replicate or confirm earlier tests, and the like. Although any research or evaluation study contains these two elements, their proportion changes as a function of the research or evaluation design. If a design is conceptually high on validity and is carried out carefully, information that derives from the study can be trusted. That trust derives not primarily from the data that is obtained, but from the circumstances under which the data were obtained, i.e., from the structure of the research design.

As an example, consider the evaluation of a program which is designed to improve the employment status of semiskilled workers. If such a study had a properly constituted randomized no-treatment control, general fluctuations in the economy would pose no threat to validity. In fact, such a study might not even require collecting data on the general economic state of the country. Although such data would be highly desirable—it could be used to increase the precision of the analysis to further theory on training and unemployment, and to study possible relationships between program success and general economic conditions—if the evaluation lacked a no-treatment group, data on the economic condition of the country would be vital. Without it, there would be no way to tell if observed results were due to the program or to other factors. In the former case, a threat to validity was solved by the logical relation among various groups in the study. In the latter case, the problem had to be solved by means of data collection.

Although one must *always* use data as a check on itself, an overwhelming imperative to do so does not exist if the design is inherently valid, and if the project is carried out according to plan. Such an imperative increases as the inherent validity of the design decreases. In other words, rival alternate hypotheses can be ruled out in one of two ways. One method is through the structure and logic of a research design. A second method is by the collection of data aimed specifically at shedding light on a particular alternate hypothesis. If one does not have a structurally sound design, one must rely on data analysis for checks on validity.

Post hoc follow-up evaluation is inherently a very weak design. As such it must contain a great deal of information that can be applied to the purpose of inspecting for the occurrence of plausible rival hypotheses to any conclusion that the evaluator might wish to draw. Further, the data must be useful as well as bountiful. Although evaluators cannot be omniscient, they can put considerable effort into determining, before a study is begun, exactly what kind of data is most likely to be useful for checking validity. One should know, for instance, that multiple measures of particularly unstable or unreliable variables are needed. The most likely nature of a dropout bias can usually be guessed, and information should be collected which might shed light on whether such a factor is in fact operating. Information will obviously be needed on the validity of questionnaires used with the population being studied, on the consistency of interviewer technique, and other similar factors. None of these suggestions (or any others) can make up for deficiencies in evaluation design, but they can give an evaluator a reasonably strong base from which inferences can be drawn concerning a program or a treatment. (Fortifying a design with supporting data was also recommended in the post hoc client-comparison situation. The major difference here is the primary need for that type of information. The general lesson is that logically weak designs are dependent upon supporting data in order to insure their validity.)

A final consideration is not to collect any more information that is necessary. The most constructive attitude that an evaluator can have is that data is a precious commodity whose collection is expensive, difficult and time-consuming. An attitude of this type will decrease that aspect of the nonresponse problem which is linked to the length of tests and questionnaires, and will also lead to more precisely formulated evaluation objectives. Although such an attitude about data is always desirable, it is particularly important in the case of post hoc follow-up evaluation. Its importance stems from the fact that often in post hoc follow-up evaluation the only source of substantive data comes through the goodwill of people who no longer have any official connection with the treatment which is being evaluated. If people's interest in a program or an evaluation is tenuous, there is no point in allowing excessive demands for information to further lower the supply of available respondents.

Of all the suggestions given so far, none is as powerful as the tactic of planning the study *before* respondents leave the program that is being evaluated. Implicit in such planning is the notion that follow-up evaluation is the method of choice of the evaluator and of other parties who have a say in developing evaluation plans. It is not a matter of casting about for a design that can be imposed after a program has been completed because a need for evaluation has appeared after the fact. The present section was written because hindsight needs for evaluation do occur and evaluators often have to work in such circumstances. Post hoc follow-up evaluation remains, however, an extremely weak method which is recommended only as a last resort. The following section will deal with optimizing the validity of follow-up evaluation that is planned while participants are still receiving a treatment, and chosen as the best method of providing the information which is of greatest interest to program planning.

Preplanned Follow-up Evaluation

In addition to the tactics suggested in the previous section, preplanning a follow-up evaluation allows the evaluator to incorporate several powerful additions to the design which will serve to increase greatly the validity of inferences drawn from data. These design elements fall into two categories: those which will increase the response rate during follow-up, and those which increase the number, type and validity of inferences which can be drawn.

Increasing Response Rate. While people are still receiving treatment, as much information as possible should be collected which might help to locate them during the follow-up period. In addition to standard information such as address, place of employment, phone number and the like, there is a great deal of information which might be useful in locating people. Consider for example, the addresses of family members, driver's license numbers, names and addresses of close friends, and so on. Information that is not collected cannot be used, and the more information one has, the greater the probability that a person will be located.

During the course of treatment participants must be informed that follow-up is an essential ingredient of the program they are in, and that they should expect to be contacted after they leave. The object of such communication is to condition respondents to believe that follow-up is important to the program and that cooperation during follow-up is expected. Although cooperation cannot be enforced by these types of communications, expectations can be set up which may help to increase response during follow-up. Many people when first contacted for follow-up undoubtedly ask: "Why should I give my time to be interviewed?" If these people have not been primed to expect follow-up contact, it is probably rather difficult to explain to them why, indeed, they should cooperate. Such problems might be lessened if the expectation of follow-up, and a sense of the importance and legitimacy of follow-up, has been instilled prior to departure. (The evaluator must wrestle with the question of whether it is ethical to instill such an attitude. One might legitimately reason that participants owe the program help in evaluation, since they benefited from the program's efforts. Unfortunately, the opposite argument can also be made, that follow-up for the sake of evaluation is not part of the treatment process and that treatment recipients do not owe information to evaluators.)

It is important to realize that the response rate problem can be solved. There is empirical evidence which demonstrates that different research tactics evoke different response rates (Astin and Panos 1969; Marcus et al. 1972). Crider, Willits, and Bealer (1971) managed to locate 99.9 percent of a sample by using data that was ten years old. Dropout bias may be detected through comparison of groups who responded only after successively increased research efforts (Eckland 1965). Intensive efforts can be invested in eliciting data from a small random sample of nonresponders. In short, nonresponse problems are not insoluble. They are difficult, time-consuming and expensive. They require careful planning. But they can be solved. (A more extensive presentation of these issues can be found in Morell, in press.)

Another tactic which may help to increase response rate is to begin follow-up a relatively short time after a person has left a treatment. The contact does not have to include long or complex data collection. At early stages, the fact of contact is probably more important than its content. A short time lag between treatment and follow-up will (presumably) serve to maintain a continuity and a sense of involvement on the respondent's part. These feelings might be extremely important in insuring a reliable source of follow-up information. Once people are well into their post-treatment existence, they may not be willing to exert the effort that is required to give accurate information on matters which they may regard as a closed chapter in their lives.

It is also important to remember that it is not necessary to ask for the same information each time a follow-up interview is conducted. Preplanned follow-up studies are likely to include several interviews that are spaced some time apart. It may well be that some variables are expected to change at a different rate than others, and evaluators might capitalize on this fact by not asking the same questions at every interview. As a consequence, the length of sessions might be reduced and the interviews would be less boring. An additional advantage is a lower danger of bias due to reactive measurement, i.e., the effect of answering a question once or answering the same question a second time.

Finally, the large and detailed literature on obtaining information from survey research should be consulted (Backstrom and Hursh 1963; Hyman 1955; Stephan and McCarthy 1958). Insuring an adequate response from a representative sample is the central issue in survey research. Although follow-up evaluation and survey research are not one and the same, both pursuits share the technical problems of obtaining data from individuals who are not formally attached to a particular program or organization. Thus the methodology that makes for good survey research is also likely to make for good follow-up evaluation.

Increasing the Richness of Data. The most crucial advantage of preplanning follow-up evaluation is that it allows one to deal intelligently with bias that may result from refusals to cooperate, or from not being able to locate some portion of the research population. Since problems of this type are inevitable, the evaluator must be able to develop a sense of the magnitude and direction of bias which may be introduced by these factors. As Baekeland and Lundwall (1975) show, there is a well-developed literature on the characteristics of people who tend to drop out of various therapeutic treatments. Although dropping out of treatment is not exactly analogous to refusal to supply research data or being difficult to locate after a treatment is over, it is not unreasonable to assume that there are major similarities in terms of the characteristics of people involved in all three phenomena. Thus the "dropout" literature might serve as an important guide in helping evaluators identify that portion of a treatment population which is most likely to be difficult to locate or interview during follow-up evaluation. By combining what is known about the progress of people during the course of treatment with what is known about the characteristics of dropouts, it might be possible to develop an understanding of the probable post-treatment status of people who for one reason or another could not be included in follow-up evaluation. As an example, Baekeland and Lundwall (1975) concluded that "social isolation" is very likely to be a factor in promoting dropping out of treatment. In many aspects of social service it may also be reasonable to assume that social isolation is a factor in poor prognosis. Thus it might be worthwhile to use available data (such as treatment records) to check on the social isolation characteristics of people who could not be located for follow-up evaluation. If their social isolation seems to be higher than the social isolation of people who were located, we would have reason to believe that our evaluation data is positively biased, i.e., that only the more successful treatment recipients were studied. Thus, the research on treatment dropouts has provided a hint as to what bias may be operating in a particular evaluation study.

Information on nonrespondent characteristics may yield quantitative estimates of the postprogram status of clients who were not interviewed. Such estimates might be based on analyses which derive from other studies that succeeded in obtaining information on the progress of the same types of people who could not be interviewed by the evaluator. As an example, consider the following hypothetical situation. A weight control program is attempting to check on their clients' postprogram reversion to old eating habits. Would it be possible to estimate the weight of clients who did not respond to follow-up inquiries? Perhaps. It is likely that our program is not the only one to have made such attempts, and that data has already been collected on the relation between postprogram weight gain and factors such as age, pretreatment weight, and program attendance. If such studies have been carried out, those already established relationships might be applied to our present case.

It must be clearly understood that attempts of this nature are fraught with peril. In the first place, the fact that information could be obtained for particular individuals is, in and of itself, a strong reason to distrust comparisons between those people and people who could not be located or interviewed. This suspicion is not (or at least should not be) allayed by apparent similarities between the groups on any number of variables, as the regression-artifact problem is always a danger (Crano and Brewer 1973, chap. 3). Second, it is not likely that "appropriate other studies" can be found which make use of all or even most of the information that might be relevant. Third, the value of these statistical techniques is strongly related to the reliability of the measurements involved, and investigators certainly have good reason to distrust the reliability of many of the measures that would undoubtedly be included in analyses of this type. Finally, the program being evaluated may really be different from others with the same objective, and it may not be legitimate to use information from one program to describe another. On the other hand, the technique proposed here is not suggested as a method of generating data concerning the evaluator's *primary* questions of interest. Information on primary issues should come from the interviews and questionnaires that are actually carried out. The "outside data" technique is proposed merely as a method of obtaining some type of reasonable estimate of bias that might be introduced by the nonresponse problem. For such purposes the cautious use of the method advocated here is certainly reasonable.

Knowledge of dropout characteristics and people's reactions to a treatment can also be used strictly on a qualitative or intuitive level. As such, the information would be used to develop an understanding of how recommendations based on follow-up evaluation data should be tempered by the amount of uncertainty generated from possible nonresponse bias. To follow up on the previous example, it may be that although no relevant data has been collected in other weight control programs, clinical experience indicates a relationship between continued weight control and factors such as age or program attendance. Even in the absence of quantitative data, much might be learned from an inspection of the age and attendance records of nonresponders to follow-up requests.

However estimates of nonresponse effects are made, they must be made by people who have an intimate understanding of the evaluation study and of the treatment which is being evaluated. Qualitative understanding is an essential ingredient in even the most rigorous research designs (Campbell 1974). Such understanding is even more important in cases where conclusions must be based on incomplete and imperfect information, because without qualitative understanding it is very difficult to temper research conclusions with a sense of what is reasonable or plausible.

The strategy of starting follow-up relatively soon after people leave a program has implications for the type of inferences that can be drawn from data as well as for increasing response rates. Some respondents will undoubtedly drop out of sight or refuse to cooperate sooner than others. It may well be that people who become nonrespondents soon after they leave are different from those who fail to respond only some time after they have left a program. Differences of this nature may result from pre-entry differences among treatment recipients, from differences in how people were treated during the course of treatment, or from factors that arose after treatment was completed (or of course, from interactions among these factors). In any of these cases, lost data may have different implications depending on when or why the loss occurred. By starting follow-up soon after people leave a treatment the evaluator might be able to check on whether varied loss of response factors are indeed operating, and if so, what they might be. As an example of why such follow-up is important, consider two simplified (although not entirely unlikely) reasons for nonrecovery of follow-up data. In the first case, refusal to provide follow-up data is solely a function of satisfaction with treatment. In the second case refusal to cooperate is a function of both satisfaction with the treatment *and* length of time since treatment was provided. Although both of these situations will result in positively biased data, their implications for understanding a treatment are profoundly different. In the first case, the amount of bias will stay relatively constant. In the second case, the program will tend to look better and better as time goes on, since by the end of the data collection period only the most satisfied treatment recipients will be providing data. The only hope of detecting problems of this nature comes from beginning follow-up as soon as possible after treatment has ended.

A final tactic for increasing the richness of follow-up evaluation data is to split potential respondents randomly into several groups so that each person is not interviewed at every data collection period. This technique will reduce the problem of measurement reactivity, ease the burden on respondents, and yield at least some information on possible interactions between the act of evaluation and the influence of the original treatment.

Summary: Validity Problems in Follow-up Evaluation

Follow-up evaluation is often chosen because the need for evaluation is seen only after a treatment or a program has been in operation for some time. Situations of this nature provide almost insurmountable methodological problems due to biases that are very likely to be operating, but whose effects cannot even be guessed at intelligently. If studies of this type must be done, they should be organized around the general principle of limiting the scope of the study to as narrow and homogeneous a section of respondents as is possible. Such limiting allows maximum resources to be invested in increasing response rates, collecting cross-validating data, and determining (as best as possible under the circumstances) the magnitude and direction on any bias that may be operating. Homogeneous samples also make analysis less complex by cutting down on the number of factors that have to be studied.

If follow-up evaluation is planned before respondents leave a treatment, there is far more opportunity to assure future cooperation of respondents, to collect data that will allow meaningful post-treatment comparisons, and to obtain trustworthy information on inaccuracies and biases that may be operating. These opportunities must be exploited to the fullest by making intelligent decisions concerning the type of information that is most likely to be important and the structure of data collection that will allow powerful checks on measurement reactivity, response bias and factors which effect noncooperation by potential respondents.

VALIDITY ISSUES IN MODALITY TEST EVALUATION

Of all three types of evaluation, modality tests are the most directly concerned with establishing causal links between a program's actions and its impact. If anyone is seriously interested in knowing which elements of a program are effective, to what extent they are effective, or precisely what results ensue from particular aspects of a program, modality test evaluation is unquestionably the method of choice.

Because of the modality test method's emphasis on causal links, traditional discussions of experimental and quasi-experimental design are most appropriate here. These discussions are based on the notion that the validity of a research conclusion is threatened by the presence of plausible alternate hypotheses, and that the strength of a design is determined by the extent to which such hypotheses can be ruled out. The literature on social science methodology is replete with prescriptions for determining the validity (or at least the "validity potential") of an experimental or a quasi-experimental design, and there is no point in repeating them here (Campbell and Stanley 1966; Cook and Campbell 1976).

A crucial problem which has received less than adequate attention is the matter of delineating specific factors which inhibit the implementation of powerful modality test evaluations, and how those problems might be overcome. Although there are numerous discussions of factors which inhibit the conduct of evaluation, there have been few attempts to develop a systematic linkage between the nature of modality test evaluation, the structure of social service, and the types of objections that emanate from various parties to an evaluation endeavor. Without such a perspective it is difficult to foresee the types of problems that are likely to arise and to prepare strategies for dealing with those problems.

The dynamic that causes most of the problems for the implementation of modality test evaluation is based on three related elements. First, the foundation of the problem is that modality test evaluation designs are very susceptible to serious weakening as a consequence of relatively minor tampering with their structure. (One might claim that they are not robust.) The second element is that modality test evaluation is more highly dependent upon close evaluator-staff cooperation than are the other two forms of evaluation. Finally, of all three types of evaluation, modality tests are the most likely to generate resistance by staff who are not directly involved in the design or management of the evaluation. Thus we have delicate evaluation design, a need for close evaluator-service staff cooperation, and a high probability of staff resistance. It is no wonder that one finds few high-quality modality test evaluation studies.

Delicacy of Modality Test Evaluation Designs

Modality test evaluation must give far more serious consideration to the conceptualization of independent variables than do the other two forms of evaluation. This is because modality tests are particularly concerned with questions of causation and in order to draw causal inference, one must have a very clear idea of what possible causal agents are being dealt with. Few people would be satisfied to know that a large, complex and ill-defined treatment program produced a particular effect. Considerations of efficiency and scientific curiosity demand more precise information.

In order to actualize these considerations, one must invoke the standard elements of a powerful research design. These include the carefully controlled administration of specific treatments to specific types of individuals, the construction of at least some type of control or comparison group, elaborate methods of determining who receives treatment and who gives treatment, and the like. Any deviations from these procedures make inferences from data considerably more tenuous, as the validity of the study is very highly dependent on the logical structure of how treatment is provided and data is collected.

As an example, consider a study that I am presently conducting with clients in methadone maintenance programs.[5] The study is a randomized field test of a particular method of teaching interpersonal problem-solving skills (Platt and Spivack 1973). The design involves several methadone clinics, each of which will have three groups: an experimental group which will receive the problem-solving training, a "special attention" group which will receive extra counseling which is not specifically linked to problem solving, and a "regular treatment" group which receives only normal clinic treatment.

If this study is to succeed, many potential problems must be attended to. For example: The experimental group must receive exactly the training developed to increase problem-solving skills. If some other treatment is given, it will be impossible to know if the program we set out to test is or is not working. Thus, we must exert a great deal of control over curriculum, training, and the actual content of each group session. The special attention and regular treatment groups must *not* receive specialized problem-solving training. Otherwise, it will also be impossible to know if any problem-solving gains are worthwhile relative to other activities which people could have engaged in. Thus we must be sure that the experimental treatment is not spontaneously adopted by clinic personnel. Assignment to various groups must be truly random. Otherwise there will be no guarantee that the experimental group did not start out with a better (or worse) prognosis than the other groups. Finally, data on all subjects must be collected at appropriate intervals. Otherwise it would be difficult to check on differences among groups which are tied to rate of change, rather than the absolute amount of change. All four of these problems have an important element in common. They are solved primarily by exerting strenuous efforts to make sure that the logic and the structure of the experiment remain intact. The main problem is not the collection of extra data to rule out threats to validity, but of making sure that the experimental plan is carefully followed.

Dependence on the logical structure of a design is not as crucial with client-comparison or follow-up evaluation because their chief concerns are with the description of dependent variables, i.e., with how people change rather than with the causes of change. Whenever causal analysis is not a major concern, validity tends to become a function of the amount, type, and quality of data collected rather than of the structure of data collection. (This statement is meant to point out differences of emphasis among various types of evaluation and must not be construed as dispensation for sloppy or inadequate data collection.) Client-comparison and follow-up evaluation are essentially descriptive studies and as such, small changes in a data collection plan are not likely to have profound effects on the entire body of conclusions that one might draw, provided that adequate comprehensiveness and redundancy have been built into the data collection scheme. A small change in the design of an experiment or a quasi-experiment, however, may raise a host of plausible alternate hypotheses that cannot be accounted for adequately and greatly weaken attempts at causal explanation. Further, it is not particularly easy to build into an experiment back-up systems which would provide a basis for causal inference when other elements of the experiment fail.

The Importance of Evaluator-Staff Cooperation

Special types of problems are inherent in any situation where the workings of an ongoing social service agency take on the additional role of independent variable in an evaluation research design. These problems stem from competing demands for control of the day-to-day operations of an agency. Administrators need such control in order to insure efficient organizational functioning. Evaluators need control in order to insure the proper conduct of their work. Further, it is by no means likely that these two sets of demands will be consonant. The evaluator's position is made even more difficult because evaluators are not likely to be in authority positions which allow them to influence directly the day-to-day functioning of a service organization's members. A consequence of these two factors is that evaluators can exert little control over the ''independent variables" in their research. In essence, the evaluator is able to implement changes only (or at least mostly) through the cooperation and goodwill of a group of people who are not particularly interested in nor committed to evaluation research.

The true-to-life situation is of course not as simple as just depicted. With the possible exception of the purest of laboratory research, nobody has full control over research design or over the precise makeup of independent variables. A great deal of applied research that is not strictly speaking evaluation is carried out in real world settings, and all these studies must contend with the different needs and interests of all parties involved. In essence, we are speaking of a continuum. At one end is the researcher with control over a budget, a position of "director," and co-workers whose primary interest and allegiance are to the conduct of a particular piece of social research. At the other end is an evaluator whose position is similar to an insignificant appendage on a large complex organization. Our unfortunate evaluator does not have institutionalized power and must rely on the good graces of people whose chief priorities and time commitments are independent of (if not antithetical to) matters concerning modality test evaluation. Most evaluation in social service settings is far closer to the second pole of the continuum than to the first.

Although one can always find exceptions, the evaluator, more than most other researchers, is put in the position of one who must ask favors instead of one who is able to dictate solutions. This situation puts particular importance on the evaluator's ability to teach people about the value of their work, and to persuade people that any deviation from a preset evaluation procedure really will decrease the value of the analysis. The final requirement is particularly difficult. Most social scientists had to go to school for a long time in order to be socialized fully into the "proper" beliefs concerning control groups, random assignment, the consistent application of experimental treatments, the special restrictions imposed by the need for statistical analysis, and the like. There is no reason to assume that others will quickly or easily assimilate these beliefs.

The term "evaluation" implies that research is being conducted on the normal day-to-day actions of an organization rather than on an isolated segment of a program which can be separated from the regular conduct of business. Modality test evaluation is particularly intertwined with "normal business" because of its concern with testing the effects of an agency's programs. We will now turn to an explanation of why precisely at a time when the need for cooperation is greatest, the likelihood of such cooperation is lowest.

Staff Resistance to Modality Test Evaluation[6]

The reasons for evaluator-staff friction can be categorized into five specific types of problems. These problems will be reviewed briefly and possible solutions will be proposed.

Interference in Standard Operating Procedures. Most administrators and service providers in the area of social service lead hectic work lives. Case loads are typically too high, funding is typically too low, reports and forms line up in a never-ending procession, and crises, both large and small, abound. Conscientious evaluators take these problems into consideration and try to make their demands as minimally bothersome as possible. Unfortunately very few research undertakings can be made totally unobtrusive. Some demands for staff time and effort must almost always be made. Service staff are often in a uniquely advantageous position to serve as data collectors and generators. Agency staff provide the service that is acting as the independent variable in the evaluation, and consequently they must often perform special tasks with regard to the type of treatment given, methods of treatment delivery, or the selection of those who receive particular types of treatment. These tasks demand interaction with the evaluator, special efforts during the workday, and more things to do in a fixed amount of time. All too often these tasks are not perceived by agency personnel as a legitimate part of their jobs, and there is almost never any special compensation for the performance of evaluation-oriented tasks. The issue is not whether cooperation with evaluators is a legitimate part of one's job, or whether special compensation should be given for such work. The point is the perception of the already harried worker who is asked (or told) to do even more work.

Evaluation Apprehension. Few people like to be evaluated or tested, and it is reasonable to expect such dislike to extend to participation in program evaluation. The dislike for evaluation, however, goes beyond psychological discomfort that comes from being studied or measured. As a start, it is clear that not all programs are evaluated and there are large differences in the rigor of evaluation for the programs which are evaluated. Political influence plays a part. Powerful well-established programs have too many advocates and supporters to have their effectiveness or founding principals questioned. Controversial programs or social experiments whose advantages are not established, however, are more susceptible to the scrutiny of the evaluator, and perhaps it is just these programs that should be left alone to try new ideas and to find out what works.

Second, there are good reasons to believe that social service organizations cannot live up to their advertised potential. Etzioni (1969) has pointed out that organizations have two sets of legitimate goals. One set involves stated goals of service. A second set includes organizational maintenance. Unfortunately, the latter type of activity is often not recognized by evaluators, who base their work on the implicit assumption that all of an organization's energies are aimed at achieving the goals which are best advertised—those dealing with public service.

Another reason why organizations fall short of their stated goals may be that people who support a program fall into the trap of over-advocacy, a situation where advocacy leads to exaggeration (Campbell 1971). It is easy to see why organizations do not wish to be evaluated on the basis of claims that may have emerged from such a process. Finally, there are arguments to the effect that given the nature of social problems and the political system, social service programs cannot significantly reduce present problems (Rossi 1972; Weiss 1970).

Although these factors may be operative in any evaluation context, the problem is not quite as acute with follow-up or client-comparison evaluation because these approaches do not usually entail a direct test of a particular social program. Modality test evaluation does entail such direct testing and as a result, evokes the full force of the evaluation apprehension dynamic.

Interference in Program Philosophy. Administrators and service providers in social service usually have some degree of freedom to shape a program in the manner which they perceive will do the most good. This freedom is never complete, as a host of political, sociological and economic forces always impact upon decisions concerning treatment tactics and philosophy. These factors notwithstanding, program employees do have some chance to exercise their judgment. Such judgments are often based on deep-seated personal and professional beliefs concerning social service; people justifiably guard whatever little freedom they may have in this matter. Evaluators in modality test situations often find it necessary to make demands for special types of treatment to special categories of people, and for the uniform application of specified treatments. These demands represent yet another infringement on social service workers' freedom to act according to their philosophical beliefs concerning their profession, and it is quite reasonable for such infringement to be resented.

Problems of Goal Definition. One of the first things that an evaluator tries to do is to get program staff to define their goals and objectives, and it is difficult to find an evaluator who has not found this task extremely difficult. Many reasons have been given for this problem, ranging from the difficulty of articulating one's motivations, to evaluation apprehension, to deliberate subterfuge. To complicate matters one might legitimately claim that the reason people have difficulty in articulating the goals of their social service organizations is because social service organizations do *in fact* have diffuse, obscure, and continually shifting goals. (Patton [1978] provides an excellent analysis of this problem.) Each member of an organization is likely to have unique interpretation of the organization's function; there is a continual flux in the needs of those who are served by organizations, and the political climate to which organizations must respond is constantly changing. If there is any truth at all in this argument, it is easy to understand the hesitancy of social service workers when they are asked to concretize goals which are inherently diffuse. At best, the task is extremely difficult and is overlaid by the problems that are imposed by evaluation apprehension. At worst, the task is impossible. The nature of modality test evaluation, however, demands that this task be accomplished. Without doubt, the evaluator and the other parties in an organization will have their difficulties over such matters.

Summary: Blocks to Implementation of Valid Modality Tests. Four factors are operating which tend to generate opposition to modality test evaluation.

These factors are: dislocation caused by the conduct of evaluation; evaluation apprehension; interference by evaluators in a program's treatment philosophy; and, problems inherent in defining program goals. Unfortunately, these factors generate the greatest difficulty at precisely the time evaluators and service agency personnel must work in closest harmony, i.e., when modality test evaluation is being conducted. It is at that time when evaluation designs are most vulnerable to serious damage through small changes, and when agency personnel are most likely to want such changes. Invalid modality test evaluations do not arise primarily through ignorance concerning proper research methods. The literature on evaluation methodology is detailed, comprehensive and insightful. Rather, problems arise because of the difficulty of implementing the powerful evaluation designs whose nature we understand so well.

SUGGESTIONS FOR SUCCESSFUL IMPLEMENTATION OF MODALITY TEST EVALUATION

Three categories of suggestions will be proposed to help the evaluator implement valid modality test evaluation. (Although many of these suggestions will be useful with any type of evaluation, they are particularly important here because of the close evaluator-agency interaction that is necessitated by modality test evaluation.) These suggestions include the evaluator's approach to the task of evaluation, issues related to the planning and content of evaluation, and issues related to the evaluator as an organizational change agent. The following section is not meant to provide detailed step-by-step advice. It is meant to set out the general directions which evaluators must take if they are to implement successfully modality test evaluation.

Approaches to the Evaluation Task

Initial Attitudes Concerning Evaluation. Evaluators are vocal and perceptive in their understanding of factors which inhibit the utilization of evaluation information. Unfortunately this understanding usually manifests itself after evaluation has been carried out and results have been discarded. Evaluators seem to be much better at carrying out a postmortem than they are at avoiding the occurrence of problems.

Part of the difficulty may lie in the fact that evaluators realize the resistance they may run into when proposing an evaluation and consequently are reluctant to put their product in any but the most favorable light. Another way to view the issue is to consider the evaluator as an advocate for the conduct of evaluation. From this perspective, problems are bound to arise because advocacy is very likely to involve inflated or exaggerated claims for the procedures which are being advocated (Campbell 1971). Consequently, evaluators are likely to be viewed as naive by service providers and administrators. These harassed professionals know full well the problems of implementing and carrying out programs. They are too well aware that evaluation information, no matter how valid or relevant, is not likely to be useful to them in their work. Although some evaluation information can be put to good political or practical use, this is not likely to be the case with modality test evaluation. Such information takes a long time to collect and analyze. Further, modality tests are not likely to yield suggestions which can be easily implemented. Thus evaluators who propose modality test evaluation are likely to be perceived by a service agency's personnel as being naive about the true worth of evaluators and evaluation.

The initiation of evaluation is a complex social process in which all parties are involved through a mixture of self-interest, compulsion from various sources, free will and curiosity. The mixture is likely to be such that evaluation is never welcomed wholeheartedly by the service organization in which the evaluation must be carried out. Given this background, the initial attitude of evaluators must be that evaluation will be designed so that information obtained will be as *potentially* useful as possible. The emphasis must be on "potentially useful," because the usefulness of information is influenced by a host of factors which are beyond the evaluator's control and perhaps even beyond the evaluator's knowledge. Evaluations must be designed which, under the most likely conditions, are most likely to be useful. No other promises can be made and no less should be attempted. If evaluators take such an attitude in the initial phases of design it is likely that their credibility will increase and the problem of over-advocacy will be tempered.

In essence, evaluators must take the attitude that evaluation must take place, that at least to some extent an evaluation can be made to fit needs of the organization being evaluated, and that beyond a "theoretical fit" between evaluation emphasis and organizational needs, very little can be promised in the way of utility or relevance. This approach is based on the assumption that in the initial phases of evaluation planning, evaluators exhibit unrealistic perceptions which lower the probability that an organization's staff would be willing to cooperate with complex modality test evaluation plans. A further assumption is that a change in these perceptions will increase the likelihood that modality test evaluation will be carried out.

In line with the reasoning outlined above, one must also consider problems which arise due to the overuse of concepts such as "relevance" and "utility." Relevance is a complex concept that has differential saliency to people with varying perspectives. Many evaluators enter a situation with the conviction that the act of evaluation, by its nature, has value. This attitude can be attributed partially to the general belief we all have in the worth of our actions. Another part of the problem lies in the fact that evaluators may take too undifferentiated a view of the concept of relevance. Evaluators seem to feel that their work will help agencies solve problems, and that as a result, evaluation should be supported. Unfortunately this may not be completely true even in the most favorable circumstances, i.e., when evaluators work "in-house" or are specifically called in by an organization in need of assistance. Organizations are complex entities and it is abundantly clear that not all parties to an evaluation have the same needs and interests. Relevance is dependent on one's time perspective, on one's position within (or without) an organization, and on one's opinions as to what is important, interesting or worthwhile. Many evaluators fail to take these different perspectives into account when they approach an evaluation situation. Consequently they do not anticipate objections to their work that arise from many quarters. They are blinded to the fact that while their evaluation may be relevant to one group, it may be irrelevant or counterproductive to others.

I have already argued that most threats to the validity of modality test evaluation spring from constraints imposed by the people with whom the evaluator must cooperate. In the present case, trouble springs from failure on the part of the evaluator to anticipate objections raised by particular parties to an evaluation. This failure to anticipate springs directly from the evaluator's sense of the relevance of the evaluation, and from the implicit assumption that what is accepted as relevant by some groups will be perceived as relevant by all groups. Not all evaluation is useful, and what is useful to some may be counterproductive to others.

Conflicts that arise from these differences are most likely to manifest themselves when close cooperation between evaluator and social agency is needed, for it is in such cases that evaluators are most visible, most intrusive, and most threatening.

The initial attitudes of evaluators certainly play only a small part in the implementation of evaluation projects. On the other hand, nothing starts without a beginning, and we know how fragile "beginnings" can be.[7] Further, initial attitudes reflect a basic philosophy about evaluation which pervades people's work and which sets a framework for actions and expectations that deeply influence concepts of what evaluation is and the worth of the work that evaluators do.

The Helping Relationship. It is often said that being helped is an active rather than a passive process and that in order to be helped one must cooperate with one's helpers. Many evaluators fail to convey a sense that cooperation from an agency is a legitimate expectation once the potential value of an evaluation is acknowledged by an agency. Cooperation is not to be sought after as a supplicant, but something to be negotiated under the assumption that an initial right for cooperation already exists. Evaluators lose an important advantage if they fail to recognize the force of their requests, or if that force is not allowed to play a part in shaping the evaluator's attitude toward his or her work.

Although there is no specific prescription as to how the right to assistance can be exploited, there are several general principles which can be followed. First, the evaluation must be designed so as to be perceived as worthwhile by at least some of the members of the organization in which the evaluation is to be carried out. Thus the evaluator should formulate questions which are relevant to an organization's members. Once formulated, that relevance must be communicated. Second, the notion of "helping" as a cooperative venture must be made explicit. Obligations of those being helped to cooperate actively with their helpers do indeed exist, but it is not likely that such obligations will be overtly perceived. Evaluators might do well to bring this issue to light at appropriate times and in gentle tones. The argument is likely to carry particular force when dealing with people who are themselves involved in helping professions, and this encompasses a large number of contexts in which evaluators carry out their work.

The Validity of Objections to Extra Work for the Sake of Evaluation. There is no question that modality test evaluation often necessitates extra work for the staff of the organization in which the evaluation is carried out. Although many evaluators recognize this fact, it is quite likely that the objections are not given the attention they deserve. It is as if evaluators do not really believe that minor modifications in an organization's standard operating procedure can be as disruptive as is often claimed. After all, evaluators say, it can't be *that* difficult to administer an extra questionnaire, or to make small changes in an intake interview procedure, or to make a few extra phone calls to clients. Changes in how clients are taken into an organization and allocated to treatments, or in how patient information is recorded shouldn't be such a major burden on people or organizations. These changes do not seem like much to ask and they will greatly increase the validity of an evaluation. Why should people object to such obviously worthwhile changes? It is not unlikely that many evaluators are given to think along these lines.

The problem is that in order to carry out such actions service personnel often have to change their mental set as to how work is to be carried out or what work is to be done. Even if there was no actual extra work involved, changing work patterns involves emotional energy that may be difficult to expend given the harassed and harried work lives of many social service providers. Further, changes in work patterns can be extremely difficult if they have to be integrated into numerous other tasks that must be performed during the course of a day. This is true even when small changes are required. How much more so in the case of large changes? Add to these problems the resentments that often arise when evaluators are perceived as making demands that are not legitimate or as infringing on the prerogatives of service personnel, and the true magnitude of the evaluator's demands begins to be seen.

Evaluators do not perceive their demands as serious intrusions into the psychological, physical and temporal worlds that make up the work lives of social agency personnel. Until those perceptions are changed, evaluators are bound to run into trouble. The demands of evaluators may indeed be legitimate, but even when such legitimacy exists, demands must not be made in a cavalier manner that fails to recognize the impact of those demands on people who must carry them out.

Summary. This section has dealt with three factors concerning the attitudes of evaluators toward their work. These attitudes relate to feelings concerning the value of evaluation; a conception of "helping" as a cooperative process; and an appreciation of difficulties involved in asking people to change their work routine. "Correct" attitudes on all these matters cannot guarantee cooperation. Although it is questionable as to whether they can have any effect at all on the eventual resolution of difficulties, one must not dismiss these considerations as trivial or unimportant. The conduct of evaluation is a process which necessitates close cooperation between many different people in many different roles, all of whom have their own needs and priorities with their attendant attitudes, beliefs and feelings concerning evaluation. People do take attitudes, beliefs and feelings into account when they make decisions, and it is reasonable to assume that these factors play a part in decisions concerning cooperation with evaluators.

Planning and Content of Modality Test Evaluation

If valid modality test evaluation is to take place, evaluation designs must be developed which mesh the objectives of the organization being evaluated with the objectives of the evaluator. The methods by which this can be done cut across the boundaries of any specific evaluation or research methodology, as they deal mostly with what an evaluator decides to study and how those decisions are made.

Determining Evaluation Objectives. Several forms of evaluation have recently been proposed as alternatives to traditional experimental or quasi-experimental designs. An important common theme in these methods is an attempt to make systematic use of informed opinion concerning the value of a particular treatment or organization as an alternative to data that is generated by more traditional research designs. Since all evaluation must start with effective planning, and since planning involves weighing people's subjective opinions, these methods suggest a basis on which the goals and purposes of any evaluation can be specified. Once goals are specified the evaluator can pursue the evaluation of those goals with any appropriate methodology or evaluation technique.

The "adversary model" argues that traditional methods of research cannot deal with the complexities, vagaries and unpredictable forces that are typical of events in most programs which may be in need of evaluation (Levine 1974; Levine, Brown, Fitzgerald, Goplerud, Gordon, Jayne-Lazarus, Rosenberg and Slater 1978). The model further claims that the types of decisions that must be made in evaluation are far more similar to the decisions that are made in the courtroom than those which are made in the scientific laboratory. Another assumption of the model is that judicial techniques of knowledge gathering and decision making have been validated through the historical development of the system. Consequently, the adversary model proposes that the evidence relating to a program's impact should be evaluated in much the same manner as information is weighed in a court of law.

The Decision Theoretic approach as advanced by Edwards, Guttentag and Snapper (1975) suggests a multistage system of setting evaluation objectives and determining whether they have been met. The method involves an elaborate method of scaling input from diverse sources in order to determine goals. It then proposes the use of Bayesian statistics to determine the extent to which goals have been met and to adjust prior opinion about an organization in light of new information.

These methods of evaluation provide detailed methods by which goals can be clarified, specified and evaluated. Other detailed methods of accomplishing similar objectives can be found in the literature which is specifically devoted to the problem of goal formation (Davis 1973). All of these systems provide detailed steps by which goals can be determined. Evaluators might use these methods in their entirety. More likely, evaluators may use these techniques, not as originally intended—to evaluate programs or to set goals—but as methods for determining the content of an evaluation endeavor. What types of people and problems can a treatment reasonably be expected to help? How much help can be expected? What information is most important in explaining what an organization does or does not accomplish? These and many similar questions must be decided during the planning stages of an evaluation. They are issues which intimately relate to the value of the evaluation, the effect of the evaluation on an organization's credibility, and the amount of work that program personnel will have to carry out once the evaluation is implemented. Given such a profound importance of evaluation planning, the evaluator would do well to look toward systematic methods of integrating and weighing diverse opinion. Such methods could be immensely beneficial in designing an evaluation which will have the greatest value to the largest number of interests. Without such attempts, there is little chance of implementing an intrusive, highly visible and disruptive modality test evaluation.

The suggestion of admitting all relevant opinion does not imply that an evaluator should merely do what he or she is told to do by members of the organization which is being evaluated. Evaluators are responsible for their work and they must do what, in their expert opinion, they consider right. Further, there are other parties to an evaluation besides the evaluator and the object of the evaluation. As an example, funding agencies may dictate the reason for an evaluation, the content of the evaluation and perhaps, the methodology of the evaluation. These factors notwithstanding, good evaluation practice necessitates the use of the informed opinion of others. The systematic and careful use of that opinion will not only increase the strength of an evaluation design but it will also increase the likelihood that the design will be implemented.

Evaluation as an Information-Generating Mechanism. Inherent in any well-planned modality test evaluation is the capacity to generate large amounts of detailed information. An organization may be in need of specialized information which it cannot collect due to deficiencies in resources, expertise or personnel. Evaluators might be able to trade some of their data collection ability for cooperation in the implementation of modality test evaluation. The data collected under such circumstances would not have to be directly related to the evaluation project in question. It would have to be of direct relevance to the organization and unobtainable by them through any other means.

Multiple Measures of Success. This suggestion involves a method of preserving the scientific integrity of an evaluation and still greatly increasing the probability that an evaluation will give an agency some positive results to advertise to the outside world. The method makes use of multiple measures of success in three ways. First, the "strength" of a treatment can be measured in temporal terms. How long do desired effects last? Second, effect strength can be measured in conceptual terms, i.e., one can search for intermediate steps leading to a desired change. As an example, programs designed to increase student performance may include measures of success motivation, study habits, and classroom behavior. Finally, outcomes might be investigated which may be desirable even if not related to a program's primary purpose. To extend the previous example, the evaluator might measure affective components of an educational program which is primarily aimed at increasing student performance on cognitive tasks. All of these measures share an important element. They are likely to show some positive effects of a program without hiding any of a program's basic faults. Early gains may attenuate, but those early gains are documented. Increases in student performance may be minimal, but improved study habits and self-image are still worthwhile achievements.

This technique is scientifically defensible because evaluators have a legitimate interest in the "power" of treatments. There is wide variability in the ease with which various desirable outcomes can be brought about, and it is reasonable for the evaluator to seek information on the ability of a program to effect those outcomes. An important extra benefit of conceptualizing evaluation this way is that the program under study has a high probability of being able to claim attainment of at least some positive goals.

The Evaluator as Change Agent

The problem of instituting evaluations in organizations is only a subset of the general topic of bringing about change in ongoing organizations. There is an extensive literature on that subject, and the lessons learned from the study of organizational change might be applied to good effect by evaluators. There are methods of using knowledge and expertise in order to gain influence in an organization. There are models for analyzing organizations and determining the most effective tactics for instituting change. Techniques are available for discovering where institutional power lies, how it can be obtained, and how it can be used. There are methods to gain allies and to defuse opposition. In sum, there is an extensive literature on the problem of how to bring about change from a variety of positions within and outside organizations. (Excellent sources for this literature can be found in Bennis, Benne, Chin, and Corey 1976; Benveniste 1972; Fairweather, Sanders, and Tornatzky 1974; and Lippitt, Watson, and Westley 1958.) Modality test evaluators, like it or not, are often in the position of having to bring about organizational change. The implementation of modality tests often necessitates changes in organizations, and it is not reasonable to assume that all sectors of an organization will graciously support those changes. Many changes are threatening (legitimately so), and evaluators must face that reality. If an evaluator is convinced that a modality test is necessary and worthwhile, he or she must be willing to pursue actively those activities which will allow the evaluation to take place.

Summary: Implementation of Valid Modality Tests

Valid modality test evaluation depends on the successful implementation of well-thought-out evaluation plans. Major factors which inhibit the implementation of such evaluation involve the attitudes of evaluators towards their work, failure to include the opinions of all relevant parties in determining evaluation objectives, difficulties in identifying relevant questions, lack of equity in the use of evaluation resources, failure to negotiate properly the terms under which evaluation will be carried out, and failure to use change agent techniques to insure evaluation implementation.

Even if all the necessary conditions are met, successful implementation of evaluation cannot be guaranteed. An evaluation endeavor involves a complex interplay among many different groups, numerous individuals and various formal organizations. The flow of power, influence and personal needs are so complex that precise prescriptions for success are impossible. Still, general principles can be discerned which, if followed, will increase the chances of success.

CHAPTER SUMMARY

"Validity" is the second element of the "type-validity-usefulness" typology which makes up the central thesis of this book. Since each of the three types of evaluation (client-comparison, follow-up and modality test) are designed to answer primarily different questions, it is not legitimate to compare the validity of one type against that of another. Although one might well be able to make such comparisons on a general scale of validity in social science research, it avails us nothing to make such an attempt. In fact, such an attempt would be counterproductive since it would blind us to the notion that at times one type of evaluation is more appropriate than another to answer a particular question of interest. Thus evaluators must look at each type of evaluation as unique. They must try to maximize the validity of each type within whatever limits of validity exist in a particular situation. The present chapter has been one attempt at this goal. (Table 3.1 summarizes the major concerns about validity which characterize each type of evaluation.)

Table 3.1 Summary of Major Validity Concerns
in Each Type of Evaluation*

Client Comparison	Follow-up	Modality Test
Use of psychological variables to predict behavior	Bias due to systematic failure to locate respondents	Vulnerability of designs to small changes
Specification of criteria for success in treatment	Bias due to systematic failure to obtain information from respondents	Resistance to the implementation of evaluation:
Comparison of success and failure patterns for people in and out of treatment	Fallibility of people's memories of past events	1. Interference in standard procedures
	Appropriate use of data as a quality check on itself	2. Evaluation apprehension
Post hoc reconstruction of pretreatment data		3. Interference in program treatment philosophy
Choice of secondary studies for the purposes of validation		4. Problems of defining goals
		Rival hypotheses to causal inference
Problems of use of pre-existing records for evaluation data		

*As has been emphasized in the text, the topics listed in each category reflect theme and emphasis, and are meant to convey a sense of general directions for developing valid evaluation. They are not meant to be mutually exclusive. The fact that a topic is mentioned in one category does not necessarily imply that it can be disregarded when other forms of evaluation are being planned.

Although one cannot specify a particular "minimum acceptable standard of validity," there are principles which will help evaluators establish standards. These standards emerge from the identification of potential threats to validity in a proposed study, personal values concerning the use and importance of evaluation, and consideration of the professional climate of opinion in which the evaluator is working.

Client-comparison evaluation cannot be viewed as a quick and easy method which can be employed whenever an evaluation is needed but adequate plans have not been laid in advance. Pretreatment information is important, as are sources of cross-validation for as much information as possible. The problem of meaningful definitions of success and failure is crucial to any attempt at categorizing people according to treatment outcome, and adequate thought must be given to defining these concepts. These conditions are not easy to meet in an adequate manner. Consequently, client-comparison evaluation should be employed only if it is the method of choice to answer the evaluation questions which are of greatest importance.

The most serious problem with follow-up evaluation is bias that may be introduced as a result of losing respondents. In order to minimize such bias, evaluators should restrict their evaluation to as homogeneous a sample as is practical, condition treatment recipients to expect to participate in follow-up evaluation, obtain data which might allow an estimation of the type and size of bias that may be operating, and collect data in a manner which imposes as little as possible on those who must be interviewed.

Of all three methods of evaluation, modality tests most closely approximate classical experiments and quasi-experiments. Since adequate methodological discussions already exist as to how such research should be conducted, the present chapter dealt with threats to validity which arise as a result of failure to properly implement evaluation plans. It was assumed that far more knowledge exists on the subject of planning valid studies than on the implementation of those plans. Further, poor implementation can have particularly serious consequences for modality test designs. While the other types of evaluation rely primarily on data analysis to rule out plausible rival hypotheses, the validity of modality tests is most dependent upon the logical structure of their designs. That structure is easily flawed if evaluation implementation plans go awry.

Four factors were identified which generate opposition to evaluation on the part of personnel in organizations where evaluation might take place. These factors are: resentment of interference in standard organizational procedure, evaluation apprehension, interference in treatment philosophy, and problems of defining goals in social service. It was suggested that if these problems were to be overcome, evaluators would have to operate on three levels: their attitudes concerning evaluation, techniques of planning the content of evaluation studies, and the use of organizational change agent techniques to implement evaluation studies.

NOTES

[1]One might argue that social programs should be forced to allow modality evaluation to take place. Arguments for this point of view might be based on the need to increase the quality of social and human service, the need to solve social problems, and ethical issues relating to the use of public funds. Although these arguments might carry a good deal of force, the inherent value of varied

approaches to evaluation cannot be denied, nor can one ignore organizational or procedural realities which influence the conduct of evaluation.

[2]The value-loaded nature of research is a complex topic which has been studied from a variety of perspectives. For those interested in precisely how an investigator's values affect the conduct of research, the following sources are recommended: Allen 1976; Argyris 1975; Beit-Halahmi 1974; Harré and Secord 1973; Kaplan 1964, chap. 10; Lakatos and Musgrave 1972; Weiss 1975. Allen deals specifically with the problem of ethics in evaluation, and consequently touches on the matter of how the implications of evaluation information might be influenced by the evaluator's unique approach to an evaluation problem. Argyris; and Harré and Secord deal with how basic theoretical perspectives of social psychologists have a profound influence on the type of research that is conducted and consequently, on what is discovered. Beit-Halahmi speaks from the point of view of a clinical psychologist and discusses how particular levels of analysis and conceptual frameworks reflect political values, and how those biases might work to support a particular social system. Kaplan presents a philosophy of science analysis of how personal values operate to influence the conduct of social science. The Lakatos and Musgrave volume presents various analyses of Kuhn's (1971) theory of scientific revolutions. The relationship between questions asked, information discovered and implications for further research plays a central part in these arguments. Although the problem is not directly related to the social consequences of evaluation, it does convey an excellent understanding of how basic orientations to a particular research problem affect investigations of that problem. Weiss presents an analysis of how political factors affect the conduct of evaluation and how those who perform evaluation are, of necessity, part of that political system.

[3]The case as presented here is quite obviously overstated since most evaluation will have the same fate as the vast majority of other scientific and technological investigation. It will be put on a shelf to gather dust and to be read by the occasional student working on a thesis. On the other hand, social programs *are* part of a sociopolitical process, the possible use of evaluation as outlined here *is* a distinct possibility, and evaluators must act on the assumption that their information will be used as part of that process.

[4]A far more detailed explanation of follow-up research as an evaluation strategy can be found in Morell, in press b.

[5]This research is being carried out with the assistance of a grant from the National Institute of Drug Abuse (Grant#1R01 OAO1929-01). Principle investigators are Eugenie W. Flaherty, Jonathan A. Morell, and Jerome J. Platt.

[6]The following section is abstracted from Chapter 6 of this book, which deals in detail with the dynamics of conflict between evaluators and those who operate or plan social service programs. Only those issues most pertinent to modality test evaluation are presented here.

[7]Many thanks to Frank Herbert who put a statement to this effect into the mouth of one of the characters in his science-fiction tale, *Dune*.

4

Usefulness of Evaluation

INTRODUCTION

This chapter will set out a conceptual structure designed to help evaluators determine the usefulness of any particular evaluation plan. First, the nature of a "usefulness continuum" will be outlined and the different types of usefulness will be defined. Methods of determining the usefulness of different types of evaluation will then be detailed.

There is a large body of literature on the subject of "research utilization" (National Institute of Mental Health 1973, vols. 1, 2). For the most part this literature consists of sociological and psychological treatments of various aspects of the question: What factors determine the extent to which results of a research study will be attended to and utilized by decision makers? Typically these studies focus on one or more of three categories of variables which influence utilization: the subject matter of the study, the organizational context in which utilization is attempted, and the psychological factors which determine the perceptions and actions of decision makers. The research utilization literature does not address questions relating to the theoretically maximum utility that can be gained from a study, given the best of all implementation situations. That quantity is a function of the design of an evaluation plan rather than of the sociology or psychology of the research situation. Since the matter of the psychology and sociology of research has already received extensive coverage, and since the emphasis of this book is on the design of evaluation, the present chapter will concentrate on how to develop evaluation plans which, if implemented properly, will yield the most useful possible information.

THE USEFULNESS CONTINUUM

There are four different uses to which evaluation results can be put. First, evaluation can be used to establish realistic expectations for what a program can and cannot accomplish. A great many social service programs are established out of value-based beliefs concerning how particular types of action can accomplish needed and hitherto unattained objectives. The Synanon method of drug abuse rehabilitation is an excellent example. The move to less traditional modes of education during the 1960s is another, and the claimed advantages of the community mental health movement is a third. It is quite likely that some advantages flow from such innovations, but it is equally likely that advantages are not all that are claimed, and that unintended negative consequences also ensue from such action. (In this regard Campbell's [1971] thesis that any advocacy necessarily involves exaggerated and inflated claims is highly instructive.) Thus, one use of evaluation is as a method of determining the advantages and disadvantages which can be realistically expected from a social innovation.

Second, evaluation information can be used by a program's employees to improve service rendered. If evaluation is to be used in this manner, the evaluation design must investigate elements which are under the control of the program's personnel. An out-patient psychiatric clinic, for example, cannot influence general community events that may affect the severity of mental disorders. Similarly, a school system does not have very much control over those learning factors which are a function of parent-child interactions.

The third use of evaluation is to aid in long-range planning. In this case, the information is likely to be used by higher-level policy planners who are in a position to make (or dictate) fundamental changes in the way that a particular social service is carried out.

Finally, evaluation information can be used for the political purpose of attacking or defending a program. Although the political use of evaluation stems from a complex process which is largely beyond an evaluator's control, it is reasonable to assume that the design and subject matter of an evaluation can in fact influence the way in which evaluation will be assimilated into the political process.[1]

Given these varied purposes for evaluation, one element of the usefulness continuum is the number of different uses that any given evaluation can serve. Although the relationship between amount of usefulness and number of purposes served might not be clearly discernable, it does seem safe to claim that usefulness increases with the number of purposes served by any single evaluation study. Another element of the usefulness criterion is the extent to which a particular evaluation can actually help with a given aspect of usefulness. As will be seen, this quantity depends largely on basic decisions about the conduct of evaluation, and is determined by factors such as the clarity of results, the amount of information conveyed, and other similar factors.

USEFULNESS OF CLIENT-COMPARISON EVALUATION

Realistic Expectations

The ability of client-comparison evaluation to help with the problem of setting expectations stems from its potential as a method of screening clients prior to treatment. Screening may convey a sense of who will succeed to what degree, and thus helps keep expectations for program success within the bounds of reason. Several conditions must obtain if maximum utility is to be gained from an evaluation used in this manner. First, the variables on which people are differentiated must have predictive validity. There is no reason to assume that a variable which is an accurate post-treatment differentiator of successful and unsuccessful clients will necessarily predict prior to treatment how people will fare. If a measure does not have predictive validity it can be of only limited use to administrators or service delivery personnel.

Second, variables must be in a form which allows data collection by personnel who are not primarily researchers. Evaluators have specialized skills and resources which allow them to collect and interpret data which are not normally available to service programs. Evaluations which deal primarily with such esoteric information are sure to generate information that cannot be made part of the daily workings of most social service organizations.

Third, the characteristics in question must be accurately measured before a person enters treatment. Practical considerations of time, work force or resources may make it impossible to obtain certain types of information during an intake process or very early in the course of a treatment. Examples of measurements that exhibit such difficulties include those which necessitate detailed observation, the administration of complicated tests, a search of diverse existing records, or interviews with third parties. No matter how much predictive ability such measures may have they will be of only marginal utility to social service organizations that do not have the resources to collect the information. The issue is practical: Can we predict, and are the tools of prediction accessible to nonexperts?

The evaluator is charged with furnishing social service programs with methods by which they can screen potentially successful clients from those who are not likely to benefit from a treatment. In order to accomplish that task the evaluator must employ as many variables as possible which meet the three requirements set forth above. The reason for using the greatest possible number of measures is to increase the accuracy of prediction as much as possible. Unfortunately a basic conflict is inherent in this type of evaluation situation. Careful measurement of a large number of characteristics is necessary to insure accurate prediction, but such measurement will also increase the work load of already overworked service providers and administrators, and as the work load increases the potential utility of the prediction system decreases. That is why the condition of easy use by nonexperts is so important. The development of methods of prediction can only be accomplished by a comprehensive client-comparison evaluation carried out by evaluators who are specifically funded to mobilize the necessary resources and to perform appropriate analyses. Although the development of methods of prediction is a complex evaluation task, the evaluator's job is to present a simple finished product which can be used by people who are not social scientists. Attaining such a goal is almost surely impossible, as evaluation is a complex task which does take specialized skills and abilities. Evaluation cannot be completely "given away." But planning client-comparison evaluation with an eye toward easy implementation by nonevaluators is apt to produce studies which are most likely to be helpful to the personnel of social service organizations.

Improved Service

Improving the quality of service by means of client-comparison evaluation involves considerably more than constructing an effective screen which will keep potentially unsuccessful clients out of treatment. Crucial to the improvement of service is the differentiation of clients on the basis of variables which influence success and which are also under the (at least partial) control of the organization which is providing service. Unlike the screening situation, the requisite information does not necessarily have to be available prior to treatment since it is the process of treatment that is under consideration rather than pretreatment decisions. Thus the emphasis shifts from the time of availability of the information to the amount of control which can be exercised over a treatment factor.

There is still another important conceptual difference between comparison for the sake of improving service and comparison for the sake of screening. When one is interested in screening there is no need to seek data on individuals who are not actually serviced. When attempting to improve service, however, it becomes very important to investigate the problem of individuals who should be treated by an organization but who never reach the "boundary of action" of the organization in question. Part of planning involves the determination of appropriate target populations, and it is important to determine the correspondence between those actually treated and the intended recipients of treatment.[2] Client-comparison evaluation for the sake of improved services must deal not only with the differences between successful and unsuccessful cases but also with differences between "cases" that never were and cases that actually did materialize.

Clearly the collection of this type of information involves special difficulties.

The evaluator must be able to determine the location of those who should be receiving service but are not. Once unserviced groups are found, methods of data collection must be devised. Such methods usually involve some type of outreach effort, and outreach efforts by their nature are labor intensive and difficult, as respondents must be dealt with who are unlikely to be interested in the research. The evaluation endeavor is further complicated because it is not likely that an evaluator will find agreement concerning the legitimate boundaries of the client population of any given organization or service. Funders, administrators, service providers, and the general public are likely to have very different opinions about who should receive a given treatment or service. The evaluator must cull from conflicting opinions a definition of the population to be studied, determine the variables that are likely to shed light on the problem of nonattendance, and collect the data from people who are probably not particularly interested in helping with the evaluation effort.

In sum, client-comparison evaluation can be useful either in its ability to increase a program's effect on those who receive service but do not benefit from it, or by attempting to determine why people who should be receiving service are in fact not receiving service. In both cases the design and the approach of the evaluation must differ from a study whose purpose is to determine, before entry into treatment, who is most likely to benefit from a service. The prime objective of a screening evaluation is to determine a combination of variables which will optimize success in prediction of treatment outcome and which will minimize the work load on service staff who must collect data. A second consideration is that data must be available prior to a person's entry into a program, or very early in the course of treatment. Client-comparison evaluation for the sake of improving service quality has a different set of constraints. In such cases the prime requisites are to collect data on variables that not only differentiate successful from unsuccessful clients, but which can also be manipulated by the organization which is providing the service. In addition, the evaluation must deal successfully with all the problems associated with determining which populations an organization should be treating, discovering the correspondence between populations who should be treated and populations who are actually treated, and measuring variables which may shed light on ways to bring the two into correspondence.

Long-Range Planning

Goals for social programs emerge from a perceived need, and it is not enough to temper those goals with a sense of what can actually be accomplished and then to let the matter rest. Although it is unlikely that goals which have emerged through a political process will ever be fully met, it is reasonable to try to extend achievements beyond the boundaries of what is immediately possible. Evaluation can be an invaluable tool in helping with such efforts. The place of evaluation in these efforts is different from its place in assisting with the development of realistic expectations or its role in improving service over a short term. In the former two cases primary consumers of evaluation information are those who are directly responsible for service delivery. It is they who are most likely to be able to act on matters regarding the screening of potentially successful and unsuccessful clients, or the changing of day-to-day program functioning to improve the quality of service. When long-range planning is involved, the input (and perhaps the impetus) of outside forces and agencies is needed. In any social service context, factors which affect outcome are likely to fall into three general categories: those that can be manipulated by the program itself; those which are not open to change or influence; and those which might perhaps be influenced given a sufficiently large investment of time and effort in the right areas. The third category of factors cannot be influenced by an established program because when programs are set up they are given a fixed amount of resources, an established mandate, and a well-defined sphere of action. Although it is assumed that these will be sufficient to solve the problem at hand, truly effective solutions often lie beyond the scope of the resources, mandates and spheres of action as originally determined. Because individual programs do not have substantial influence over those factors which might be most crucial in bringing about needed change, the primary consumers of evaluation information concerning long-range change must be those policy makers who are not involved in the day-to-day administration of programs, but who are able to introduce basic modifications into organizations and programs.

Political and social realities are such that service agencies have relatively little latitude in determining the makeup of their clientele. Take for example community mental health centers which are influenced by community boards, the National Institute of Mental Health, state and local governments, third party payers, and the policy of Congress as determined by a legislature which responds to innumerable forces. Each of these groups has some influence over who will be served by mental health centers, and each will be swayed by different types of arguments. Thus client-comparison evaluation must choose differentiator variables which will be especially meaningful to particular organizations or groups. While community boards might be most interested in variables which relate to community adjustment and levels of functioning, the National Institute of Mental Health may be interested in long-range efforts at reducing the incidence of psychopathology. Third parties involved in subsidizing the cost of treatment may be most concerned with still another set of factors—those which influence the cost of treatment. Thus, maximum benefits are gained when client-comparison evaluation is carried out as a systematic search for particular differentiators which are most likely to be of interest to well-defined influential groups. Although such an effort might not (and should not) consume all the resources of an evaluation plan, maximum policy setting utility will be gained when client-comparison evaluation plans contain at least some systematic efforts at satisfying well-identified groups and interests.

POLITICAL USES: GENERAL INTRODUCTION[3]

Assuming that a program does indeed have some merit even if it does not meet its intended goals, those who have vested interests in the program are faced with the problem of defending their work against the inevitable attacks of failure that will be leveled against it. To a large extent the outcome of such struggles will depend on public opinion, political influence, the state of social service funding, and numerous other factors which have nothing to do with evaluation. But it is also true that information derived from evaluation can be put to use as part of the armament which is used in the defense of a program. Further, each of the types of evaluation which are presented in this book have different contributions to make to this effort. The aim of these sections on "political usefulness" will be to show what each of these contributions are, and to point out the special elements that must be built into evaluation design if these contributions are to be made in the most powerful manner possible.

In a great many cases, attacks against a program or an organization take the form of arguments to the effect that the organization or program is falling short of its mandated goals. Usually these arguments claim either that the appropriate populations are not being served or that only part of the target population is being reached, and that a large percentage of those who are being served are being served poorly.

In almost all these cases there is unquestionably some validity to the criticism. It would be foolish for advocates of a program to advance claims that such criticisms are invalid. Good evaluation, however, can be used as part of an intelligent defense of the program. The tactic involved in such arguments is to acknowledge that part of the attack is correct but argue that the program still has some value and that the existing program can do a better job than alternatives which might be proposed.[4] Although evaluation information cannot supply all the necessary elements of such a defense, it can generate a sound basis for that part of the argument which rests on pointing out benefits which have ensued. Each type of evaluation supplies a different aspect of this type of information, and special elements must be built into each type of evaluation if it is to be maximally useful for generating that information.

Political Uses: Client-Comparison Evaluation

Client-comparison evaluation allows a program or organization to identify those elements of the population who do indeed show improvement as they move through some particular procedure or operation. Thus client-comparison evaluation will allow a program's proponents to acknowledge that all may not be as successful as it should be, while at the same time making it clear that some specific worthwhile change is in fact taking place. As a consequence of such information, any indictment of the program must be recast as an analysis of why only partial success has been attained, and global condemnations are de-escalated to discussions of specifics.

There is, of course, no guarantee that a program will succeed even to a limited and partial extent, and it is entirely possible that evaluation will do nothing more than confirm such a state of affairs. This is by no means an undesirable set of findings because programs may indeed be lacking, and discovery of their failings is an entirely legitimate function of evaluation. On the other hand, dedicated planners do need help in intelligently defending programs which are, in their best professional judgment, important and worthwhile. That too is a legitimate function of evaluation.

As a first step the evaluation must be designed to collect information on as many different categories of people as is practical. The finer the categories, the greater the chances of detecting unique effects on small subsections of the treated population. An important consequence of this tactic is that information must be collected which allows the necessary categorizations to be drawn. Much of this information may relate to the pretreatment status of treatment recipients and might be unobtainable after a person has entered a program or a treatment. Thus anticipation and prior knowledge of meaningful categories of treatment recipients becomes a vital first step. As this type of knowledge decreases, so does the probability of obtaining evaluation results which might be used in defense of a program.

A second important step in maximizing the political usefulness of client-comparison evaluation is to choose multiple change measures which exist at different levels of analysis. These should ideally include psychological measures, behavioral change measures and demographic or sociological change measures. Further, it would be advantageous to collect such information not only for an individual who is being treated but also for significant others in the lives of those who are being acted upon by a program. The use of different types of variables is based on a concept that has already been introduced; namely, that any given program may be effective in one category of measurement but not in others. By increasing the categories of measurement it is possible to increase the probability that some type of positive effects will be detected. The suggestion of collecting data on significant others is introduced in the same vein. It is entirely likely that impacting the life of an individual will result in worthwhile changes in the lives of others, and, in terms of defending the value of a program, knowledge of such efforts might be extremely useful.

A final consideration in maximizing the political usefulness of client-comparison evaluation is the use of previously obtained information to shed light on those populations most likely to be positively affected. As an example, consider the "social isolation" case cited in the chapter on validity. Clum (1975) found that hospitalized psychiatric patients who were married had a better prognosis than those who were not married. Knowing this, evaluators working in mental health settings might do well to consider a marriage variable when searching for distinct groups of clients who improved during treatment. Another example can be found in the evaluation of work incentive programs. Goodwin and Tu (1975) have concluded that although there is a continual fluctuation of people above and below the poverty line, low income families headed by black females are particularly prone to stay within poverty levels. Thus, evaluators in work incentive and similar programs would be well advised to analyze data for such groups separately. If data were combined, the picture to emerge would be one of decreased program effectiveness. Here too, client comparison information provides a sense of how data should be analyzed if program success is to be highlighted.

The presentation of such evidence will give a program's detractors further pause for thought and will inhibit the extent to which blanket condemnations can be leveled. Further, it is more difficult to criticize when one must accompany the criticism with an explanation which must be more powerful and acceptable than one which has already been advanced. A program that engages in this tactic will be able to claim that it is doing the best job that can be expected under the circumstances, that it is indeed accomplishing part of its objectives, and that the reason for its limited success lies with factors beyond its control.

In sum, maximum political utility from client comparison evaluation will be obtained under two conditions. First, as many different meaningful categories of success as practical must be developed. Once the dimensions of "client type," "multiple measures of outcome" and "effect on significant others" are taken into account, there is an enormous opportunity to detect worthwhile change. Second, categories must be developed which allow evaluation results to be tied into already existing theories of change. An important consequence of an evaluation conducted along these lines is that a program's critics will tend to be turned away from global attacks and into precise criticisms of specific treatment dynamics. Such criticisms are likely to be far less devastating or bitter than generalized critiques of entire programs.

USEFULNESS OF FOLLOW-UP STUDIES

The most important use of follow-up evaluation involves the study of how the effect of a given treatment or program changes over time. Numerous factors are constantly influencing the life of any individual and it is most unlikely that those factors will leave a person exactly as he or she was at the time when a treatment was terminated. Thus the importance of follow-up evaluation lies in its ability to assess a program's effect within the context of a person's continuing life experiences. Further, follow-up evaluation can help assess the complex relationship which exists between a treatment and a person's life experiences. Two issues are important here. First, social service attempts to bring about long-lasting changes in people's lives. Thus, the best follow-up evaluations are those which are specifically designed to explain program effects within the context of complex life-style factors.

Second, another important function of follow-up evaluation is to obtain information on the formation, persistence and extent or unintended consequences (both positive and negative) of attempts at change. Here too, special elements of design must be built into an evaluation if the nature of these unintended consequences is to be understood.

Realistic Expectations

Follow-up evaluation can be useful in determining three different (but almost certainly related) categories of realistic expectations concerning the effects of a program or a treatment. First, evaluation can determine the extent of attenuation or snowballing of treatment effects over time. What is the rate of change? Are there any sharp jumps in the amount of change, and if so, when do they occur? Second, one can investigate the occurrence of unanticipated consequences of a treatment. Given the complexity of social service programs of all kinds, and given the numerous unforeseen factors which arise to influence a person's life, unforeseen consequences of social service action are quite likely. If one is really interested in understanding the value of a social service program, information on such unintended consequences must be taken into account.

The determination of change of effect rates and of the occurrence of unanticipated consequences do not necessarily involve understanding the dynamic by which observed changes take place. They are in a sense "parameter estimation" studies whose value lies in the measurement of states of nature, without any particular emphasis on why or how those states came into being.

Third, it is important to understand how or why observed long-term changes take place. A full understanding of post-treatment change involves not only a realistic sense of what will happen, but also a realistic sense of the dynamic by which those events occur.

A crucial common element in all three aspects of using follow-up evaluation for developing realistic expectations is that the object of the investigation is understanding the behavior of individuals in complex social settings. The evaluator is not interested specifically in the effect of a particular treatment or action, but rather in the interplay between that action or treatment and the post-treatment day-to-day behavior of treatment recipients. Consequently, maximum utility can be gained from follow-up evaluation *only* when a variety of techniques are brought to bear which are specifically designed to analyze complex, uncontrolled social behavior. Even if the original treatment was carried out under rigorous experimental conditions, the follow-up participants in the study must employ these "real world" analytic techniques. Otherwise the dynamic of post-treatment change will be understood only in a very partial manner. Although the original experimental design may give the evaluator excellent information on the lasting power of a specific treatment or the effects of several well defined variables, it is not sufficient to supply information on the complex process of post-treatment change on the effects of unintended consequences, and on the amount and types of changes that take place on numerous factors that were not of primary interest in the original experimental design.

One appropriate methodology has already been introduced—Levine's (1974) adversary model, a system which identifies relevant information and processes it according to the logic by which information is processed in judicial settings. (Further details can be found in the preceding chapter.) Another promising approach involves the applications of social, anthropological and ethological methods to the conduct of evaluation (Parlett and Hamilton 1976). A third useful methodology makes use of the social ecology approach as manifest in many studies in community psychology (Lehmann 1975). (Social ecology studies are based on the tenet that behavior must be studied in its social context and that psychological issues can indeed be explored in this manner.) Finally one may take a sociological approach to the analysis of social settings (Lofland 1971). Sociologists have long been involved with the precise analysis of behavior which occurs in naturalistic settings, and evaluators might do well to learn from their experiences.

While any evaluation might benefit from these specialized techniques, they are particularly vital to the study of complex naturalistic behavior, and such behavior is the chief concern of follow-up evaluation. Hence the introduction of these methods here, for without an emphasis on interactions between treatment effects and natural life conditions, follow-up evaluation loses its unique advantage and its unique perspective.

Improved Service

It is to a program's considerable advantage if any changes it institutes are aimed at bringing about the greatest amount of positive change that can be had for a given set of resources.[5] Follow-up evaluation can make a particularly important contribution to this goal because only with follow-up evaluation can one get an accurate estimate of the total effect that a treatment has over relatively long periods of time, and such estimates are vital in making decisions about the worth of a treatment.

Thus follow-up evaluation will be optimally useful for improving service if it meets two conditions. First, as in the case of client-comparison evaluation, the research must concentrate on factors which can be influenced by the service-providing organization without major changes in its mandate, budget, or scope of operation. Second, the innovations suggested by the evaluation must be of such a nature that cost and efficiency factors can be assessed when proposed changes are planned.

These conditions for optimally useful evaluation clearly necessitate considerable planning of an evaluation prior to the implementation of the program which is to be evaluated. Specific types of information must be recorded in a manner which makes their use accessible and flexible. Further, despite one's best efforts there is bound to be considerable variation in the availability, accuracy, and relevance of cost-related data. A planner or an evaluator may well be faced with a situation in which a particular change is under the control of a program but accurate cost-effectiveness information is lacking, or a situation in which accurate cost information is available for changes that are not under the control of the program. There are few enough important variables which can be influenced by a service organization. With the additional requirement of having good cost information the number of factors left for study is smaller still. Consequently it becomes very important to identify and obtain information on all factors which are available for study, and such a process cannot take place without a thorough evaluation planning process prior to program implementation. A further complication which necessitates planning and foresight is the requirement of integrating cost analysis with the more traditional elements of social science research.

In sum, follow-up evaluation has a unique advantage in that it can supply an estimate of the "complete" effect of a program.[6] If such information is to be maximized, however, the data collected must point to changes which are under the control of the program in question and which are also open to an analysis of the cost of past and proposed actions. These requirements greatly reduce the number of variables which will be useful, increase the complexity of the analysis, and increase the importance of early planning of evaluation designs. If these conditions are met, follow-up evaluation can be an enormously powerful method of improving the quality of service which is provided.

Long-Range Planning

Because of the ability of follow-up evaluation to provide a fairly complete picture of the extent of a program's impact, it is uniquely suited to help those who are in positions to make judgments concerning the makeup and direction of social programs. In this regard follow-up evaluation can be particularly useful in planning for integration of various aspects of service delivery—an endeavor which is beyond the power of any single service organization, and which cannot be adequately planned without the long-term effectiveness data which emanates from follow-up evaluation.

How do unintended consequences which are generated by one agency or program affect the work of some other agency or program? How might the attenuation/snowballing phenomenon be bettered by the combined action of several services, and how would each service have to change in order to take full advantage of such cooperation? What is the value of a program relative to other programs which compete for public funds? All of these questions and many more like them can be answered intelligently only if one is able to obtain an overall estimate of the benefits and disadvantages of a program, and such an overall estimate can come only from the extended time frame of follow-up evaluation.

As in the client-comparison case, the key to maximum usefulness is to identify successfully the priorities and interests of the groups which influence an organization's future. Once such an identification is accomplished, the evaluator must then determine the type of information which will be most relevant to those groups and design an evaluation which will supply the necessary information. The crucial difference between the follow-up and the client-comparison case is the uncertainty introduced by follow-up evaluation's extended time frame. Follow-up evaluation cannot be as timely as other forms of evaluation because by its nature the data must be collected over a relatively long period. (Unless of course one chooses the much less preferred option of post hoc follow-up.) The initial conditions and concerns which prompted the evaluation are likely to have changed, and it is difficult to know what types of policy various organizations may attempt to set in the future. Thus it becomes much harder to know which sets of concerns should be addressed by an evaluation. On the other hand, long-lasting effects can offer dramatic support for a program, and knowledge of these effects might have a profound influence on program planning. Although achieving such success may not be likely, the possibility cannot be ignored.

As a consequence of these considerations, evaluators must engage in a three-step process when planning follow-up evaluation. First, they must determine the most appropriate time frame for their evaluation given their resources, other evaluation demands, and a sense of what is likely to happen to program effects with the passage of time. Second, the evaluator must determine the groups which are most likely to be interested in evaluation results *at the time when those results will be available*—a time span that may last from months to years. Finally, the evaluator must guess at the specific types of information that the previously identified relevant groups are likely to find most important for decision making. The recommendation being made here is to attempt the systematic solution of problems whose solutions are extremely uncertain. The recommendation is based on the assumption that concerted efforts are bound to produce favorable results more often than haphazard attempts.

Political Uses

It is to a program's immense advantage to demonstrate that it has brought about lasting or continually increasing benefits to the population it is charged with serving. Unfortunately most attempts at constructive social change end in effects which diminish over time. To compound the problem, the public is far more likely to attend to the disappearance of positive effects than it is to applaud positive changes which last for a relatively short period of time. As a consequence of this situation, treatments which are actually quite successful relative to the difficulty of the problem they are trying to solve may be seen as inefficient, ineffective, and nonproductive. Although the results of evaluation are certainly not enough to insure a change in this view, they might be useful as part of any arguments mounted to dispel such negative judgments. To this end data from follow-up evaluation might be used in two ways. First, it can be used to show that a program does indeed have beneficial results and that those results last for at least some time. Evaluation data is extremely important in this regard because failures are likely to be far more dramatic than successes. (One need only consider the publicity given to failures in prison release and other similar programs for socially deviant populations in order to be convinced that this is indeed the case.) Consequently a program's advocates must be ready with defensible and understandable data which can be used to defend program performance.

The second important use of follow-up evaluation is to help form arguments to the effect that attenuation of a treatment's influence is due to the action of factors which are quite clearly beyond the control of any given program, agency or organization. Although any follow-up evaluation might be useful in this attempt, several elements must be built into the evaluation design if maximum political usefulness is to be gained. As a first step one must have an understanding of what information will be most useful in explaining a program's effect. In many instances this type of information must include pretreatment measurements which would be lost forever if they were not made in time. A knowledge of what information will be most useful may be very difficult to obtain since such understanding is based on knowledge of the dynamics of people's life situations and the interaction between those factors and the effect of treatment. Very often both theory and common sense are inadequate guides when such decisions must be made. Consequently, a provision for open-ended field investigation of these issues must be built into follow-up evaluation. These efforts require far more than collecting psychological information at various points in time. They must be capable of detecting unforeseen factors and of yielding a rich variety of information concerning the life-styles of past treatment recipients. If information of this type is available, it may be possible to formulate arguments as to why the attenuation of program effects can reasonably be attributed to factors outside the program's sphere of action. Data which is collected for this purpose must yield information on several different levels of measurement—psychological, sociological, economic and behavioral. It is entirely possible that the rates of change of effects will differ for each of these realms of measurement, and it is to a program's greatest advantage to find and point out all the longest-lasting effects.

Finally, the evaluation must deal with information which is likely to hold sway in the political decision-making process, and there is no guarantee that such information will be particularly useful for the task of planning better service or improved treatment. Consequently the potential political value of follow-up evaluation must be considered as a separate factor when an evaluation is planned. The overlap between politically useful evaluation and evaluation which is useful for treatment improvement must be considered, and the relative value of such information must be assessed.

MODALITY TEST EVALUATION

Of all types of evaluation, the modality test framework offers the best opportunity for drawing inferences concerning the effect of a program or the impact of its various parts. In its classic form modality test evaluation approaches true experimental design. These designs are the most powerful methods of drawing causal inference. But even in cases where modality test evaluation is not designed along experimental lines, it is a far better tool for collecting information on the effect of programs that are either client-comparison or follow-up evaluations. Client comparisons are far from any type of causal inference because it is extremely difficult to relate the characteristics of client subgroups with particular aspects or activities of a program. The focus of client-comparison evaluation is on the careful description of people rather than on any links that might exist between people and program. Follow-up evaluation does concern itself with the effects of a program, but its prime focus is on untangling, sorting out and trying to understand the complex influences of that impact on post-treatment behavior. Although important information can be gained from such an endeavor, it is not likely that such information will have any direct bearing on the importance of specific elements of a specific program. Follow-up evaluation may shed light on effects which have ensued from a complex relationship between program and life, but that is far different (though perhaps no less important) from precise information on the size of specific effects which emanate directly from a well-defined action.

Modality test evaluation is uniquely suited to assess four elements of program functioning. These are: the relationship between program activity and program impact; the size of effects brought about by program activity; the dynamic by which program activity brings about change; and causal inference concerning the activities of a program. The present section will attempt to show how modality test evaluation can best be used for these purposes.

Realistic Expectations

The main question here is: Given a specific program or treatment as it currently exists, what effects can be expected? This information is particularly valuable since it involves direct observation of program activities rather than the study of residual effects during follow-up, or a comparison of different types of clients. Information obtained by a modality test is directly relevant to the problem of knowing what to expect from an action, and is not clouded by interactions between program activity and past treatment or life-style. It is the basic information on which all other inferences about a program should be built.

When the development of realistic expectations is the sole question of interest, effort does not have to be spent in determining the process by which change is brought about or in relating change to previously developed explanations concerning the problem in question. Thus all the resources of the evaluation can be brought to bear on the problem of estimating the size of various effects of a treatment. To this end as many facets of change as possible must be accurately measured. The greater the number of types of change that are accurately measured, the more detailed the picture of realistic expectations which can be developed. The point is to conceptualize as many facets of change as possible so that the picture which emerges will be balanced and complete. This can only be done if input on possible program effects is solicited from as wide a variety of concerned people as possible. It may well be that possible effects which might be postulated by one group of people would be overlooked entirely by some other group. Take for example the various perspectives of client groups, administrators, and policy makers from various levels of decision making, the different theoretical orientations of various professionals, and the differing viewpoints of different types of clinicians. It is likely that each will have a different opinion concerning the impact of any given treatment.

There are certain objectives of treatment on which evaluators will find general agreement. But any treatment or program is likely to impact people's lives in many more ways than are manifest in those commonly agreed upon objectives, and it may take the unique perspectives or knowledge of people with special backgrounds to alert evaluators to the possibility of such impact.

Improved Service

Just as in the other types of evaluation, the key to improving service by means of modality tests is the ability to exercise control over the factors which are being studied. In the present case, however, control (or at least influence) over treatment factors takes on an importance beyond the practical matter of whether a program will be able to implement any changes which might be suggested by an evaluation. Because of its special emphasis on the activities of a program rather than the behavior of a program's clients, modality test evaluation is particularly suitable for conduct in an experimental or at least a quasi-experimental mode and consequently, yields causal inference concerning why treatments work as they do. The greater the control exercised by the evaluator, the greater the likelihood that a rigorous design will ensue which will yield causal information. Such information cannot fail to help planners develop a sense of how treatment can be improved.

If modality test evaluation is to be maximally useful in helping to improve service, another constraint, over and above that of control over variables, must be imposed. The factors which are studied by the evaluator must be embedded in an already well-developed structure of theory and commonsense understanding. It avails little to know that a treatment is influenced by a factor which we do not understand and cannot explain. The importance of pre-existing knowledge frameworks is based on arguments from the philosophy of science which indicate that any research must be embedded in theory or at least in explanatory structures; and these arguments are augmented by factors which are special to the evaluation research situation.

In terms of the philosophy of science, four factors must be considered. First, the usefulness and adequacy of any scientific explanation is dependent upon the specific need for the information—the value of an explanation is (at least partially) dependent upon the situation for which the explanation is needed (Sherwood 1969). Second, understanding a phenomenon cannot be solely dependent upon the information that is generated from a given research endeavor; research data is necessarily based on—and embedded in—a complex network of implicit untested assumptions (Campbell 1974). Third, no single experiment can ever decide a scientific issue or debate—"critical experiments" are only labeled as such in retrospect; in truth a complex process of research and sociological dynamic is involved in deciding scientific debates (Lakatos and Musgrove 1972). Finally, data alone will not allow an investigator to extend his or her understanding beyond the most immediate implications of data—if data is to be useful in any but the most limited context, a theory is required as a guide (Bruner 1957). Taken together, these arguments indicate that "atheoretical evaluation" is not likely to yield information which will act as a valuable guide to future action, i.e., to the improvement of service. (Arguments against atheoretical evaluation which emanate from the literature which specifically deals with evaluation can be found in: Riecken 1972; Suchman 1969; Weiss 1970.)

In addition to these general considerations of the importance of theory there are three reasons why contextual and theoretical knowledge is particularly important in the case of modality test evaluation research. First, programs which are designed to meet a social need are likely to be far more complex phenomena than one might ideally wish as the target of a scientific (or even a technological) investigation. Researchers often have the luxury of constraining the phenomena they study in such a way as to simplify the conceptual issues involved in formulating explanations. Although simplification is a necessary element of any research investigation, evaluators are not as free to exercise such options as are many other social researchers. Evaluation almost always involves the study of a complex phenomenon which can be changed in only very limited ways in order to meet the methodological or conceptual requirements of the evaluator. Since the phenomena which are studied by evaluators cannot be simplified by any "internal" manipulation, a kind of conceptual simplicity must be imposed on the phenomena by already existing knowledge and understanding. Which elements of a treatment or program can be ignored and which must be accounted for in efforts at interpreting evaluation data? Which possible explanations or classes of explanations can be discounted and which must be considered? Although all research has these problems and all research needs "external" knowledge to help make such decisions, reliance on such knowledge is to a large extent a function of the complexity of the phenomena under study. Evaluation problems are highly complex and consequently understanding them is very dependent on previously existing theory and explanation.

Another important reason for the importance of conducting evaluation within a highly developed context of previously developed theory and explanation is based on problems of performing replication studies in the field of evaluation. Replication is a crucial element in the research endeavor because it allows the researcher to check on factors which may limit the generalizability or the validity of any single study, as well as provide a method of increasing the statistical sensitivity of any analyses which are performed (Keppel 1973, chap. 24). A third important reason for replication is to check on the possible effects of factors which arose during the conduct of the research, which came to light after a study was started, and which if properly understood would be of considerable value in analyzing a phenomenon under investigation. In this case, replication involves a partial modification of previous research designs so that previous findings will not only be corroborated but also clarified.

Unfortunately the possibility of implementing replication in the field of evaluation is extremely low.[7] Social programs are implemented and terminated for reasons which are quite apart from the needs of evaluation. Since further research cannot be counted on to clarify or validate an evaluation study, all efforts must be made to use other conceptual tools which might help in providing a meaningful analysis of evaluation data. Valid research design is one such tool. Maximum exploitation of previously developed knowledge is another. As the use of such knowledge increases so too does the probability of using evaluation data for constructive purposes.

A final factor to consider is that a knowledge of precisely how or why a particular effect exists is more likely to be useful to planning improved service than is the mere knowledge that some particular effect does in fact exist. It is unlikely that the elements which are necessary for discovering subtle treatment dynamics will be built into the evaluation of a social program. This problem occurs because the makeup of social programs represents a compromise between the needs and interests of many different parties among whom evaluators play a small and relatively powerless role. Thus the only way that evaluators can shed light on treatment dynamics is to embed the factors they study in as powerful a context of already developed understanding as is possible. Evaluation is primarily an attempt to determine whether particular treatments fit into already understood dynamics. If evaluation is seen as an attempt to study new dynamics then it is bound to yield results with only limited ability to point out new directions for the improvement of service. This is so because political and social constraints make it extremely unlikely that evaluation of social programs will be carried out in a methodological framework which will allow new theories to be developed on the basis of valid causal information.

In sum, the scale and context of program evaluation make it an undertaking which is quite different from a great deal of other social science. These differences have to do with the complexity of phenomena which are studied, the political nature of social programming, and the limited possibilities of conducting further clarifying research. Because evaluation as a research endeavor is put in an extremely unfavorable position as a result of these factors, it becomes important to use the full power of already existing conceptual frameworks for help in the development of correct and useful analysis of evaluation data.

So far the discussion of maximizing modality test data for the improvement of service has dealt with matters of the amount of control which can be exercised over variables and the need for studying the effects of factors which are already well understood. A third issue which must be considered is the amount of change that a factor is likely to bring about. It stands to reason that evaluation should concentrate on studying aspects of treatment which have the highest potential to bring about the greatest amount of change. As an example, consider the evaluator in a drug or correctional setting who has a choice of concentrating his or her efforts on investigating the effects of various types of psychotherapy, or on determining the effects of efforts to increase people's family support systems. It is not unreasonable that an evaluator will have to make such a choice because of limited resources or desire to limit intrusion into the daily workings of an agency, or for a variety of other possible reasons. Thus the evaluator is faced with a fundamental choice which will largely determine the types of recommendations which can be made to program planners. Considerations which might influence the evaluator's decision include the length of time that any positive change can be expected to last, the amount of potential constructive change that is inherent in the factor being studied, and other similar considerations. Given that evaluators have to limit the number of factors they can study, it seems reasonable to provide information on those factors which have the greatest potential to bring about the largest amount of constructive change.

Thus the problem of picking a focus for modality test evaluation which is aimed at improving service must involve a consideration of which factors are backed up with the most highly developed explanatory structure, the extent to which factors can be manipulated by the evaluator, and the potential of a factor to bring about desired changes. A final matter is, of course, the extent to which one can measure the variables of interest in a valid and reliable manner. Although one would be hard pressed to develop a formula which would provide an optimal weighting of these factors, it is safe to say that unless each of them is considered during the planning of an evaluation, the resulting study will not be optimally useful in providing information which will lead to program improvement.

Long-Range Planning

The higher up one goes in the hierarchy of decision making, the more one is primarily concerned with behavioral outcomes which are directly tied to the stated objectives of a program or treatment rather than with "intermediate" outcome. This happens because the higher one goes on a policy-making level, the greater the amount of funds that one is responsible for and the wider the political constituency to whom one must answer. As an example, take the case of drug abuse rehabilitation. At any decision-making level a concerned individual should be interested in the psychological well-being of the drug abuser and his or her family, the relation between drug abuse and crime, the amount of illicit drugs that are consumed, the expense of treatment, the financial effects of funding or not funding drug abuse programs, the amount of improvement that a program can bring about, the length of time that such improvement lasts in a given individual, and a host of other factors. It is also clear that the extent to which people are concerned with each of these factors will quite legitimately vary with the scope of their responsibility and the constituency to whom they are immediately responsible. Further, as a person's role changes so too does his or her ability to bring about specific types of changes in a program or a treatment.

An important consequence of these differing concerns and abilities to institute change is a variability in the nature of evaluation information which will be considered most relevant. Although these considerations are important in the planning of any type of evaluation, there are added complications where modality testing is concerned. As we have seen, the availability of pre-existing explanatory structures is of particular importance in modality test evaluation, and as the evaluator shifts his or her audiences along the decision-making hierarchy, there must be an accompanying shift in the *level of explanation* which is most appropriate for the variables of greatest interest. In other words, there is a shift in the types of theory and explanation within which one must attempt to interpret evaluation results. A program administrator, for example, might be most concerned with the relationship between program activities, small behavioral changes and psychological well-being, while a person who is charged with developing social policy might be more concerned with the amount of money invested in a program and highly visible behavioral changes in a program's clients.

These differences go beyond the fact that people in different roles have different interests and responsibilities. The difference also exists in the types of causal explanations and the levels of conceptualization that are necessary to understand and work with any given phenomenon. Although there is an interdependence among these various levels of understanding, there is also a reasonable amount of independence among them. Consequently there may be clearly different foci of interest concerning the types of explanations that will be considered useful and acceptable.[8] Further, research designs will change as there are shifts in the variables of interest and the levels of explanation that are needed to deal with those variables.

As an example, consider the evaluation of an educational program designed to help school children with poor reading skills. Teachers may be most interested in how the program affects study behavior, classroom deportment and the individual reading skills of each student. Principals and school boards may have a somewhat different concern. To them, the important question is whether in total, students in a school or school district are improving in their reading. The individual gains that are of such vital concern to classroom teachers becomes less salient to school administrators. Other shifts in concern take place at other levels. Those who set educational policy might be most interested in the program's effects on movement into other types of educational settings, on employment, and on other factors which may be felt in a community. These shifting emphases require the evaluator to employ different designs and different conceptual frameworks. Teachers' concerns might require observational studies and theories of classroom dynamics. The administrators' needs might be best met with standardized reading tests and theories dealing with the etiology of reading deficits. The policy planners may require information based on demographic information and behavioral/economic theories dealing with the relation between educational ability, educational level, and general success in life. Although people at each level may share some of the concerns of people at other levels, there are distinct shifts in emphasis. Such shifts require the evaluator to choose different variables, theories, and levels of explanation.

If evaluation is to be useful for long-range planning those who design evaluation must determine which level of understanding will be most useful for the decision makers who have long-term control over the direction and content of the program in question. Once that level is chosen and the basic framework for analysis is thereby determined, the evaluator must then choose variables for study which meet the four criteria set forth in the previous section: control, explanatory context, capacity to effect constructive change, and validity of measurement.

Although an evaluator's audience is likely to comprise people from many different levels of decision making, it is reasonable to assume that the *primary* audience for an evaluation can be determined. It is also safe to assume that if evaluation results are clearly irrelevant to the sphere of action in which that primary audience operates, the likelihood is that evaluation will have only minimal impact. Although one can never predict precisely who will "discover" and use an evaluation study, it does not seem reasonable to count on such discovery as the basis for the utilization of evaluation information.

One might well argue that concerted action is needed on many levels if substantive change is to be brought about, and this argument is almost certainly true. But it is also true that the type of action that any single person can take is sharply limited by his or her role and expertise. A clinic director may be able to upgrade the quality of service in his or her clinic but cannot influence integration between social programs or the extent of funding for ancilliary services. Each individual can influence people in different positions, but influence is far different from direct responsibility. Evaluation cannot be maximally useful unless it yields suggestions for change which are within the immediate realm of responsibility for the primary consumers of the evaluation information. Matching types of analyses with an evaluation audience's ability to act is the primary issue in maximizing the use of modality test evaluation for long-range improvement of services.

Political Usefulness

Although any type of evaluation might be useful in demonstrating that a program has resulted in some desirable outcome, modality test evaluation is particularly well suited to the task by virtue of its emphasis on specific program activities rather than on a program's clientele. Only with modality test evaluation can the evaluator point to links between specific outcomes and aspects of a program which one wishes to defend. There is a complication to this approach because not all positive outcomes are equally desirable and any program is likely to have several objectives—both stated and unstated—all of which are important and worthwhile. A further complication arises because once the points of view of various parties and constituencies are taken into account, there is a large increase in the number of possible objectives that an evaluator might consider as politically important elements in an evaluation.

If maximum political use is to be made of an evaluation, one must judge the extent to which evaluation can be used to enlist the support of the numerous groups who may take an interest in the program or treatment which is being evaluated. A second consideration must be the benefit which can be derived from the support of these different groups.

The defense of a program does not necessarily have to proceed by means of satisfying or enlisting the aid of the most powerful groups who are involved. This is fortunate because it may well be that some of the most powerful groups are also the most difficult to please. Consider for example the evaluator who would like to demonstrate to the Law Enforcement Assistance Administration that a particular type of rehabilitation program is worthwhile. Although it is likely that the rehabilitation program in question will improve people's self-image, coping skills and motivation to succeed, it is most unlikely that the program will have the type of effect on recidivism which would make law enforcement policy setters sit up and take notice.

Fortunately for the advocates of social programs, no single group has complete or total control over the course of social programming. There is a complex pattern of control and influence among these various groups and the goodwill of some groups may act as a buffer against the disapproval of those who are ostensibly in positions of greater influence or power.[9] Further, it is likely that evaluators can produce data which would be considered as favorable by at least some of the interests involved in deciding the future of any given program, treatment, or organization. Since one cannot please all people all the time, maximum political utility of evaluation depends upon a careful analysis of who the various interested parties are, the extent to which each can help, and the probability that evaluation will yield results which will be of value to those groups.

In conclusion, two important issues must be emphasized. First, the evaluator cannot guarantee that data will have the desired effect on any given party. All he or she can do is plan an evaluation which is *potentially* usable or of interest, i.e., to maximize the probability that the information will be acted upon. Second, evaluators must confront the serious ethical question of whether they conceive of their work as an attempt at defending social programs. Several considerations must be taken into account in such decisions. "Objective" methodologically defensible information about programs is a necessity for intelligent decision making. A reasonably large amount of public resources are undoubtedly wasted on ineffective programs. Evaluation is not and cannot be a neutral or value-free process. Implicit assumptions are always present, and those assumptions do effect what an evaluator will find. There is only a very low probability that evaluation will indicate that any program is unambiguously successful. If evaluation information is utilized, it will be as an element in a value-loaded sociopolitical process. With these facts in mind, the evaluator must search his or her conscience and determine if an evaluation should be aimed at a defense of the program under study, and if so, how such attempts should be weighed relative to the other legitimate functions that evaluators might assume.

CONCLUSION

Although the usefulness of information derived from an evaluation cannot be foretold or guaranteed, there are ways to plan evaluations so that the probability of usefulness is maximized. The first step in this process consists of identifying the various types of usefulness which can derive from evaluation data. Although no categorizations will be sharp and clear, four basic uses can be discerned: as a tool for setting realistic expectations for a program or treatment; as a method of helping organizations to improve the quality of service which they deliver; as a guide for long-range planning; and as a political tool in the sociopolitical decision-making process. The evaluation design concerns which an evaluator must consider will differ depending on which aspect of usefulness is to be maximized. Further, the type of evaluation which is to be conducted (client comparison, follow-up, modality test) will also influence strategies for increasing any given aspect of usefulness. (A summary of the particular advantages of each aspect of evaluation appears in Table 4.1).

The techniques of maximizing different aspects of usefulness are by no means mutually exclusive, although they do compete for the limited amount of resources which are usually devoted to evaluation. Consequently, evaluators must carefully determine what they want their evaluation to accomplish, and they must

Table 4.1. Summary of the Primary Themes in the Use of Evaluation Information

	Client Comparison	*Follow-up*	*Modality Test*
Realistic expectations	Screening to find clients who can actually be helped	Attenuation effects Snowballing effects Dynamics of long-term change	Magnitude of changes which can be expected from a program
Improved service	Differentiation of clients on factors which 1) influence success, and 2) are under control of the program	Effectiveness, efficiency and cost of "total" change resulting from program	Cause-and-effect information on factors which are under the control of the program
Long-range planning	Discovery of success differentiation factors which can be used by the groups who determine a program's clientele	Service integration information	Cause-and-effect information of interest to planners, funders, and citizen's groups
Political utility	Highlighting groups who were helped by a program	Determination of length and amount of nonobvious but important changes Explanation of why attenuation of gains are beyond a program's control	Cause-and-effect information on politically sensitive factors

assess the extent to which time, effort, and money should be devoted to each aspect of evaluation usefulness.

The unique skills of evaluators allow them to see relationships and options which may not be obvious to administrators, managers, or policy makers. Evaluators have an obligation to explore such options, but there is no point in making suggestions which cannot be implemented or acted upon. Hence the evaluator needs to determine feasible alternatives, to be sensitive to political realities, and to pitch evaluation studies to the range of action which can be taken by relevant parties.

NOTES

[1] These four uses for evaluation constitute what might be called primary uses, as they are the major considerations when evaluation is planned. Evaluators would do well, however, to consider a whole range of secondary uses of evaluation. For example, consider the effects of asking clinical staff in a mental health setting about the medical assistance or insurance status of their clients. Such questions may increase clinicians' awareness of the funding structure of their organization. Similarly, a variety of questions may increase awareness of problems which are of great concern to an organization's administration, but of minor direct concern to service delivery personnel. Other benefits of evaluation might be increased morale on the part of staff who receive feedback based on data they provide, opportunities for formal and informal in-service training, and the like. It is difficult to assess the value of these benefits, but they may be important for cooperation among organizational units, work efficiency, and other similar factors. Although these effects should not dictate evaluation design, they should certainly be considered whenever possible.

[2] Methodological and procedural issues in determining who needs specific types of treatment are discussed in the following sources: Kay 1978; Struening 1975; Warheit, Bell, and Schwab 1974, Kay and Struening represent the social area analysis perspective on determining population needs of social services. The Warheit, Bell and Schwab volume is a comprehensive review of needs assessment approaches.

[3] The discussion of political uses for evaluation in this book will center on methods by which programs or organizations will be able to defend their credibility, value, and worth. This orientation is based on the assumption that evaluations are not likely to find large and dramatic success among social programs (Rossi 1972; Weiss 1970); and that evaluation results notwithstanding, many programs do in fact accomplish some good. The question of course is whether the amount of good accomplished is worth the cost. Evaluation can contribute to such a determination by providing accurate data on a program's accomplishments. In so doing, however, evaluation is also likely to cause considerable difficulties for organizations which are not accomplishing spectacular results but which are doing all that can be done to solve a problem. Hence emphasis here is on the political use of evaluation to defend programs' credibility. Evaluation might well have the unintended consequences of limiting programs which perhaps should be continued or expanded. This section is written in an attempt to lessen that unintended negative consequence. It must be emphasized, however, that this *cannot* and *should not* be the only use for evaluation. Hard questions about program effectiveness must be asked, and evaluation must be used to that end.

[4] In essence this amounts to what is called in debating a "comparative advantages analysis." For an explanation of the logical structure of this type of argument and an explanation of how it relates to various other methods of argumentation, see Freeley 1976.

[5] There are many ways by which such a determination can actually be carried out and the relative merits of each technique must be weighed for each new situation. At the simplest level one needs only

a good estimate of the benefits and disadvantages of a program to which a personal set of values and a general sense of cost can be applied. Numerous other systems, all more complex and all more or less applicable to social and human services, can be applied. A review of these techniques together with relevant bibliographies appears in Tripodi, Fellin, and Epstein 1971, chapter 4.

[6]Strictly speaking, the picture can never be "complete" because an evaluation cannot extend for an infinite period of time. An arbitrary cut-off point must be determined past which no data is collected. One would like to extend a follow-up for a long enough period so that a reasonable sense of the performance of a program can be determined and an estimate of future performance can be projected, but some cut-off must be made and information is, therefore of necessity, incomplete. The picture will be incomplete along other dimensions as well, since information is not likely to be collected on all relevant factors. Another aspect to the matter is that the chief product of any research seems to be the generation of new questions, so from three points of view at least, information must always be only partial.

[7]Actually the situation may not be quite as bleak as is depicted here. If an evaluator is interested in investigating programs or treatments which for one reason or another have already become accepted, then multiple instances of treatment probably can be found because such programs are likely to be implemented on a wide scale. Unfortunately there is also likely to be considerable variability in precisely how a given modality is implemented, the actual service delivered, the clientele served, the competence of the staff, and numerous other factors. Even if an evaluator could overcome the obstacles involved in implementing evaluation at many different sites, there would be serious questions as to whether each site represented a replication of a particular type of treatment or whether several different treatments were under investigation. Still, replication of evaluations of widely implemented programs is within the bounds of possibility, especially if one has sufficient knowledge to make intelligent decisions about the "sameness" of different programs.

In cases where the evaluator is primarily interested in new or innovative programs, the possibility of replication is very small indeed.

[8]An analysis of levels of theory and analysis would lead the discussion too far afield to be presented here. Such matters should be of considerable interest to evaluators because they have much to say about the type of analyses which should be attempted, and the types of explanations which should be developed to explain the actions of social programs. A good introduction to the problem is presented in Bunge 1967, chapter 11.

[9]I am alluding here to the complex sociopolitical process by which social programs are instituted, continued, modified and terminated. Although a detailed discussion of these matters is beyond the scope of this book, evaluators would do well to develop a sensitivity and understanding of such processes. For those interested in pursuing the matter, the following work is recommended: Gilbert and Specht 1977. The book deals with the planning of social welfare programs, and Part 3—"Interactional Tasks: Perspectives on Planning as a Sociopolitical Process"—should serve as an excellent introduction to the problem.

5
Evaluation as Social Technology[1]

INTRODUCTION

So far I have argued that the value of outcome evaluation can be increased if type, validity, and usefulness are considered separately as distinct aspects of any given evaluation plan. Each of these three elements contains implications for the other two, but those implications will not be clear unless each component part is analyzed separately. There is another aspect of the problem which must also be considered, namely, the basic philosophical model of knowledge seeking upon which outcome evaluation is based. This is a consideration which cuts across elements of type, validity and usefulness, and deals with basic approaches to social research. How are questions formulated? How are variables chosen? What decision rules are used to weigh evidence, draw conclusions, and make recommendations? The answers to these questions reflect a philosophical model of research, and the model chosen can have far-reaching effects on the ultimate value of any research project. There are three main aspects to the argument about to be developed. First, there are crucial differences between scientific and technological models of knowledge development. Second, these differences have profound implications for the practical value of research. Third, evaluation is far more of a technological than a scientific pursuit.

Evaluators strive to make their work as useful for decision making as possible.

94

This desire is not an aberrant phenomenon in the history of social science, as there is a long tradition of trying to make social research responsive to the needs of society. It seems reasonable to consider the "evaluation usefulness" issue as part of this tradition, as there is no reason to assume, a priori, that evaluation is uniquely different from all other aspects of social research. In fact, a survey of critiques of relevance in social research will prove extremely enlightening and applicable to the case of evaluation. It will become clear that a good many of the problems which impede the relevance of social research will be lessened by reconceptualizing evaluation as a technological rather than a scientific process.

WHY IS SOCIAL RESEARCH NOT RELEVANT? A REVIEW OF CRITIQUES

There are four types of explanation for the lack of relevance of social research.[2] Each type presents a different aspect of the problem, and all have some bearing on the choice of appropriate evaluation activity.

Cultural/Historical/Sociological Roots of Irrelevance

The course of social research is profoundly influenced by the greater social milieu in which the work is embedded, and theories generated in one setting are not easily transplanted to other settings. Further, those who perform social research can be said to have a "culture" all their own with shared values, a unique vocabulary, special interests, relatively distinct boundaries, its own reward system, and many other aspects of social groups. The needs and objectives of those who share that culture are often at variance with the needs and objectives of other groups. Even when there is agreement, communication is often difficult, and serious misunderstandings are common. All of these issues contribute to the problem of lack of relevance.

Gergen (1973) argues that while the methods of social research may be scientific, theories are often based on "acquired dispositions" which reflect the thinking of society about particular issues. If there is any truth to this statement, the relevance of social science will depend at least in part on the speed and direction with which social scientists change their theories relative to changing contemporary history. Irrelevance is likely if the change processes for society at large are out of step with the change processes within the social scientific community.

Moscovi (1972) makes essentially the same point. He argues that the content of American social psychological theories are uniquely American, and as such are not applicable to countries with other social systems or different basic mechanisms for organizing economic and social life. Our theories are culture bound and are not necessarily applicable when transposed to new surroundings.

For both Moscovi and Gergen, social theories are a reflection of the culture in which scientists work, and consequently, any change in the cultural context may lead to a lack of "fit" between existing theories and their surrounding societal context.

Another aspect of the culture problem lies in differences between scientists and the rest of society in terms of vocabulary, goals, epistemological beliefs, reward systems, time frame for work completion, and the like. Morell (1977b) has developed the notion that these differences amount to a "culture gap" between social scientists and the administrators of social programs.

This "culture gap" is an important aspect of the lack of relevance because the social scientists' work simply does not fit into the world of program planning and administration. There are too many differences in terms of requirements for knowledge, beliefs in the quality of different types of knowledge, questions which are considered important, and reward systems.

As an example of this problem, Lorenzen and Braskamp (1978) have conducted research which indicates that of three different types of information—political, cost benefit, and scientific—administrators in mental health settings attend only to the cost-benefit data. Their evidence suggests that this may be true regardless of the nature of the problem for which the information is collected, or the "true" best fit between problem and information. Unfortunately our best theories of client success in mental health settings do not involve cost-benefit issues. Although some work has been done in this area (for example, Newman, Burwell, and Underhill 1978), cost-benefit aspects of client improvement in mental health are certainly not the major thrust of current mental health research. In this case both the theories of mental health upon which evaluations are based, and the major interests of evaluators, seem to be at variance with the needs and interests of decision makers.

In sum, one important reason for the lack of relevance of social science may lie in a lack of congruence between the body of social scientific knowledge and the requirements for knowledge which emerge from the larger societal context.

Irrelevance Imposed by the Basic Strategies of Science

The basic goal of science is to discover what is true (Popper 1965, chap. 3). This goal is pursued by means of theory development and through research. There are inherent elements in both of these strategies (theory development and research) which may result in the inapplicability of social scientific work to the understanding of in vivo social phenomena. I will deal first with issues related to methodology and then turn the discussion to the constraints imposed by the nature of theory.

Many arguments have been advanced to the effect that the most powerful scientific procedures are also the hardest to apply in a manner which will be applicable to nonresearch situations. Argyris (1975) claims that many experiments require the researcher to exert a high degree of control over his or her subjects, and to advocate one particular, limited, well-defined course of action. He further argues that experiments involve minimal amounts of real time learning by both subjects and researchers. Argyris' argument is that because of these constraints, results obtained from experimental research may not be applicable to similar, but nonexperimental situations.

Tajfel (1972) cites conditions under which experiments will be applicable to real world situations, but the conditions he requires are rarely met. As examples, Tajfel believes experiments must be interpreted in light of knowledge about the social science context of research and the effects of researchers' and subjects' expectations on research results. This type of information is rarely available and difficult to obtain.

A different approach to the problems caused by research methodology is taken by Edwards, Guttentag, and Snapper (1975). Their basic claim is that there are fundamental limitations imposed by the traditional approach to hypothesis testing, and that those limitations preclude evaluation from providing a "usable conceptual framework and methodology that links inferences about states of the world, the values of decision makers, and decisions" (p. 140). This critique was developed specifically within the context of evaluation, but presumably it would also apply to other (but not all) applied research situations.

While some of the problems of lack of relevance in social science emanate from the methodology of science, still others emerge from the nature of scientific theory. An essential element of theory building is the development of models of phenomena which *are* and *must be* simpler than the actual working of that phenomenon under natural conditions. (See for example, Kaplan 1964, chap. 7.) The "simplistic models" idea is based on the notion that all events are caused by a very large (in fact, an infinite) number of factors. Although some of those causal factors may be much more immediate and powerful than others, the actual number is limitless. Since it is beyond human capacity to explain an infinite number of factors, our models will always reflect a simpler picture of reality than is actually the case. Another aspect of the problem is practical. Our models are often likely to exclude factors which we may know influence an event. Those factors are left out because including them would obscure the relationships among particular variables of special interest. Given the scientist's need to construct simplistic models of reality, it is by no means surprising that those models often fall short when called upon to predict or explain events which occur in uncontrolled, unsimplified settings.

Another aspect of the problem is that theories can be said to have the properties of range and accuracy (Bunge 1967). Range refers to the number of elements which the theory explains. Accuracy refers to the precision of those explanations. Bunge advances the notion that there may well be a trade-off between these two dimensions, and that an increase in one may well lead to a decrease in the other. If there is any truth to this assertion, it is easy to see why many theories in science are found wanting when called upon to explain social events. The complexity of real life events may result in a lack of consonance between the artificially simplified event for which a theory was developed, and the uncontrolled event which must be explained. In a sense, the range of the theory may be extended beyond the precise range for which it was originally developed, with an attendant decrease in the accuracy of explanation. Since many theories are usually based on simplistic situations, or are developed for specific contexts, the use of theory in diverse practical settings is very likely to result in a stretching of the theory's range, with a consequent decrease in accuracy.

Callahan (1962) has documented a dramatic example of the misapplication of theory. In a carefully reasoned and well-researched analysis, he has shown that a considerable drop in educational quality resulted from the wholesale transfer of business mangement concepts into the field of educational administration. Such transplanting was rampant in the early part of this century, and in Callahan's judgment, the results were tragic. Callahan does not argue that good management practice should be excluded from educational administration. He does claim that management requirements are different in education and in the profit-making sector, and that theories developed in the latter cannot be transposed in wholesale fashion to the former. In a sense, the range of business management theory was stretched considerably. The resulting predictions from that theory were not only inaccurate, but extremely counterproductive.

In sum, there are certain requirements of scientific methodology and theory which are likely to result in a lack of applicability of scientific findings to the general course of events. Although it is conceivable that these problems may be ameliorated, it is impossible for them to be eliminated, as they derive from fundamental aspects of the scientific research enterprise.

Irrelevance as a Function of Choice of Topics for Study

One important criticism about the irrelevance of social research is that researchers are devoting their time to the study of the wrong variables. This is not an issue of the relevance of theory to a particular time and place, nor is it an issue of methodology. It is a criticism of the choice of topics of study—a critique of people's interests and priorities. Goodwin and Tu (1975), for instance, wonder why more psychological studies are not done concerning attitudes about taxation, or on other policy-relevant matters. A second example may be drawn from income maintenance research. Berk and Rossi (1977) criticize the evaluation of such programs for an overemphasis on "work disincentive," and for downplaying factors such as effects on improved health, or the enrichment of leisure time. They argue that although information on work disincentive may meet the major priorities of Congress, it may not make for an accurate assessment of income maintenance programs.

A common theme runs through all of these arguments. Social research as it is presently constituted has not yielded explanations that are useful in understanding or predicting complex social systems or behavior, and the reason for the failure is based on a mistaken choice of problems, variables, or questions.

Irrelevance as a Function of the Impotence of the Social Research Enterprise

Arguments have been advanced to the effect that evaluation research has not been helpful in solving social problems simply because the social research enterprise does not have the power to help with such problems. Rossi (1972) for instance, claims that many current social problems are extraordinarily difficult to solve, and that only small gains can be expected from attempts at their solution. He argues that much of what is easily done has already been accomplished, and that which is left is highly resistant to solution. Rossi (1972, p. 226) cites the example of illiteracy:

> Dramatic effects on illiteracy can be achieved by providing schools and teachers to all children: Achieving a universally high enough level of literacy and knowledge, so that everyone capable of learning can find a good spot in our modern labor force, is a lot more difficult.

If there is any truth to Rossi's assertion, it is little wonder that research has not been helpful in pointing directions to solutions. There may be no good solutions, and all the science and all the research in the world will not change that fact.

A similar problem is alluded to by Carol Weiss (1973) in her writings on the political nature of evaluation research. Weiss argues that attempts to solve social problems are forged in the political arena, complete with all the vested interests and influence patterns which are part and parcel of the political decision-making world. If there is any truth to her analysis, scientific knowledge will be related in only the most tangential manner to attempts at solving social problems. The reason for the weak and indirect relationship is that political dynamics allow only those solutions which are based on single-cause models. Any research which indicates the need for solutions based on multiple-cause models will be disregarded. In this case, research is irrelevant not in the sense that it cannot point to better solutions, but in the sense that it will not be called upon to do so.

Another aspect of the problem is that our best methodologies may be least appropriate to the problems at hand. Berk and Rossi (1977) argue that the methodology of applied social research is far more highly developed for the study of individuals than it is for the study of organizations. They cite the case (p. 81) of studies of alienation, where:

> . . . there is a conventional scale for measuring the alienation of individuals, but not for the alienating tendencies of work organizations.

To the extent that meaningful solutions to social problems will emerge from studies of social structure, evaluators find themselves with inadequate methodological tools for the work they must do.

A FRAMEWORK FOR SOLUTIONS

Each of these criticisms of lack of relevance in social research has some validity, and each sheds light on a different aspect of the problem. Taken together, they constitute a formidable obstacle to the conduct of relevant social research on a systematic and ongoing basis. An efficient way of overcoming this obstacle is by means of a single overriding framework which could lead to a solution to each of the variety of problems involved. If such a perspective could be found, we would have a powerful and simple means of furthering the development of relevant social research. The purpose of this chapter is to argue that the technological approach to research is just such a model.

There are important differences between science and technology, and many problems of relevance will be solved or lessened if social research is based on the technological model. In particular, that aspect of research called "outcome" evaluation will benefit from such a formulation. The next section will detail the crucial differences between science and technology. The discussion will then show how the technological model will help evaluation avoid or reduce the problems which cause irrelevance in social research.

DIFFERENCES BETWEEN SCIENCE AND TECHNOLOGY

A review of the literature on the nature of science and technology reveals four types of differences between the two enterprises. Each difference has its own implications for the use of evaluation, and each highlights different aspects of the relevance problem.

Theory in Science and Technology

An analysis of scientific and technological theory by Bunge (1967) makes it clear that there are profound differences between theory as a guide to practical action and theory as a model for understanding nature in as truthful and accurate a manner as possible. In fact, the requirements for good theory in each realm are often incompatible, if not antithetical. Incorrect or inaccurate theories often lead to correct predictions, as often has been true, for example, in the case of weather forecasting. Thus, although accurate prediction may be a valid criterion for judging the value of technological theory, it may be misleading as an aid in the discovery of truth.

Testing theories for truth or accuracy must often take place in settings which are deliberately removed from the noise and distractions of naturalistic settings, as such distractions may make it impossible to investigate subtle (or even not-so-subtle) relationships among variables. Further, the truthseeking endeavor does not put the scientist under any obligation to test his or her theories under naturalistic conditions. In terms of truth-seeking work, there is no logical imperative to do so. On the other hand, the ultimate test of theory as a guide to action is whether the theory proves useful in the face of the very same real world noise which is deliberately removed from the truth-seeking endeavor. Consequently the developer of technological theory is duty bound to test the practical consequences of his or her theories.

The difference is crucial because it relates to the way in which researchers orient their thinking, choose their projects, and organize their work efforts. When truth seeking is the goal, work may or may not force researchers to confront issues of practicality. When guides to action are being sought, practicality becomes a central, organizing principle of an entire research effort. Technological theories may still have to be developed in artificial settings, but they *must* be evaluated in light of real world events. This is not true in the case of science.

The search for guides to action might actually be hampered by seeking too much truth. As Bunge (1967) points out, lens designers rely on the wave theory of light—a theory which has been outdated since early in the twentieth century. The wave-particle theory of electromagnetic radiation, with its attendant quantum mechanical considerations, is far more true than is the outdated wave theory. But the use of quantum mechanics would enormously complicate the job of the lens designer, have no practical benefit for the design of better lenses, and waste enormous amounts of time. (On the other hand, if only practical needs were taken into account, the development of quantum mechanics would have been greatly impeded.)

As an example, in the behavioral sciences, consider an evaluator's use of psychotherapy change measures which are reliable and valid, and whose validity is based on a well-tested theory of psychopathology. Those very same measures may also be impractical for use in ongoing service agency settings. The reasons for such impractability may be many. Measures may be accurate only if used by specially trained personnel. A measure may be time-consuming and not fit with the hectic schedule of service providers, thus leading to improper use of the measure. A scale may be usable only in abbreviated form because of limitations of space on existing forms or the programming requirements of a management information system. Those problems take on considerable significance if an evaluation objective is to develop an ongoing evaluation system for use within an agency. In such cases the feasibility of a measure becomes at least as important a factor as reliability and validity. In fact, it might be useful to sacrifice some scientific rigor for the sake of practical application. The result of such a trade-off may be a measure which does not give the highest possible quality information, but which will be extremely useful to program planners, administrators and service providers. As in the case of lens design, the "scientifically better" or "more true" approach has less practical value than the "scientifically inferior" method.

In sum, the differences between technological and scientific theory relate to issues of prediction, contexts of application, and strategies of theory development. In all these cases it is likely that theories which are useful in a technological sense might be counterproductive to the development of theories which are powerful guides to action.

Search and Decision Strategies

There are important differences between science and technology in terms of how problems or variables are chosen for study, the requirements for accuracy of results, and the type of evidence which constitutes a solution to problems or questions.

The Choice of Topics. Given that all phenomena have an infinite number of causal factors, which aspects of a problem should be studied in any given research setting? The criteria for answering this question are different for science and technology, and as a result different aspects of a problem are likely to be studied depending on whether one approaches the issue from a scientific or a technological viewpoint. The technologist will be interested in those causes which are most immediate, or most powerful, or most manipulable within the constraints of a specific real world context of action. The scientist will be most interested in studying those causes which will clear up a conceptual difficulty, or which will help determine the truth of a speculation, or which will advance the development of theory.

There is no reason to assume that scientific and technological criteria for choosing variables will necessarily lead to the same point. In fact, it is easy to see how the search for truth may focus attention on variables or phenomena which have little or no practical value. Consider the example of the search for cross-situational consistencies in behavior. Efforts at understanding and predicting behavioral consistency have considerable theoretical importance in social psychology, and enormous efforts have been put into research on the topic (Bem and Allen 1974, Mischel 1973). The general (and highly simplified) conclusion is that cross-situational consistencies in behavior probably do exist, but only in highly constrained circumstances. Further, the prediction of people's behavior requires careful assessment of various aspects of social situations and, probably, of individuals as well. Given the amount of precise information needed to predict individual behavior, it does not seem reasonable that theories of behavior consistency will have much practical use in understanding highly complex social programs. Even if all the necessary measurements could be made (which is not likely at this point in our social psychological knowledge), it is not likely that they could be made in the hectic world of social service. Service providers are too busy, measurement tools are too delicate, and the client population is too diverse. There *are* legitimate and important theoretical issues to be studied in the area of behavior consistency, and the topic does have considerable importance. On the other hand, theories of behavior consistency are not useful guides to the choice of variables in evaluation settings, the scientific value of those theories notwithstanding. Given the amount of substantive debate and measurement problems involved, a consideration of variables important in behavior consistency research is almost certain to focus attention on issues which have minimal importance for people who plan large-scale programs.

Levels of Accuracy. Once problems are chosen it becomes necessary to decide on the level of accuracy which will be accepted for results and solutions. Here too, technology and science are different. Within the limits of available instrumentation, the person engaged in the scientific search for truth must attempt to make results and solutions as accurate as can be obtained. (This does not mean using inappropriate measures, such as angstrom units for astronomical research. It does mean an attempt to be as precise and accurate as possible within the problem context in which research is being conducted.) The applied researcher, on the other hand, has the liberty of specifying, in advance, an acceptable degree of accuracy (Ackoff, Gupta, and Minas 1962). Further, that degree of accuracy can be considerably less than the greatest amount of accuracy which is attainable. In other words, those engaged in applied research can specify the precision of a solution which is "good enough," and that determination usually depends on practical considerations which result from the context in which research results must be applied. The search for truth, on the other hand, does not allow such liberties.[3] Scientific results are never good enough unless they are as good as they can be. The technologist who operates on the scientific model is likely to invest time, effort, and resources in pursuing levels of accuracy which are unnecessary and, perhaps, even misleading as guides to practical action.

A good example of this problem can be found in the area of psychological testing. Clinicians have long known that the full battery of psychological diagnostic tests (WAIS, MMPI, etc.) provide far more detailed and multifaceted information than can possibly be used for overall assessment. When judgments have to be made, much information must be glossed over or ignored. The area of diagnosis is simply too imprecise to make good use of all the information which the science of psychometrics is able to provide. When complex tests are used, some information must be ignored. Every jot and tittle of a psychological profile cannot demand attention. From a scientific point of view, however, precision and multidimensionality are much to be desired. Specific research hypotheses about personality cannot be investigated with imprecise tests, and small differences among groups of people may have major consequences for one or another theory of personality.

Types of Evidence. A third important difference between decision strategies in science and technology deals with the relative importance of refutation and confirmation. Agassi (1968) points out that traditionally science relies heavily on the concept of refutation. Since it is impossible to investigate all possible instances of a phenomenon, it is impossible to state unequivocally that a particular assertion is true. On the other hand, it takes only one disconfirming instance to demonstrate that an assertion is false. Thus in the search for scientific truth, disconfirmation and the refutation of assertions are much more important than confirmation or attempts to prove that hypotheses are true.[4] Not so in the world of technology, which is tied at least as much to the practical world of political decisions as it is to the realm of science.

A further element in Agassi's (1968) argument is that the conduct of technological investigation often involves the commitment of resources to the solution of a problem of considerable social significance. Resources are always scarce, and decision makers are in great need of guidance as to which of a number of innovations are likely to be most successful. The aim is not to prove things true, or to show that one solution is certainly the best, but to eliminate the worst alternatives and to choose from the ones which are likely to prove most beneficial. In that sense, confirmation becomes a very important concept. Each time a solution has been shown to lead to an acceptable outcome, the faith of the public and of decision makers in that course of action will increase. Technological endeavors may be seen as efforts at confirming expectations about particular programs or course of action, while the chief role of science is to provide empirically testable explanations about states of nature. The main criterion for a good technological study is its potential to accurately affect our perceptions of the probability of success of a particular innovation. In contrast, the main criterion for a good scientific study is its potential to test, via the mechanism of disconfirmation, assertions about the true state of nature.

According to Agassi (1968) these differences can lead to important practical problems if the wrong model is followed. In science, standards of criticism can be raised as high as possible in any given situation. The more stringent the criticism, the better, as it is truth which is at stake. In technology, however, it is possible to raise standards of criticism too high, and in so doing, impede the implementation of needed innovations.

Summary. The search and decision strategies of science and technology are different in three crucial areas. Differences exist between them in terms of how problems or variables are chosen for study, in the ability to specify levels of precision and accuracy, and in the importance of designing research so as to confirm expectations of success or to disconfirm a stated hypothesis. These differences add up to entirely different methods of approaching problems and conceptualizing important issues.

Key Elements and Goals in Science and Technology

Agassi (1966) believes that as a minimum technology includes elements of applied science, problems of the implementation of research findings, and issues relating to the maintenance of existing systems. Wiesner (1970, p. 85), in a discussion about making psychology more relevant to the problems of society claims that:

> Technologists apply science when they can, and in fact achieve their most elegant solutions when an adequate theoretical basis exists for their work, but normally are not halted by the lack of a theoretical base. They fill in gaps by drawing on experience, intuition, judgment and experimentally obtained information.

Sporn (1964), in an analysis of the nature of engineering (a field which is certainly closely related to technology) echoes the sentiments of Weisner. Sporn claims that engineering empiricism can provide a guide for action in cases where a theoretical base is lacking. To do so, the practice of engineering must include elements of science, tools, methods, systems and social organization.

Writings on the question of goals in science and technology make it quite clear that the objectives of the two endeavors are not the same. Skolimowski (1966) claims that the goals of science are to investigate reality, enlarge knowledge, acquire truth, and study "what is." Technology, on the other hand, seeks to increase the efficiency of given techniques, create a reality of our own design, and in general, is far more concerned with what "ought to be" than it is with investigating "what is."

The difference between science and technology is best summed up by Jarvie (1972) who wrote: "The aim of technology is to be effective rather than true, and this makes it very different from science."

In a discussion of the methodology of engineering, Walentynowicz (1968) argues that while scientific achievement lies in the truth of a statement which might be made, engineering success is the effective solution to a proposed problem. Further, the solution must be acceptable within the constraints imposed from four sources: a particular body of knowledge, a given set of skills, a well-defined point of view, and the constraints imposed by available resources.

Although it may be argued that factors such as the lack of theory, limitations on freedom of action, and the need for nontheoretical information are operative in *any* research, a crucial difference still exists between science and technology. The entire scientific enterprise is geared toward overcoming these limitations in order to further the search for truth. The raison d'être of technological work is to maximize solutions which must operate within practical constraints.

Summary: Differences Between Science and Technology

Although science and technology share many surface similarities, an investigation of the logical structures which underlie each endeavor reveals quite clearly that they are *not* one in the same. (A summary of crucial differences appears in Table 5.1.) Scientific theory is very different from technological theory. Search and decision strategies are different in each realm. Rules for the acceptability of

Table 5.1. Summary of Differences between Science and Technology

	Science	Technology
Theory	Main use is as a guide to truth	Main use is as a guide to practical action
	Emphasis on understanding	Emphasis on prediction and control
	No obligation to test in practical settings	Must be tested for usefulness in practical settings
Search and decision strategies	Study of factors which explain conceptual strategies	Study of factors which are immediate, powerful, and manipulable within practical contexts
	Accuracy must be as high as possible	Accuracy determined by limitations of action in real world settings
	Emphasis on refutation	Emphasis on confirmation
Key elements and goals	Theory development	All factors which help as guides to practical action (theory, intuition, experiment, social systems)
	Truth, "what is"	Efficiency, reality of our own design, "what ought to be," effectiveness

evidence differ. The goals of science and technology are different. Taken as a whole, these differences have far-reaching implications for the ways in which scientists and technologists choose problems, invest their efforts and resources, select audiences, evaluate evidence, and make recommendations. These differences are not merely alternate routes to the same place. Because of the differences between science and technology, it is quite likely that each approach will lead to entirely different strategies for the study of social problems. Further, it is likely that the subject matter of each investigation and the conclusions arrived at will also differ greatly.

So far this chapter has reviewed two main areas—critiques of relevance in social science, and the differences between the technological and scientific methods of approaching research. It remains to be shown how these problems can be reduced if evaluation research is conceptualized as a technological rather than a scientific enterprise.

ADVANTAGES OF EVALUATION AS SOCIAL TECHNOLOGY

As we have seen, basic critiques of the relevance of evaluation (and social science in general) revolve around four issues: cultural/historical/sociological factors; constraints which result from the basic approach of science; the choice of topics for study; and impotence of the social science enterprise. We have also seen that differences between science and technology revolve around questions of theory, search and decision strategies, goals and key elements. This section will attempt to synthesize this information so that evaluation can become a powerful factor in the solution of social problems. The discussion will deal first with issues of culture and history, and then collectively treat issues of constraints inherent in the basic approach of science, the choice of topics for study, and the general impotence of social science research.

Cultural/Historical/Sociological Irrelevance

This critique operates on two levels. First, there is a difference in perspective which divides evaluators from the decision makers, policy setters and administrators with whom they work. (This issue will be elaborated in Chapter 6.) This division is characterized by differences of vocabulary, belief in the power of research techniques, reward systems, objectives, and priorities. Second, there is a more general difference between the needs and social/philosophical orientation of society at large, and the theories and perspectives of social scientists. Gergen (1973) and Moscovi (1972) discuss this issue in terms of the relevance of social psychological theories to other countries and other social systems, but a similar dynamic operates in the relation between evaluators and the society in which they are embedded.

Both aspects of the problem point to the need for a mechanism which will bring the thinking and theorizing of evaluators into line with the needs, priorities, and goals of the society that surrounds them. One promising solution is the development of evaluation along the model suggested by technology rather than that suggested by science, as technology is far more responsive to the demands of its social environment than is science. This increased responsiveness is manifest in all aspects of differences between science and technology—theory, search and decision strategies, goals, and key elements.

Irrelevance Based on Theory. The value of technological theory is directly related to the usefulness of the theory as a guide to practical action. As such, technological theory must be developed within a context of responsiveness to practical issues. Theories which are true but irrelevant or weak in the real world of everyday action will be discarded, a tendency which may not exist in the scientific world where theories are judged by testability, influence on understanding states of nature, and contribution to clearing up conceptual difficulties. To the extent that evaluators plan their work on the basis of scientific theories, they run a risk of gaining knowledge about social programs which is valid, but which may also be irrelevant as a practical guide to action.

As an example, consider the evaluation of an educational program which is guided by theories of the relationship between subtle teacher-child interactions and academic achievement. Such a theory is likely to lead to the study of many interpersonal factors which may be difficult or impossible to substantially manipulate in nonresearch settings. Although the information which would be gained may be true and accurate, it would not be particularly useful to those who plan educational programs, administer schools, or teach classes. In contrast, consider the variables which would have been chosen had the evaluator operated on theories which relate curriculum and textbook content to academic achievement. These factors are relatively easily manipulated, and such information might be extremely useful in changing educational programs for the better.

Search and Decision Strategies. Similar problems exist when search and decision strategies are based on the scientific rather than the technological model. Variables are chosen in science for their ability to suggest theories which are accurate reflections of the true states of nature. Unfortunately, the variables which are most important for such knowledge may not be the same as those variables which are the more powerful determinants of real world events. In fact, small unexplained aberrations in the prediction of an event are often the best clues to the discovery of new truths and the furtherance of theory. Consequently a scientific orientation to the choice of problems and variables may lead to factors which are irrelevant to people whose chief interest is discovering powerful solutions to serious practical problems.

As an example, consider the debate over race and intelligence (Brody and Brody 1976; Jensen 1973). The hereditability of psychological characteristics is certainly an important issue for our understanding of individual behavior, psychological makeup, and the relationship of individuals to social systems. Consequently there is a good deal of scientific justification for studying the topic. But does the topic have any practical value for those who plan educational programs or social policy? One could cogently argue that it does not. Our society is very much based on an ethic which encourages each person to realize his or her highest potential. As a result of this ethic, much of our educational system is geared (at least ideally) to educate each student to the best of his or her ability. We know that many black children have higher IQs than white children. This is an indisputable fact which clearly emerges from the very evidence which is used to demonstrate overall racial differences. In fact, the overlap in IQ is considerable. If the average black-white IQ difference is 15 points, and the standard deviation for intelligence tests is between 15-17 points (both commonly accepted figures), 16 percent of the black population has a higher IQ than the *average* score for whites. The number of black children who have higher IQs than whites is even greater. The implication of these figures is that many students (both black and white) stand to be done a considerable disservice by an educational planning system which pays too much attention to overall differences in intelligence among racial groups. The important point is that the disservice will occur even if the average difference figure is correct, and regardless of whether the difference is caused by hereditary or environmental factors. Thus we have a case of a scientific psychological problem which deserves attention, but which may mislead educational planners if they allow their priorities to be influenced by the issue.

A related issue is the specification of acceptable levels of accuracy. An important aspect of applied research is the identification of specific levels of accuracy which will satisfy the need for a solution to a practical problem (Ackoff, Gupta, and Minas, 1962). By making such decisions evaluators automatically gear their work to the requirements of those who are primarily responsible for implementing innovations. Failure to set levels of accuracy explicitly may lead to a mismatch between accuracy obtained in an evaluation study and the accuracy that is needed by decision makers and program planners. Too much precision is useless and distracting because it does not reflect the actual amount of influence which can be brought to bear on a problem. (As in the case of diagnostic testing, where more detailed information is provided than can possibly be used for placing individuals in various programs, organizations, or modalities.)

A final issue concerning decision strategies involves the roles of science and technology in the adoption of new plans or courses of action. As Agassi (1968) has shown, standards of criticism in science should be raised as high as possible. If this is done in the technological field, however, it is unlikely that decision makers will ever have enough confirmatory evidence to be willing to risk a new solution to a persistent problem. Thus technologists must constantly consider which level of evidence will guard against the choice of poor solutions but encourage experimenting with solutions which are among the better alternatives to a problem. If evaluators do not take this issue to heart they are likely to level too much criticism at a project without a sense of why decision makers need evaluators in the first place, namely, to perform research that will give people enough confidence in a new course of action so that further constructive efforts might be attempted.

In sum, search and decision strategies in science are aimed at developing theory which is true, at honing information to the highest possible level of accuracy, and at being as critical as possible of new ideas and of the tests of those ideas. All of these three objectives may be disfunctional in a technological sense. In technology, accurate prediction is more important than truth, levels of accuracy are situationally determined, and the function of research has a much stronger practical confirmatory function than it does in science. All of these aspects of technology force researchers to confront the needs of decision makers because technological problems are fundamentally determined by the same need context which operates for administrators and planners. The defining context of scientific problems is entirely different, as theory development is not inherently tied to practical needs.

Key Elements and Goals in Science and Technology. The planning and conduct of any research must take into consideration elements of available tools and methods, practical issues of implementation, and constraints imposed by systems and social organization. In science these elements are obstacles to be overcome in the search for truth and the development of theory. In technology they represent the researchers' response to the very same parameters and operating principles that guide decision makers in the practical world of action. In essence, the world of the technologist is bounded by the same factors as the world of administrators and policy makers. Thus the technological model of research automatically relates to the problems and needs of those who must make decisions about social programs. The universe of the scientist is not so bounded, as scientists are permitted (in fact encouraged) to construct artificial situations in which tools, resources, and the like are extended as far as possible, with no regard for large-scale everyday limitations. Consequently researchers operating on the scientific model are likely to generate information which is incompatible with the needs of decision makers.

The goals of administration and planning are effectiveness, control over situations, and efficiency, all to be maximized within the constraints of available resources, existing knowledge, and freedom of action. These objectives will be pursued by planners and administrators regardless of whether researchers attempt to help or not. Technological research is automatically attuned to the same objectives, as success in technology is determined by the extent to which resources and knowledge can be used to increase efficiency, effectiveness and control over real world settings.

In addition to identical success criteria, it is likely that pursuit of that success is done with the same intellectual tools in the world of technology and the world of everyday choice making, i.e. theory, experience, intuition, judgment and experimentally obtained information. The only difference is that the technological research approach is likely to bring a rigor to the decision process which might be otherwise lacking. Although scientists also use all of these elements in decision making, the scientific enterprise is not specifically geared to sharpening the use of those elements in others.

Thus there is a correspondence between the goals and intellectual tools of everyday decision making, and the technological approach to problem solving. This correspondence is lacking in science, which generates rewards not for how well solutions operate within practical constraints, but for how well those practical constraints are transcended in the pursuit of truth and theory development.

Summary: Technology as a Solution to Cultural/Historical Irrelevance. A telling critique of the relevance of social science is that the theories and investigations which are generated by researchers are incompatible with the requirements or basic orientation of the surrounding cultural climate. The argument is that even if the methodology of research is applicable, the subject matter of the research is not. This problem is manifest in the field of evaluation by a disparity between what evaluators study and the solutions they propose on one hand, and the needs of decision makers and the general public on the other. What is needed to solve the problem is a mechanism to make the work of evaluators compatible with the more general problem-solving needs. A powerful method of accomplishing this task is to base evaluation on a technological model. Technological work is much more closely bound to the needs of society at large than is scientific work. This relationship is manifest in differences between science and technology as they relate to the nature and use of theory, the development of strategies of search and decison making, the key aspects of science and technology, and the goals of both endeavors. In all these cases, practical factors arise which the scientist seeks to transcend in order to further the search for truth and the development of theory. The aim of technology is not to transcend those factors, but to seek novel solutions which are the best possible under the limitations imposed. Scientists are rewarded for transcending those limitations. Technologists are rewarded for working successfully within them.

Modeling evaluation on the technological system merely imposes on the researcher precisely the same constraints and sensitivities which are encountered by those who, with or without the use of research, will seek solutions to genuine societal problems. Scientists do not have those constraints, or at least, are rewarded for avoiding them. Thus while the scientific model is inherently irrelevant to practical issues, the technological model is, by its nature, responsive to changes in the need for practical solutions to practical problems. Just as planners are rewarded for their responsiveness to solutions to new problems which may arise, so too are technologists rewarded for the same responsiveness. In sum, the technological model of research is likely to bring the "research culture" and the general societal culture into alignment.

Relevance as a Function of Basic Strategies, Choice of Topics, and the Impotence of Social Research

It has been claimed that basic strategies of research do not make for practically useful information, that researchers study topics which are irrelevant in the world of practical decision making, and that in any case, the social research enterprise does not have the power to help with pressing social problems. All of these criticisms have some validity, and none can be made to disappear. On the other hand, research has the potential to discover more powerful and precise information than can be obtained from other means. Thus we are faced with the problem of finding an approach to research which will minimize the problems of applicability and relevance, and will thus allow the advantages of the research approach to be brought to bear on practical problems. Organizing research efforts as a technological enterprise will accomplish this goal.

Basic Strategies of Research. The technological model of research yields a clear difference between research which is conducted for the sake of developing new innovations, and research for the sake of testing those innovations in actual practice. This distinction provides a frame of reference which will allow evaluators to meet a great many criticisms of the relevance of their work. Discriminating between development and field testing is not an important element in science. Such a distinction is, however, a major element in technological research. The development-field test distinction touches all dimensions of differences between science and technology, and in each case the technological model yields powerful guides to increased relevance. Argyris (1975) argues that the more powerful methodological tools of social science are not applicable in many field settings. Tajfel (1972) claims that experimentation can be useful, but only if a large amount of research is carried out on factors which influence the research context. Edwards, Guttentag, and Snapper (1975) believe that the classical approach to hypothesis testing is not particularly useful for evaluation situations.

All of these critiques assume, at least implicitly, that in order to be relevant, research must be done in settings which are highly similar to the situations in which research results are meant to generalize. In other words, the research setting must be as "messy" or complex as the real world setting of interest. If this were true it may indeed be impossible (for practical and ethical reasons) to conduct adequate research on practical problems. Fortunately the history of research clearly indicates that this is *not* the case, and that the simplifications which are necessary for research can lead to practical advances. The question turns on the distinction between technological research and development on the one hand, and the field testing of new techniques on the other. The two are not one and the same.

Research and development efforts can—and usually do—take place in settings which are different from those where products will ultimately be employed. The only requirements for development research are that major elements of real world influences be approximated in the research setting, and that variables be chosen which are likely to make a practical difference within the context of those influences. These requirements constitute the essential ingredients of the research and development phase of technology, and are quite compatible with artificial research settings.

An excellent example can be found in the concept of the "lab school." In these cases, universities or research institutions help set up and run schools for the express purpose of having a context for educational research. These settings are not exactly analagous to normal school systems. Crucial differences exist in the expectations and role perceptions of staff, funding structure, the source of authority for policy decisions, selection processes for students, size of student body, and the researcher's control over everyday activity. Given these differences between ordinary and laboratory schools, there is certainly no guarantee that educational programs developed in the controlled setting will operate effectively on a wide scale. On the other hand, laboratory schools are a reasonable approximation of normal school settings, and certainly provide a useful context for the development of meaningful educational innovations.

Another phase of technological work is the field testing of proposed innovations. The purpose of field testing is to determine whether an innovation will be successful without the artificiality, special attention, and extra funding which are inherent aspects of efforts at development. Field test research is less methodologically rigorous than development research. It must be so, as the reason for field testing is to see if an innovation will function as planned when operated by practitioners under everyday conditions. It is precisely for these reasons, though, that field tests should not be carried out unless the dynamics of an innovation's workings are well understood. Without such understanding, the noise of field settings would make it impossible to attribute program effects to particular aspects of a program, or to determine why a program did not function as planned. In the language of Campbell and Stanley (1966), field test research admits a large number of plausible rival hypotheses.

Because of these rival hypotheses, data from field test research cannot be interpreted in the absence of a well-developed knowledge base. Such a base can only come from methodologically rigorous efforts during the development phase of technological research.

It may be that in the actual practice of evaluation in social service, the line between program development and field testing is blurred and that evaluators find themselves doing two tasks at once. It is easy to see why in the face of such confusion evaluation is vulnerable to the charge of not appropriately applying powerful research designs. It is difficult to extract valid development data from field test contexts, and the attempt to do so is likely to sensitize evaluation's critics to think in terms of the requirements of development research. If evaluators speak the language of development research, they are likely to be perceived as doing development research, the real nature of the work notwithstanding.

One might argue that the fault is the evaluators', as they should know better than to jam square pegs into round holes—development research designs into field test settings. It is more likely, however, that the fault lies with the system in which we are all forced to attempt solutions to social problems. Campbell's (1971) experimenting society is not a reality and we all must do the best we can in difficult circumstances. There is a political dynamic to social service funding, and evaluators are just one of the parties who are caught in the maelstrom. On the other hand evaluators do not help their image when they fail to recognize the difference between development research and the field testing of innovations—a distinction which is crucial in technology but of minor importance in science.

An excellent example of differences between development and field test research can be found in the area of drug research. Typically, the development of a new drug passes through several stages. (A more in-depth explanation of this process can be found in Calesnick 1971.) First, a likely substance is identified. This process may result from the blind testing of numerous chemical substances, or from theories of biochemical action, or from some combination of the two. Once a substance is identified as a likely candidate, it is tested on animals for efficacy, negative effects, potency, and the like. These animal tests are conducted in a fairly rigorous manner, with the use of control groups, strict regulation of dosages, and careful attention to time schedules. If the new drug still seems useful, it may be tested on humans through the use of controlled clinical trials. These trials are also conducted according to a methodologically rigorous research plan. Ideally, the study should have a no-treatment control group, several experimental groups using varying dosages, and careful attention to drug administration and measurement of effects on the subject. In addition, such a study may also match the drug against the best-known accepted drug, and will be administered according to a double-blind format. Neither the subject nor the researcher should know which drug is being administered to whom. Research of this type is labor-intensive, and is usually conducted with a relatively small number of subjects. Finally, if the drug still seems worthwhile, it may be tested in large-scale, uncontrolled clinical trials. The final stage is needed to see how the drug will work with large and diverse populations. Such studies are also needed to make sure that the drug works appropriately when administered in the absence of close research scrutiny, and in the normal working context of every-day clinical medicine.

From our point of view, there are several interesting facets to this process. First, chemical substances are picked only if there is reason to believe that they will make a noticeable and practical difference in the everyday world of clinical medicine. This is a technological—not a scientific—criterion.

Second, both development and field test studies are employed. The animal research and the randomized clinical trials are necessary in order to develop precise expectations of what the drug will do. Uncontrolled research could not produce such knowledge. There is wide variation in people's reactions to drugs. The same drug may operate differently in different populations. Individual medical history may influence a drug's effect. Individual behavior—such as seeking other medical treatment—may affect drug action. Because of factors such as these, uncontrolled trials—no matter how large—could not supply accurate and valid information on drug action. Thus, randomized controlled trials are needed in order to develop a knowledge base which will allow the effects of a new drug to be understood.

Third, controlled clinical trials are not sufficient for making decisions about using a drug as part of general medical practice. The use and effects of a drug may differ in closely controlled circumstances and in general medical practice. Thus wide-scale research is needed to approximate the usage of the drug in general practice.

Fourth, the uncontrolled clinical trials would never be acceptable as the sole methodology for testing a new drug. On the other hand, those uncontrolled trials, if used within the context of an already developed knowledge base, can supply crucial information. Without that information, a decison to employ the new drug could not be made.

Scientists who are primarily interested in understanding biochemical mechanisms would not choose to study a substance only because it might be useful in clinical medicine. Given a choice between a substance which makes a practical difference and a substance which might elucidate an unknown chemical mechanism, the scientist would choose the latter. The technologist, on the other hand, would choose the substance which would make a practical difference. Scientists would not feel compelled to conduct uncontrolled clinical trials. Technologists must conduct such trials.

There is no reason why similar dynamics should not operate in the area of education, or income maintenance, or the development of mental health programs, or any other area of social endeavor. Development research could be used to establish a knowledge base which once established, would allow the interpretation of information from wide-spread trials. Both are needed in order to develop useful social innovations.

In sum, the methodology of social research can be rigorously exercised in the cause of evaluation as long as the distinction between development research and field testing is maintained. Although this destinction is a major element in the technological model of research, it is not crucial in the scientific model. Valid development research can be conducted if three conditions obtain. First, variables must be chosen for the express purpose of being powerful enough to make a discernable difference in the settings where they are destined to operate. Although the technological model is sensitive to this requirement, the scientific model is not. Second, the research setting must include the most powerful or important factors which might mitigate against the proper action of experimental variables or programs; scientific research attempts to screen out such factors. Finally, research settings must be simplified enough to allow observation of the relationships among important variables. If these conditions are met, there is a good chance of obtaining valid information which has a reasonable chance of directing meaningful action in real world settings. As to whether such results can be translated effectively into the real world, that must await the classic field test.

Field testing is a special form of research which by its nature cannot employ the more rigorous methodological techniques. Consequently, field test research cannot be adequately interpreted in the absence of an already well-developed knowledge base. There are better and worse ways of conducting field test research, but critics of such research cannot employ the criteria used for judging development studies. Field test research must be criticized within its own frame of reference.

Once a technological model of research is adapted, the ambiguity between development and field testing disappears and the requirements for choosing appropriate research designs become clear. Rigorous experimental or quasi-experimental designs are appropriate for development research, while less powerful techniques must be employed during field testing. Each type of research can vary greatly in methodological quality, but critiques must be confined to appropriate frames of reference. Part of the ambiguity between the two types of research is due to the political reality which forces evaluators to carry out both types of work simultaneously. Another part of the problem is failure to conceptualize research as clearly belonging to one or the other category. The scientific model of research blurs this distinction, while the technological model casts the development-field test distinction in sharp relief.

The Choice of Topics. Still another reason why technological models should be invoked in evaluation is that the scientific world is a very special existence in which priorities are not set with practical value in mind. In a sense, there is no obligation to conduct field tests in order to assess practicality. It might be said that science is very much an art in which the aesthetic criteria are truth and theory development. This is not to say that science is immune to sociological forces, as this is clearly not the case. Scientists are influenced by the priorities and needs of the world around them, funding priorities do indicate the research which will be done, and science is most certainly subject to fads and fashions. There is, however, a crucial difference between the influence of societal forces on science and on technology. In the case of science, there is no *logical* connection between practical societal needs and the topics of scientific investigation. Such factors are intruders on the logical structure of science. Science as a pursuit could exist without such forces, if only the world would let it. Not so in the case of technology, which, by its *essential nature* must be responsive to practical needs. This difference shows up in the nature of theory, in the choice of topics, and in the methods of both endeavors. This is the crucial reason for adapting the technological approach to evaluation, as on all levels, it orients the researcher to an interface with practical issues, theories, laboratory models, and variables which make a difference in the real world. Most important, the criteria of truth and potential to help with theory development—the aims of science—are likely to lead *away* from practical concerns, or at least, any correspondence between the two is at best coincidental.

Impotence of Social Research. Rossi (1972) claims that social research may simply be too weak an enterprise to solve current social problems. Those problems are so difficult and unrelenting that current knowledge is simply not up to the challenge. Weiss (1973) believes that the problems may be solved, but only if programs are designed and funded to deal with the multiple causal factors which we know to be operating. The current political process of program funding does not recognize this reality, and until it does, many social problems will defy solution. How might evaluation help in a world of difficult problems and inadequate solutions? Again, the technological model comes to the rescue. To date, theories in social science have not addressed powerful variables set in a context of factors which are important in the real world. One reason for this state of affairs is that scientific theories are not developed for the express purpose of guiding social innovation. Bunge's (1967) notion that theories have both range and accuracy is useful here. As the range of any specific theory is stretched, its accuracy decreases. It may be that the use of scientific theories to address practical issues necessitates stretching the range of those theories, and as a result accuracy suffers. We would be far better off with theories specifically aimed at explaining factors which make a difference in the real world.

As an example, consider the case of the multicausality of social problems.

Weiss (1973) has criticized policy makers for funding programs which are based on single-cause theories even though we are certain that those problems must be dealt with on a multicausal basis. Although program funding may be based on single-cause models, program evaluation need not follow the lead. Evaluators might measure many of the likely determinants of a problem even though the program being evaluated is designed to influence only one of those many factors. Such an evaluation might begin to give us a sense of which factors are truly important in a practical sense, and might point the way to theories of social action which are useful for program planning. For instance, the evaluation of a program designed to increase reading speed by teaching pattern recognition might include collateral measures of parental support for students' participation, achievement motivation, study habits, and the like. The same is true for mental health, drug abuse, corrections, and many other areas of social programming. Numerous social, psychological, and economic aspects of a problem may be incorporated into the evaluation of programs based on single cause models. The power of inference may not be as great in such situations as we might wish, but the information may still be useful, and likely to lead to theories which explain program effects in naturalistic settings.

Efforts of this kind may lead to predictions which are not as accurate as those of scientific prediction, but as Ackoff, Gupta, and Minas (1962) have pointed out, technologists have the luxury of setting limits on the amount of needed accuracy. This luxury is not shared by scientists who, in their search for truth, must try always to be as accurate as possible.

We have seen that technology includes several elements which are not shared by science. These include experiment, intuition, experience, and judgment. Although scientists certainly use these intellectual tools in their work, scientific efforts are not primarily aimed at expending effort to systematically sharpen others' ability to use those tools. Technologists, on the other hand, do make such efforts. An excellent example of this process is Guttentag's work in decision theoretics, where the major thrust is sharpening the ability of program personnel to make accurate judgments about their intuitions, observations, and opinions. (See for example: Edwards, Guttentag, and Snapper, 1975.) Operations research is another example where the main thrust is to help with the prediction of events regardless of the causal factors which are involved. As a consequence of its special emphasis on experiment, judgment, intuition and experience, technologically based evaluation is likely to help administrators and policy setters choose appropriate programs, see the importance of programs based on multiple causation, and choose from all available alternatives those programs which have the highest potential for success.

Evaluation alone is by no means equal to the task of finding radically new and powerful solutions to social problems, nor is it likely to change funding mechanisms in a pronounced manner. It can, however, make a contribution to this effort, and such a contribution is a natural outgrowth of the technological model which has, as integral elements, far more than truth seeking and theory development. Although conscientious scientists may also make such efforts, their attempts flow from a sense of civic responsibility rather than from the inherent nature of their work and their research. The logical structure of scientific work is not geared to finding successful practical innovations, and it is not surprising that civic responsibility has not transcended the limitations of logical structure. A concerted effort at employing a technological model of research might lead to powerful innovations which could work within present funding limitations.

Conclusion: Advantages of Evaluation as Social Technology

Rather than being a unique phenomenon, evaluation research is merely the latest manifestation of long-standing efforts at making social research relevant to the problems of society. As such, the shortcomings of evaluation must be understood within a larger framework which encompasses the more general issue of why social science has not been as socially relevant as it could or should be. Critiques of the relevance of social science revolve around four themes: the relation of theory to changing social needs, fundamental limitations of methodology and theory, the choice of inappropriate topics for investigation, and the difficulty of social problems relative to the weakness of social research. To some degree at least, all of these problems inhibit the usefulness of evaluation, and all become less serious when evaluation is conceptualized as a technological rather than a scientific endeavor.

Although there are many surface similarities between technology and science, profound differences exist between them which have direct and serious implications for the social relevance of research. (These differences are summarized in Table 5.1.) Differences involve the nature of theory, research strategies, the dominant intellectual tools of both endeavors, and the goals of each. Taken together, the differences mean that technology is more responsive than science to the task of developing practical innovations. The use of theory, the choice of research topics, the reward system for researchers, the organization of resources—all are attuned to developing successful course of action for those who have the responsibility of solving everyday practical problems. The central theme of science is not organizing resources for successful practical action, but rather, organizing resources for the development of theory and the discovery of truth. The scientific goals are independent of the technological goals, and on many occasions they are antithetical.

Evaluation is a form of social research which emerged from a need to test the value of society's efforts at solving social problems. As such, evaluation must generate information which will be useful to decision makers. If evaluation is to fulfill that role, it must operate on a model which is attuned to maximizing solutions within a context of ever-changing political, social and economic constraints. The scientific model, with its main goals of advancing truth and theory development, is attuned to surmounting those constraints by developing artificial situations which interact as little as possible with the practical world. Although scientists as individuals (or in groups) may be interested in helping with practical issues, the logical structure of their work is oriented toward goals which are, at best, irrelevant to the development of innovations which will survive the rigors of wide-scale implementation. Hence the need for conceptualizing evaluation as technology, a system in which the reward structure and the use of resources are intimately attuned to the issues involved in developing and testing practical innovations.

For the sake of clarity, the discussion so far has cast the scientific-technological distinction in the starkest possible contrast. One must not think, however, that there is no interplay between the two endeavors, that evaluation has no relation to social science, or that evaluators should not be concerned with matters of truth or theory development. Powerful interplays between science and technology do exist, and evaluators must consider those interactions. The main point in this chapter has been that, as a dominant mode of organizing activity, it is not productive to conceptualize evaluation as science, nor to assume that the search for truth and theory development will lead to successful practical innovation. Because of evaluation's highly specific and applied focus, the organizing theme of evaluation research must be technological. Now that the point has been made, the discussion will turn to the complementary aspects of science and technology. This will be done in order to obtain a sense of how the entire social research enterprise can be brought to bear on the solution of social problems.

INTERRELATIONSHIPS BETWEEN SCIENCE AND TECHNOLOGY

What is the relationship between social technology/evaluation and social science? What does each body of knowledge hold for the other? Is there a role for social science in helping to solve social problems? These issues cannot be ignored, as an over reliance on technological evaluation to the exclusion of social science is likely to stultify the search for substantive innovations which may help solve social problems.[5]

In an analysis of the differences between science and technology, Gruender (1971) argues that because the range of scientific study is limited, it is entirely possible that technologists will, in the course of their work, discover important inconsistencies in scientific theory. These inconsistencies may pose crucial problems to scientists, who would then have to redirect their thinking or research. Presumably, a similar process could also work in reverse. Scientists may discover facts which are inconsistent with technological theories, and which may direct the technologist into modifications or corrections which would improve guides to practical action.

Bunge (1963) claims that scientists and technologists are able to inspire each other, not because of any logical relation between science and technology, but because both endeavors are critical and analytic; and in a later work (1966, p. 128), because:

> . . . knowledge considerably *improves* the chances of correct doing, and doing *may* lead to knowing more (now that we have learned that knowledge pays), not because action is knowledge but because, in inquisitive minds, action may trigger questioning.

Another reason why the scientific aspects of social problems cannot be ignored is that there are crucial junctures when interaction must take place if substantive progress is to occur. In the usual course of business, new technology flows from old technology, and not from science (De Sola Price, 1965). There are, however, cases where technological limits are reached and where further progress is impossible without a basic, new, fundamental understanding of a phenomenon. According to Feibleman (1961) these are the times when technology must turn to science. But which body of science is sought at such times? De Sola Price (1965) makes it clear that avant garde technology does not turn to the newest scientific developments when help is needed. On the contrary, such events are rare exceptions. In general when technology is in need of help from science, it is the generally known, or ambient, body of scientific knowledge which is invoked. (The same also holds true in reverse. When scientists need technological help they do not turn to the very newest developments in technology, but rather, to the generally known and understood body of technological knowledge.) Thus it becomes vital for social science research to continue, for in the absence of continuing scientific progress, the limits of technological understanding and action will remain stationary, or at least, stultified.

A classic example of scientific contributions to the practical world of program planning can be found in the works of Jean Piaget. Piaget considers himself a "genetic epistemologist" (Rosen 1977). The essence of genetic epistemology is the study of the acquisition of knowledge. It is a theoretical pursuit which deals primarily with how people develop the ability to know and to understand. It was not developed for the express purpose of practical application. Piaget's theories, however, have had enormous impact on curriculum development in education, to the extent that one can find mathematics textbooks which are specifically based on theoretical concepts developed by Piaget and his colleagues. (As an example of such a book, see Copeland 1970.) Prior to Piaget's theoretical work, the best efforts of educational technologists resulted in curricula which were not responsive to the actual ability of children to process abstract concepts. It is quite likely that many of those curricula demanded that children produce at a level which was impossible for them. It is not likely that these problems would have been brought to light by people in the business of developing curricula. It took knowledge which came from highly abstract and theoretical sources to do the trick. Although that theory was based on empirical research, the research was intended to further theory, and not to help with practical problems of education or curriculum development.

Thus the argument in evaluation is not "science or technology," as both are indispensible aspects of efforts to achieve practical solutions and workable innovations. The issue is one of emphasis. If one is engaged in evaluation, the focus of the work is likely to be narrow, well-defined, and intimately tied to the working lives of service delivery personnel, administrators, and policy makers. Given this focus, the most powerful approach for conceptualizing problems and organizing work is the technological model. Technological theories concentrate on factors which make a difference in the real world. Technological research recognizes important differences between the development and field testing of innovations. Technology is specifically aimed at helping decision makers with all the phases of knowledge—theory, experiment, experience, intuition and judgment. Above all, technological action is guided by the same practical constraints which impinge on practical innovation, and success in technology is determined by the extent to which solutions are optimized with those constraints.

NOTES

[1] I picked a lot of brains in my efforts to find specific examples of issues which I discuss, and many thanks go to the people who helped with this effort. In alphabetical order, they are: Michael Kean, Hugh Rosen, Myrna Shure, Jerry Siegel, Glen Snelbecker, and George Spivack. In addition, I would like to thank Lois-Ellin Datta for her excellent overall critique of this chapter.

[2] Actually, there are five types of critiques. The fifth is an explanation proposed by George A. Miller (1969), in a discussion about the relevance of psychology. He argues that although psychology is relevant to practical problems, the relevance is not of an "instrumental" nature, i.e., the practical relevance of psychology does not depend on turning scientific concepts directly into technological applications. He claims that although a relatively direct transposition may be done in the physical sciences, it is not likely in the case of psychology. As an alternative, he proposes a type of relevance which manifests itself not through technological products, but through influencing public conceptions of what is humanly possible and desirable.

I am not dealing with this critique in the body of the chapter because my chief interest is not whether psychology (or any social science) has technological relevance, but whether evaluation can be useful if it is built on a technological model. In that sense, Miller's point is not relevant to arguments presented in this chapter. I mention it here for the sake of completeness, and because it might be useful for people who are concerned with other aspects of the relevance issue.

[3] The phrase "the search for truth" is not original. It constitutes the subtitle of a fascinating work by Mario Bunge (1967) on the philosophy of science. The full title is *Scientific Research: II. The Search for Truth.*

[4] This is a very brief and simplistic statement of the issue. All theories have some disconfirming instances, and isolated instances of disconfirmation are by no means sufficient to destroy a theory. A detailed discussion of the issue can be found in Lakatos and Musgrave 1972. Disconfirmation is much more important in science than it is in technology, but the reader should not think that single instances of disconfirmation play a major role in the development of scientific theory.

[5] Actually, this is a statement of faith in the potential power of social science. It may be that, except for a few exceptions, social science will never be useful in finding solutions to practical social problems. Finch (1961) points out that until the sixteenth century, science and engineering were very

different activities which had very little to do with each other. It was not until then that scientists began to develop theories which were powerful enough to be of use to engineers. What stage are we presently at in terms of the relation between social science and social technology? The answer is not at all clear, and there are no guarantees about the course of future developments.

6

Implementation of Evaluation: Dynamics of Conflict and Suggestions for Change[1]

INTRODUCTION

No matter how well armed with knowledge of research design, evaluation, or principles of information utilization, evaluators are not likely to enjoy an easy coexistence with administrators and policy makers. There will always be problems in implementing evaluation studies, and these problems are bound to cause friction among the interested parties. Most evaluation takes place (at least in part) within existing service delivery systems, and powerful forces are at work which limit the suitability of such organizations for evaluation activity. The main contention of this chapter is that frictions can be minimized if evaluation is organized along the lines suggested by the previous chapters of this book, namely, as a technological endeavor consisting of three basic characteristics—type, validity, and usefulness. The argument will proceed in three steps. First, the historical and sociological roots of evaluation implementation problems will be set out. Second, possible solutions will be proposed. Finally, I will try to show how the three-dimensional typology of evaluation, together with technological perspectives, can be used as organizing principles for all methods of reducing conflict due to the implementation of evaluation.

Attempts at explaining the reasons for friction between evaluators and decision makers are not new. The rise in popularity of evaluation has raised many people's consciousness concerning this matter, and a good deal of attention has been paid to the problem (Aronson and Sherwood 1967; Bergen 1969; Bloom 1972; Caro 1971; Mann 1965; Rodman and Kolodny 1964).

These analyses have attempted to point out areas of difference between the groups, and sometimes to propose solutions. They have not, however, proposed a systematic typology of problems and solutions that are grounded in the structure of social research and service delivery. Such an attempt is necessary because evaluation is part of the social research tradition, and because the problems involved are rooted historically and sociologically in the larger question of interactions between social research and social service delivery in this country. Without the larger perspective, it will be difficult to understand the persistence of problems or to see a way clear to solutions. Consequently it is important to explore the roots of problems, to propose a structure within which the issues can be understood, and to propose solutions based both on mutual understanding and on substantive change.

BINDING FORCES BETWEEN SOCIAL SCIENCE AND SOCIAL SERVICE

Social service agencies and social science are bound together by ties of mutual need, historical tradition and outside pressure. As a first step it is necessary to investigate the nature of these ties and try to sort out the problems that exist because of them.

Mutual Need. Although theory and explanation are not one and the same, explanation is one of the major components of theory (Brown 1963). Explanation in turn is only meaningful within a well-defined context (Kaplan 1964). Thus, in a sense the nature of our science is defined by the contexts within which we attempt our explanations.[2] Further, once a body of knowledge is developed, there also develop strong forces for working with and within that body of knowledge (Kuhn 1971). There is already a strong tradition of social research within service agency settings. As examples, one need only consider the research which has been done in school systems, mental health facilities, health care delivery systems, and day care settings. As a consequence of these facts, it is likely that social scientists will continue to perceive an ongoing need to do research within service agency settings.

Social service agencies, on the other hand, are constantly attempting to maximize the benefits of their services.[3] Although any given agency may or may not be interested or involved in research, service agencies must in the long run look to research for the improvement of their services. Such improvement cannot take place without the research, testing, and analysis that social scientists can provide. As examples, one need only look at attempts to discover the etiology of reading problems, the characteristics of effective therapist-client relationships, or the major components of social and vocational rehabilitation (Bond and Tinker 1973;

Reagles, Wright, and Butler 1970, 1972; Truax and Carkhuff 1967). It is also likely that administrators perceive their agency's funding to be related in some manner to the quality of service that is dispensed. To the extent that this is so, administrators have an additional reason to cooperate with researchers. (The notion that quality of service is not a primary concern of administrators will be discussed later in this chapter.)

Social scientists need social service agencies as unique laboratory settings while social service agencies need the investigative and methodological skills of researchers.

Tradition. One of the hallmarks of our age is the notion that science is a powerful and useful tool and that this tool should be used to help us in all our endeavors. A consequence of this belief is that considerable prestige evolves to one associated with the use and furtherance of science. Although one cannot escape the impression that our scientific ardor has paled in the last few years, the thesis that science is central to our lives and highly valued is certainly still true. Another common belief is the simple notion that one should help solve social problems if one can. These beliefs impel social agency administrators to seek (or at least accept) the help of researchers. Similarly, researchers are impelled to try to help.

Outside Pressure. The idea that science should be applied toward the betterment of the human condition seems firmly entrenched. This notion exists within social service agencies, in the ranks of the scientific community, and among the general populace. More important, it is held by the powers that hold the purse strings. It is painfully obvious that most research ideas are not funded. It is equally obvious that those who control the money also control the existence and direction of most social service agencies. Given such financial control and given the belief that science should help solve social problems, there exists strong pressure for close interaction between social service agencies and social scientists. The recent emphasis on evaluation research is merely a formalization of this belief.

Thus we have a combination of four forces: the need for research settings, cultural values, desire to improve one's product and financial reality. The result of these forces affects a marriage between social science and social service. The marriage, however, is mostly one of necessity and convenience. Little love and much friction exists between the two parties. The friction is manifest in many ways. Difficulties in implementing evaluation, difficulties in getting evaluation results used, problems of gaining entry to service organizations for the conduct of research, resentment or hostility between service delivery and research/evaluation personnel—these are but a few examples of the types of conflict that can arise. The reader will no doubt have little difficulty in adding to the list.

These agency-research problems can be broken down into several fairly distinct categories.

SOURCES OF FRICTION BETWEEN SOCIAL SCIENCE AND SOCIAL SERVICE

Conflicts over the Type of Research or Evaluation That Is to Be Conducted

These conflicts include disagreements concerning relevant theories, differences over specific topics for research, and differing notions about what makes a specific study "scientific." Social science theories are often perceived by nonscientists as weak and as having little potential to explain the causation or etiology of important problems (Bloom 1972). Issues and topics that are of great concern to a researcher may seem less than trivial to an educator, a social worker or an administrator. Conversely people in these professions might have great need for information that is of little interest to a psychologist, a sociologist, or an economist. Given the different perspectives (both theoretical and practical) of different professions, such disagreements are not unlikely. Further, conceptions of what is or is not "scientific" are not always agreed upon by researchers and service agency personnel. An administrator may consider a study scientific if it collects information that is objective, systematic and comprehensive, while a researcher might insist on control groups and randomization (Tripodi, Fellin, and Epstein 1971). Such differing conceptions might cause great difficulty when it comes to negotiating what a researcher or an evaluator may or may not do in an agency setting. (For an enlightening discussion of what should be included in such negotiations, see Fairweather, Sanders, and Tornatzky 1974.)

Conflicts over the Dislocation That Research or Evaluation May Cause an Agency

Such conflicts can arise in two separate contexts: a) when a researcher approaches an agency for permission to carry out a pet project, and b) when an agency approaches a researcher to do a specific job. In both these cases research will almost certainly involve some demand on staff time, some changes in an agency's standard operating procedure, and some disruption of routine. It should come as no surprise that such demands are resented.

Conflicts over the Control of Evaluation and Research

The head of an agency is ultimately responsible for everything that happens within his or her organization. Because of this responsibility it is legitimate for administrators to have a say in all aspects of their agency's functioning. The problem is that evaluators and researchers have a similar responsibility to their work, and research designs are usually very delicate and cannot tolerate much tampering. Thus conflicts over control of research are based on two (often) antagonistic sets of legitimate responsibilities.

Evaluation Apprehension

Feelings of vulnerability are aroused whenever outsiders are allowed into one's private domain. As a result almost any research is likely to arouse evaluation apprehension. Several people have advanced the idea that evaluation apprehension is grounded in the structure of the research situation. Etzioni (1969) claims that all organizations must split their efforts between two sets of objectives, stated goals and organizational maintenance. The latter are not clearly stated to the outside world but they are legitimate activities which absorb a good deal of an organization's efforts and resources.

> From the viewpoint of the system model, such activities are functional and increase the organizational effectiveness. It follows that a social unit that devotes all its efforts to fulfilling one functional requirement, even if it is that of performing goal activities, will undermine the fulfillment of this very functional requirement, because recruitment of means, maintenance of tools, and the social integration of the unit will be neglected (Etzioni 1969, pp. 103-104).

Etzioni argues that most evaluation is not carried out from this perspective. Rather, researchers tend to look only at stated goals and to evaluate on the implicit assumption that such goals are the only legitimate ones.

Wildavsky (1972) makes a similar point. He claims that essential aspects of the functioning of any agency are the stabilization of its working environment, securing internal loyalty and insuring outside support. These functions are incompatible with too much information which may indicate a necessity for changes in organizational functioning, or may cast a negative light on an organization's operations. The essence of Wildavsky's argument is captured in his introduction, where he states (p. 509):

> I started out thinking it was bad for organizations not to evaluate, and I ended up wondering why they ever do it. Evaluation and organization, it turns out, are to some extent contradictory terms. Failing to understand that evaluation is sometimes incompatible with organization, we are tempted to believe in absurdities much in the manner of mindless bureaucrats who never wonder whether they are doing useful work.

Campbell (1971) argues that any advocacy is bound to involve exaggeration and inflated claims. If this is true, and if one considers members of an organization as advocates of the goals and objectives of their organization, then we can easily understand reasons for evaluation apprehension. People do not want to be forced into defending an indefensible position, namely, that their organization is a failure unless they meet their overly stated, exaggerated goals.

Rossi (1972) and Weiss (1970) claim that of necessity, the impact of most social programs will be small. Rossi claims that :

Dramatic effects of illiteracy can be achieved by providing schools and teachers to all children. Achieving a universally high enough level of literacy and knowledge, so that everyone capable of learning can find a good spot in our labor force, is a bit more difficult. Hence the more we have done in the past to lower unemployment rates, to provide social service, etc., the more difficult it is to add to the benefits derived from past programs by the addition of new ones. Partly, this is because we have achieved so much with the past programs and partly this is because the massive efforts of the past have not dealt with individual motivation as much as with benefits to aggregates of individuals (Rossi 1972, p. 226).

According to Weiss:

Fragmentary projects are created to deal with broad-spectrum problems. We know about multiple causality. We realize that a single stimulus program is hardly likely to make a dent in deep rooted ills. But the political realities are such that we take what programs we can get through Congress (and other sources) when we can get them (Weiss 1970, p. 226).

It is doubtful that the administrators and employees of most social service programs can articulate these issues as clearly as has been stated above. It is certain, however, that they have a feeling for these issues and that their fear of researchers and/or evaluators is founded on these arguments. Feelings of vulnerability may be especially high when program evaluation per se is conducted. Almost any research, however, is likely to allow outsiders at least an informal or indirect evaluation of one's work and one's organization.

The "Culture Gap" between Researchers and Service Delivery Personnel

There is a profound difference in perspective between those oriented toward research and those oriented toward service delivery. The difference is composed of numerous elements but I believe that the most important ones can be summarized by seven main points. First, researchers tend to look for generality and similarity among discrete events or people. Practitioners tend to emphasize the unique attributes of each particular patient or client (Bloom 1972).

Second, researchers like to deal with the development of knowledge that may have long-range beneficial effects. Practitioners are usually preoccupied with immediate patient needs (Bergen 1969).

Third, inherent in the notion of research is a force toward development and change. Inherent in administration are efforts at maintaining a steady state in one's organization (Caro 1971; Wildavsky 1972). This problem is likely to be manifest in entirely different perspectives on the function of evaluation research. In an empirical study of attitudes about evaluation research, Eaton (1969) has found that while researchers take a *substantive* view of such work, administrators tend to take a *symbolic* view. Eaton (1969, p. 32) summarizes the differences as follows:

Research has two very different functions for organizations: a symbolic function and a substantive one. Science thrives on substantive research: the asking of questions, the gathering of data to explore them, the application of theory to explain the findings, and the communication of findings to others. Symbolic research, in contrast, characterizes studies of socially controversial topics. It involves ritualistic avowal of the value of research by staff members in organizational committees and in policy statements. Such a favorable verbal climate for research can be maintained as long as findings are not seen as threatening to positions of power or as questioning professional traditions or organizational policies. Symbolic research is an unintended consequence of the uncertainty element between two conflicting attitudes—the belief in the value of exploring the unknown, and the fear of disturbing positions of power or raising questions about existing agency operations.

Fourth, a researcher's status is bound up with the process of finding out and answering questions, while the status of practitioners is bound to helping individuals by the application of a specific body of knowledge. A further complication is that the status of administrators is centered on an entirely different loci from that of researchers. Administrators gain status by maintaining a smoothly operating organization. Researchers gain status by publishing research (Bergen 1969).

Fifth, parts of the cultural gap are different perspectives concerning the ethics of control groups, randomization and other accoutrements of experimental design. (There are many discussions of these issues. (For examples, see Mann 1965; Riecken and Boruch 1974).

Sixth, there is the issue of how researchers and administrators organize and conceptualize their work. Researchers are immediately interested in causal relationships that exist between dependent and independent variables. One might think that this interest is also of great importance to administrators because such knowledge can easily be translated into the question of an organization's effectiveness relative to its stated goals. Attainment of program goals is probably not, however, the real, practical, everyday concern of administrators. Most of an administrator's daily concern revolves around insuring smooth interplay between organizational units such as personnel, units, services, departments, etc. The interplay between such concerns must of course be related ultimately to program goals. But what percentage of anyone's day is taken up with concern over "ultimates"? We are all preoccupied with immediate concerns. Thus we have a situation in which the immediate concern of researchers is the distant concern of administrators, and nobody likes to be pushed into a confrontation with long-range goals when one is enmeshed in a daily battle for survival.

Seventh, there is the issue of stating clear goals and objectives. An enormous amount of energy has gone into attempts at reconciling the seemingly ubiquitous ambiguity of service agency goals with the needs of evaluators for precise statements of organizational procedures, objectives, and expected outcomes. There is good reason to believe that although the problem can be ameliorated, it cannot be eliminated or even substantially reduced. The nature of social service work may well involve goals which are *necessarily* ambiguous and constantly in a state of flux. (An excellent analysis of this problem may be found in Patton 1978, chap. 6.) If this is the case, it is little wonder that much tension is generated by evaluators' requests for well-defined, precise goal statements.

These categories of researcher-agency problems can be reordered into two categories: conflicts over the subject matter of the research, and conflicts over the disruption that is needed to carry it out. As a case in point, consider an evaluation or research project in a school setting. At least six issues came to mind which may cause friction between school and research/evaluation personnel.

1. The disturbance caused when children are removed from a class for research or evaluation purposes can be quite serious. The child misses instruction, class routine is interrupted and the attention of other students is diverted.

2. Aberrations in daily schedules can have a very disconcerting effect on the smooth flow of activity in a school. Testing children for the purposes of research or evaluation often calls for such changes.

3. Teachers often resent (rightly, I think) having to devote class time to activities other than education. This often happens when questionnaires, special tests and the like must be filled out by students.

4. Teachers also resent (again with a good deal of justification) having to devote their own free time to research work. Rating students on special scales, for instance, can be very time-consuming and tedious.

5. One type of objection over subject matter concerns the content and nature of data-gathering tools. Resistance to research may arise out of beliefs that questionnaires should not ask for information about students' private lives or home environments. Also, educators may fear that a study will cause students to call into question cherished values or raise their levels of anxiety. Further objectives might arise because of the anxiety-producing effects of research apparatus, procedures, or personnel.

6. Another objection over subject matter concerns the worth of the topic under study. As explained earlier, issues of interest to researchers or evaluators may be of little or no concern to educators.

JUSTIFICATION OF THE RESEARCH/EVALUATION POSITION

So far the drift of this argument has cast the researcher/evaluator in the role of villain. There are, however, several powerful factors that speak to the justification of evaluators and researchers.

First, very few research or evaluation projects can be totally unobtrusive. Once the legitimacy of any given piece of research is acknowledged, the probability of some inconvenience to the research context must be accepted. (This is not to say that unobtrusive research is impossible. For examples of such research see

Hyman 1972; Webb et al. 1966.) The probability of a great deal of inconvenience to the research or evaluation design is of course, a foregone conclusion.

Second, social scientists have skills and abilities that can (and should) be exploited by society at large. Society does have problems and it is legitimate to seek help from all quarters. Those who seek help, however, must realize that receiving help is not a passive process. One must actively cooperate with one's helpers. A researcher's anger and frustration is well founded when people fail to recognize this point.

Third, there are many scientific puzzles which are in and of themselves worthy of study. Pure science, the attempt to understand the world, is unquestionably a legitimate undertaking. Because of the nature of their subject, social scientists must have the cooperation of social service agencies. Some important scientific issues simply cannot be studied in any context other than the social service agency. Agency personnel must learn to accept this fact. Many social scientists lament that they do not.

Finally, a great deal of social service takes place with public funds, and receiving such funds carries with it certain obligations. One obligation is to permit careful assessments of the wisdom of the public's investment, hence the necessity of evaluation. A second obligation is to help solve social problems in more than the narrow sense of providing specific services to well-defined populations. In many cases, services that are being provided are obviously far from the ideal, and it might be argued that organizations which provide such services have an obligation to help search for more effective solutions. Participation in that search might be construed as part of the organization's reason for existence, as it is obvious that the service provided may, in and of itself, not be worth the public's investment.

So the lines are drawn. Researchers and social service agencies have legitimate demands to make on each other. Both have reasons for being unhappy with the other. The mere existence of conflicting needs and demands does not, however, fully explain the problem. There are additional factors that serve to lock both sides into their respective positions.

FACTORS THAT INHIBIT COMPROMISE

Consequences of Attempting to Be Relevant

In recent years it has become more and more important for scientists to do "relevant" research. While pure science and relevant science are not necessarily incompatible, the correspondence is very far from one-to-one. (For an excellent critique of the usefulness of research see Baumrin 1970.) Pure (or at least "non-relevant") science might well be viewed as a frill. In times of tight money and ever-growing social problems frills become less and less important. Social and economic forces generate strong pressure for research that is immediately applicable. Pressure notwithstanding, it is difficult to persuade people to surrender a cherished idea. For social scientists that cherished idea is often a nonrelevant piece of research. Thus a conflict often arises between what many social scientists want to do and what they are funded to do. This conflict manifests itself in both an overt and a subtle manner. Overtly, researchers keep trying to obtain funds for projects that interest them. Subtly, there is a tendency to try to "bend" fundable projects to the purpose of the researcher (Weiss 1970). The idea is to set up a research or evaluation project that will serve both a social need and also test a hypothesis that is of interest to the researcher. Unfortunately there is a limit to the extent to which such compromises can be effected. All too often a choice must be made, and at that point people begin to dig in and defend their positions.

Just about any proposal for work in evaluation or research can be written so that it seems relevant, and funding dynamics result in such attempts being pushed to their limits. Researchers often feel that unless they base proposals on relevance, they will never be able to study that which interests them. I do not mean to imply that deliberate misrepresentation takes place. I do believe that pressure leads one to grasp at any possible argument, no matter how tenuous, as a justification for research. The result is a loss of faith in the social science establishment. The cry of "relevance" has been heard too often. It is no longer believed.

To complicate matters, people often grow to believe their own propaganda, and social scientists are not exempt from the problem. The researcher may really believe that the results of his or her work will be useful. Such beliefs are not, however, shared by the personnel of social service agencies. The resulting arguments are often futile, acrimonious, and leave suspicion on both sides.[4]

Fear of Evaluation

For all the recent talk of constructive evaluation, administrators and staff have good reason to fear the intrusion of the social scientist. Even in cases where no evaluation is intended, evaluation is often implied. The agency's operations are being scrutinized, variables are measured which probably reflect on the agency's functioning, and reporting is done both formally and informally to the outside world. As we have seen, the administration of a social service program is likely to involve making exaggerated promises of effectiveness, a continual shift in objectives and goals, fights for funding and survival, and attempts at solving complex problems by simplistic means. It is easy to understand why evaluators might be feared by social service workers who are dedicated, competent, and realistic. Those workers know the problems, they know that they are doing the best they can, they know that every penny of funding will involve a fight, and they feel sure that close scrutiny of their work will reveal many problems, much inefficiency, and little effectiveness. It would be surprising indeed if evaluation apprehension were not a serious problem.

These are the factors that transform the basic researcher-agency misunderstanding into a simmering, often erupting, feud. It now remains to see how the feud can be settled.

SOLUTIONS TO THE CONFLICT

As a first step in increasing cooperation between the social service and the researcher/evaluation communities, it is important to identify those areas where increased understanding of the opposite party's position might lead to mutual respect and greater efforts at compromise. Although mutual understanding is by no means a complete solution, it certainly is a good place to start. Once started, more substantive and structural solutions can be attempted.

Change Based on Increased Respect and Understanding

The need for respect and understanding is most easily explained by categorizing issues on the basis of which group must take the initiative for changes in its attitude or position.

Change Needed by Researchers and Evaluators. Researchers must be made to realize and appreciate the disruption they can cause. Social workers, teachers, counselors, nurses—all have precious little free time in the course of a work day. One-half hour's time filling out a questionnaire is a half hour that could have been spent collecting one's thoughts, settling one's mind and steeling oneself against the chaos of the next few hours.

Researchers and evaluators must also take seriously the concept of relevance. Overused words lose their meaning. People who overuse words lose their credibility. Social scientists must have a clear idea as to what puzzles they are trying to solve, and they must be honest in outlining the possible benefits of the work they propose.

Finally, it is important for researchers and evaluators to try to gain an appreciation of the kinds of problems social service agencies really need solved.

Change Needed by Service Agency Personnel. Social service agencies must recognize the legitimacy of research and evaluation which may not have obvious or immediate applicability. Although I would be hard put to specify the size of the role it should play, I am absolutely convinced that such work has a value of its own, and should be carried out.

Agency personnel must realize that much social science simply cannot be carried out without their help. Any problem has a context within which it can best be solved, and social service agencies often provide the best context for studying certain types of problems.

Agency personnel must understand that almost no research or evaluation can be made totally unobtrusive. Inconvenience can be minimized but rarely can it be eliminated. Once the legitimacy of such work is accepted, the inevitability of some disruption or bother must also be accepted.

With the possible exception of the specific evaluation of a specific program, almost no research can have immediately practical results. There is always a time lag, and it is often longer than one might wish. This fact is too often missed by the directors and staffs of social service agencies.

Change Required of All Parties. Both researchers and agency personnel must understand the uses and limits of research, of science and the scientific method, and of analagous aspects of technology. Science and technology can best be viewed as methods of providing high-quality hints as to the true state of affairs about certain types of problems. They are not methods for dispensing truth or guaranteed answers, and they cannot be applied to any and every question. The problem is that researchers subscribe to the dictum: "Give a small boy a hammer, and he will find that everything he encounters needs pounding" (Kaplan 1964, chap. 1). Further, there is great pressure on administrators and practitioners to go along with a belief in the power of research even though they have good reason to mistrust it. A balanced view of how research can be intelligently exploited (which includes an understanding of where it will not work) might reduce many existing tensions.

The assumption behind these solutions is that if only communication can be established, if only each side could understand the other, all conflict would vanish. This assumption is certainly false. Changes in organizational routine cannot be eliminated; demands on people's time must be made, and the need to solve social problems will not go away. Conflicting needs of staff and researcher cannot be reduced to zero. Economic priorities will always tend to favor work on immediate problems. Time cannot be expanded to allow everything to be done. Evaluation apprehension will not disappear. The structure of the situation is such that the marriage between social scientists and social service agencies will always have its rough spots. The important thing is to minimize the roughness. Communication and understanding are not sufficient conditions to the successful completion of this task. They are, however, necessary.

I will now turn to some solutions that go beyond the realm of communication and understanding and enter the area of substantive change. These solutions will not resolve all issues, nor will they be universally applicable. They are presented in the hope that they are steps in the right direction and that they will stimulate an earnest attempt to smooth relations between social researchers and the personnel of social service agencies.

Change Based on Structure

Recognition of People Who Supply Evaluation and Research Data. In a real sense the agency personnel who supply data are acting as experts who can supply important information that cannot be gained from other sources. Ways must be found to foster this attitude in both researcher and agency personnel. One way to do this is for researchers to keep their informants abreast of the progress of the research. To the extent that research design allows, informants should be given information about why their information is useful, where they fit in the total research plan, problems that have been encountered and solutions to those problems. Intermediate and final study results should also be supplied. Simply supplying final results is not enough. Final reports may not appear for many months (at best) after the completion of data collection. The delay between stimulus and response is too long and the reward has lost its meaning. Agency personnel must be made to feel that they are important elements in evaluation and research plans. Ongoing dialog is an important element in the attainment of this goal.

Another way to foster this attitude is to pay agency personnel for their services as research assistants and data generators. Such payment lends credibility to people and should support the feeling that they are supplying a valuable service. Payment alone will certainly not suffice. The roots of the problem lie in the social scientist's attitude toward his or her assistants and subjects. Payment can, however, act as an expression of belief in one's credibility and should be used to this end wherever possible.

Education for Researchers. It is my firm belief that most researchers (especially those in academic settings) have little or no conception of the problems inherent in the administration of an organization. (Support for this belief can be gained from Weiss 1973; Caro 1971.) Perhaps certain management courses should be included in the curriculum of graduate students who anticipate doing research in social service agency settings. Other useful courses might include communication skills, the ethics of engaging in research or evaluation, and systems theory. (Justification for including these topics in the education of evaluators can be found in Ricks 1976; Sheinfeld and Morell 1977, 1978.) The aim of this training would not be to turn scientists into administrators, but to help researchers deal with administrative, programmatic and human relations issues which are bound to arise when any sort of research is carried out in service delivery settings.

Education for Administrators, Policy Makers and Service Delivery Personnel. Since part of the problem involves a cultural gap between researchers and agency personnel, steps should be taken to bridge the gap. One aspect of this solution might be workshops or seminars that are designed to teach decision makers and service delivery personnel about research in applied settings. (A similar suggestion along this line has been put forward by Scriven 1967.) Researchers have to go to school for a long time to be convinced that control groups, randomization and the like are worthwhile and important. There is no reason to assume that people who are not socialized in this manner should embrace our position.

An essential ingredient of such programs is that they carry academic credit or some other type of recognition for achievement. Professional credibility and job mobility potential are legitimate desires for social service workers, and recognition of those desires may be an important element in making the educational program work. One should expect people to act rationally and to desire practical, tangible benefits from time and effort which is put into study. This does not negate the intrinsic value of the educational program or of the knowledge gained from it. It merely recognizes the Talmudic dictum "Where there is no sustenance, there is no learning" (Mishna Aboth, chap. 3, par. 21).

Fortunately the importance of life long education is becoming increasingly recognized, and many options exist for acknowledging achievement in this area. As examples, one need only consider the concept of the Continuing Education Unit (National Task Force on the Continuing Education Unit 1974), the proliferation of institutions which confer academic credit for nontraditional learning (Chronicle Guidance Publications 1977), the medical profession's elaborate apparatus for ongoing physician education, and the numerous opportunities which exist for certificates of achievement in a variety of fields.

Programs to teach evaluation and research to agency personnel will be especially helpful in cases where career mobility and accreditation are of serious concern, and this comprises a rather large percentage of service delivery personnel. Paraprofessionals have a strong need for the status and credibility which is confered by formal training (Morell in press). Teachers' salaries are often tied to academic credits. Administrators and policy makers may seek continuing education because their efficiency and credibility depends on their ability to deal knowledgeably with many diverse professionals. All these and many others would benefit from the type of social research training proposed here.

Such courses would not (and should not) be designed exclusively to help researchers better exploit certain types of research settings. A major emphasis of the courses should be to teach agency personnel how to use social science for the benefit of their organizations. No tool can be used intelligently unless its uses, potentials and limitations are clearly understood. It is also true that tools tend to get used more often when one is an expert in their use.

In sum, special courses on "social research in social agency settings" should be designed for the personnel of such agencies. These courses must have three objectives: to explain why various elements of research designs are important for information gathering, as a channel for personal credibility and career mobility of service agency personnel, and as a way to teach agency personnel how to use the tools of research to best advantage.

Researchers as Information Generators. Another possible solution is for social scientists to make themselves valuable to service agencies by collecting information that will be of direct use to the agency. Such information does not have to be directly related to the main thrust of an effort in evaluation or social research. It does have to be information that is of direct use to the agency and which the agency would not be able to collect under ordinary circumstances. Part of any research project involves the setting up of an efficient data-gathering machine. I am proposing that some of the efforts of that machine be directed toward providing immediately useful information to the agency regardless of whether the information is vital to the research or evaluation being conducted. In exchange for allowing research, the service agency would be allowed to exploit the data-gathering potential of the research machine. Certain types of information may have great value for an agency, but be outside the agency's normal data-gathering ability. Administrators or practitioners often want (and need) information that they do not have the time, money, nor organizational resources to collect. Thus the data-gathering ability of a research project can be of very great use to social service agencies.

My suggestion is that permission and support to do evaluation and research be traded for information that cannot be gathered without the help of the researcher. This may complicate or add expense to the research. But is would also add equity to the situation that might not otherwise exist, and equity must be the cornerstone of the researcher-agency relationship.

Credit for Publications and Reports. Several people have discussed the problem of who should receive credit for research that is carried out in service agency settings (Fairweather 1967; Rodman and Kolodny 1964). Typically the issue becomes one of assigning authorship to written reports. The problem is that administrators of agencies feel that their support for the research warrants their being given dual authorship in any publications that ensue. Researchers, on the other hand, feel that such support is not enough to warrant authorship. This conflict can be turned into a method of bringing researchers and agencies into closer cooperation. The transformation hinges on the amount and type of help that administrators are willing to give to researchers. While merely lending organizational support does not warrant authorship, help with design, analysis and data interpretation does warrant authorship. Further, key agency personnel are often uniquely qualified to help with such problems because of their knowledge of the research context, their understanding of possible alternate explanations to results, and their insights into factors that may bias the study and influence outcome. Insofar as administrators (or other key people) are interested in research, an offer of joint authorship might well ensure both close cooperation and a more valid study. It must be made clear, however, that authorship will only be given for active help in many phases of a study.

Increased Relevance. As stated previously, part of the problem stems from the different perspectives of policy makers and administrators on one hand, and researchers and evaluators on the other. The immediate concern of the former involve personnel, service units funding allocations, and the like. Outcome remains an ultimate objective which tends to get lost in the daily press of business. The immediate concerns of researchers and evaluators tend to be issues that deal with outcome. The objectives of research simply do not fit in the day-to-day elements of administration or policy making. In the real world of decision making, rational information on outcome, efficiency, or effectiveness is not necessarily important or desirable. One solution might be a change in the emphasis of research or evaluation projects to make them more compatible with the clear and present needs of decision makers.

As an example, the differential therapeutic effects of family therapy and behavior therapy in solving children's psychiatric disorders is probably *not* of immediate value to a service director. This is because the effectiveness of therapy has no direct relation to the day-to-day decisions that administrators must make. The extent to which the provision of legal counseling services influences attendance at therapy sessions *is* relevant to a service director, especially if there is a need to increase an organization's case load, and decisions must be made regarding funding allocations, the hiring of particular types of personnel, or the opening of new types of services.

I do not claim that researchers must switch their fields of study. I do claim that evaluation and research must provide decision makers with information that has a reasonable expectation of being useful. Such a change in emphasis does not have to be total, nor should it. The equity principle does demand, however, that part of the research that is carried on within a host agency be of obvious use to the host.

Facilitation of Information Utilization. Cherns (1971) has suggested that our field lacks a type of professional who plays an important role in other areas, namely the "development engineer." Such people are employed for the specific purpose of searching out practical methods of applying scientific data to solve practical problems. (The chemical engineer is an excellent example.) The idea is similar to the concept of a "linking agent," a person who is charged with bringing useful innovations to the attention of decision makers, and facilitating the implementation of the innovation (Bennis et al. 1976.) The concept of "organizational change agent" is also useful here (Chin 1976). All of these concepts were developed out of a feeling that there was a missing link between knowledge about successful action and the incorporation of that knowledge into the world of practical decision making. We have pure researchers, applied researchers, and evaluators—but we do not have applications experts. Even if we had a body of scientific theory that was salient and a body of technological theory that was practical, there would still be a gap between knowledge and its practical use. An applications expert might be useful in bridging that gap.

We cannot, of course, begin to train such people; the time is not right, funding is nonexistent and jobs are nonexistent. Researchers and evaluators might, however, begin to play a limited role as applications experts in the setting where they work. If the problem they are working on has a practical application, the possibility of that application should be presented to appropriate parties in a separate report. Such a report would be different from a normal scientific publication, and might not be directly related to the original research. It would be a separate service that the investigator would volunteer. The short-run advantage would be better relations between researchers and decision makers due to the more obvious benefit that research might provide. In the long run this might have an effect on the way in which information is used and in the development of a new (and very useful) type of social science professional.

Multiple Measures and the Acceptability of Information. In cases where a research study is specifically evaluative in character, a special precaution can be taken to increase agency acceptance. It is a method of insuring that the research results will help the credibility of the organization being evaluated, without degrading the scientific value of the study. The method involves employing multiple measures of success, each measure a little further removed than the preceding one from the immediate target of a treatment. Campbell and Fiske (1959) have proposed that multiple methods be used as a validity check, but the technique can also be employed to help the research acceptance problem.

The "distance" between a treatment and an effect can be along conceptual and temporal dimensions. As an example let us say one is evaluating the effect of a particular type of marriage counseling technique. One might measure the following outcome variables: Do couples feel better after undergoing counseling? Do they feel that the potential for success in their relationship has been improved? Do they fight or argue less at increasing intervals after completing counseling? Each of these outcomes is more likely to show positive results than the outcome which follows it. It is very likely that the counseled couple will feel better. It is not particularly likely that counseling will have an effect on their lives in the long run. A measure of the immediate locus of action of a treatment is quite likely to show success. The further one is removed from that immediate locus, the lower the probability of an effect. (In a sense we are dealing with an attenuation phenomenon that exists not only over time but also on a conceptual level.) This technique is scientifically defensible because researchers have a valid interest in the "strength" of a treatment. They want to know which domains of thought, feeling and action will be affected by their experimental manipulations. A side benefit of gaining such knowledge is that the agency being evaluated will probably be able to claim some positive effects.

Mediation of Conflict. This suggestion relates to methods of structuring the interphase between social research activities and the worlds of politics, funding allocation, and service delivery. Recent history has given rise to several attempts at setting up varying types of liaison between the social sciences and other sectors of society. One example was an attempt by the Society for the Psychological Study of Social Issues to set up a special committee to provide relevant social science information to legislative committees and to publicize legislative concerns among social scientists (Moles 1973). The idea surfaced again in several ways at a recent American Psychological Association Convention in a symposium entitled "Ombudsman for Science in Government Program Evaluation." Campbell has called for the establishment of an "auxiliary legislature" to advise elected officials on matters dealing with social science and public policy (Campbell 1971). Fairweather (1967, chap. 14) argues in favor of the establishment of independent centers for experimental social innovation that would be "a central place where social innovative researchers can plan new experiments, analyze data, discuss research results with others, create demonstration teams and train new experimentalists." These centers would be unique in that they would be separate from existing institutions, include nonscientist representatives in their leadership, and only perform research that has been discussed and agreed upon by both researchers and laymen. The central thrust of such centers would be to attempt experimental solutions to society's problems.

The plan I am about to propose fits into the recent trend of attempting organizational solutions to researcher-society interphase problems. Perhaps the social research/evaluation profession should move to set up an organization whose job is to mediate between the profession and other sectors of society. Such an organization would consist of members of many elements of society and would deal with problems such as excessive demands by evaluators, inordinate tampering with research designs by administrators, guarantees of privacy, and the like. It would act as an ombudsman and/or mediator to help work out problems that develop between researcher, agency, study participants and society at large. Such an organization would, of course, not be involved in every piece of evaluation or research that is carried out. It could, however, educate, set guidelines, and explore solutions to the common conflicts that arise between social scientists and other sectors of society. Its outstanding feature would be its ability to intervene, mediate and judge, when called upon to do so. The cause of social research would be much enhanced by the establishment of such an organization, as it would serve as a conflict resolution authority in an area where no such authority exists.

ORGANIZING PRINCIPLES OF INCREASED RELEVANCE

The solutions proposed here cannot, even under the best of circumstances, eliminate all difficulties. First, the problems involve an extremely complex interplay of psychological, sociological, historical and political factors which affects all parties. Second, there are real and legitimate differences between the needs, desires, and goals of the various groups. Under foreseeable circumstances it is not reasonable to assume that these differences can be eliminated. It is reasonable, however, to assume that a combination of mutual understanding and thoughtful change can minimize the problems which do exist. In order to promote such changes, a basic shift in perspective is needed, as each change, in and of itself, might have a wrenching effect on the present system. A perspective is needed which will make the suggested changes flow naturally from the general way in which work is organized and carried out. Even if this objective is not fully met, change in that direction will be helpful.

A shift in perspective which is likely to accomplish this goal would be the organizing of evaluation according to technological principles, and in line with the type-validity-usefulness typology which was suggested earlier. The technological perspective promotes the development of practically useful theories, of studies which focus on genuine societal concerns, and a concentration on variables which make a difference in the practical world of action. The technological perspective also sets up a reward and a problem definition system for researchers which is consonant with analagous systems for decision makers. The type-validity-usefulness perspective serves as a structure which allows research to be fine tuned to the needs of its audience and to the methodological requirements of the situation. Thus, these perspectives set up expectations, orientations and motivations to produce research and evaluation information which is relevant, valid, and useful. Given this general perspective, most of the suggestions presented in this chapter become feasible.

Communication and understanding become possible because there is a common ground for conceptualizing problems and solutions. Recognition of service agency personnel's importance to research becomes possible because the nature of problems and needs to insure validity make the input of those people truly important and of obvious benefit.

Management and communication skills become a natural part of evaluators' training because those skills are needed to help define evaluation problems and fields of action. Traditional research perspectives do not require such skills because in the traditional view, research is not integrally bound to the process of practical decision making. Education of policy makers and administrators in evaluation- and research-related topics becomes practical for the same reason. Once a common field of action is defined, decision makers are likely to see the necessity for tools and concepts which will allow the full exploitation of resources which are at hand.

It becomes reasonable for researchers and decision makers to share authorship, as the two groups will be likely to work jointly on the same problems. The relevance of studies is also likely to increase because a mechanism will exist for defining problems in a practically relevant manner, and of fine tuning studies to meet the expectations and needs of administrators and policy makers.

Applications experts are more likely to find suitable material to work with, as increased relevance will mean that such experts will not have to stretch their imagination and credibility when they advocate the advantages of an innovation.

The use of multiple success measures will be far more than a ploy to reduce evaluation apprehension. This is because the technological/type-validity-usefulness orientation is likely to yield greater numbers of meaningful variables, as well as concepts of "effect strength" which will have practical value to decision makers who wish to gain a sense of what particular programs can and cannot do.

The use of mediators and ombudsmen becomes reasonable, as their task will no longer involve the reconciliation of two fundamentally opposed positions. Also, it is not likely that efforts will be put into setting up mediation mechanisms if it seems clear that such mechanisms will be ineffective.

These innovations will not flow automatically if technological or type-validity-usefulness perspectives are adopted. Further, the frictions which exist between researchers and practical decision makers are not likely to be eliminated. These perspectives will, however, set a tone and define a context of action in which the suggested innovations may have some chance of success. Social research must be relevant, valid, and powerful if it is to help solve social problems. Once it meets those requirements, efforts to relieve tension between researchers and decision makers become feasible. This chapter has been an attempt at showing why problems exist and how they may be solved. Technological and type-validity-usefulness perspectives form the foundation of those solutions, as they provide a framework in which the proposed changes become a natural outgrowth of the way in which evaluation and research activities are organized.

The proposed solutions are not equally powerful or universally applicable. Further it may not be possible to implement any of them in their entirety. They are presented in the hope that they will start us thinking in new directions. Present problems spring from a particular reward system that is embedded in an institutionalized structure of service and research. I have attempted to explain why research-agency frictions are an inevitable by-product of that structure, and to suggest a perspective that will help us to see how that structure might be changed to the advantage of all.

NOTES

[1]This chapter is a much expanded version of an analysis which was first presented in *Administration in Mental Health*. See Morell, 1977b.

[2]I do not mean to pass judgment on the relativity or absoluteness of scientific truth. I merely claim that the truths we find are at least partially determined by where we look.

[3]At least they exert some effort at trying to maximize benefits as perceived by agency personnel. The congruence between perceived and real effects is an empirical issue that is always open to question.

[4]It might be worthwhile to entertain the notion that this problem results from too many social scientists working in the field, combined with too few good research settings. As a result competition for status and publications has forced researchers to try to fit square pegs into round holes—good research design into settings that cannot support such designs.

7

Powerful Evaluation: Consequences for The Organization of Social Research[1]

INTRODUCTION

We believe that if evaluation develops along the lines suggested in this book, there is bound to be an acceleration of the already developing trend for evaluation to become a profession. Since many consequences of professionalization are not particularly beneficial, it is important to understand why problems will arise and to anticipate solutions.

Recent events have made it clear that during the past several years a new entity has been forming which can best be described as "program evaluation." As evidence of this assertion one need only consider: the number of books, journals and conferences in the field; the development of training programs; the opening of job opportunities in evaluation; the appearance of formal associations; and the pressure for evaluation that is being exerted by various government agencies. (A detailed analysis of these events can be found in Flaherty and Morell 1978.)

What are the implications of these events, what do they mean for the study and practice of program evaluation, and what might we expect in the way of future developments? Two general possibilities are likely. One alternative is that work will be organized as it has been in the past. People from different fields will maintain their primary allegiance to their original discipline, but will engage in a particular variety of work called "evaluation." A more likely possibility is that a distinct profession of evaluation will emerge, with its own intellectual tradition, its own organization, relatively distinct boundaries, and a pattern of interaction with other professions which is characteristic of the history of professionalism. The reasons for this likelihood will be explained through the use of sociological theories of professionalization. These theories provide a dynamic model which will allow us to integrate the meaning of recent events and to understand what is likely to happen. They clearly indicate that evaluation is developing into a profession, they provide cogent insights into the process of that development, and they yield predictions which seem likely and which we should be ready to welcome or to oppose, as the case may be.

EVALUATION AS A PROFESSION

A large number of writers have attempted to define the characteristics of a profession. There is quite a bit of agreement among these writers, and the consensus is best summarized in the writings of Howard Becker.

Becker (1970) finds general agreement among observers of the scene that there are six crucial elements to the "symbol" of a profession. First, the profession must have a monopoly over an esoteric body of knowledge which is considered important for the functioning of society. Second, that body of knowledge must be comprised of abstract principles rather than the result of practical experience or technical skill. Third, there must be strict control over recruitment into the profession to insure that only qualified people are allowed to practice. Fourth, control over entry into the profession must lie in the hands of the profession itself. Fifth, because of the strict control that is exercised by the profession over its own practice, any member of the professional group can be considered fully competent to practice the profession. Finally, the symbol of the profession must project an image that the profession's members have altruistic motivations and a heavy emphasis on service for the good of the client. Very similar conclusions are arrived at in a separate review conducted by William J. Goode (1969).

If the above criteria are correct, evaluation clearly cannot (yet) be considered a profession. The signs that the professionalization process is beginning, however, are unmistakable. A special body of "evaluation knowledge" is certainly on the brink of emergence, if in fact it has not already appeared (Flaherty and Morell 1978). Although no single group has claimed a monopoly on this knowledge, such a time cannot be far off. The sheer amount of material in the field is such that assimilating the evaluation knowledge base is (or will very soon become) a full-time job. Once that happens, those who devote themselves to the pursuit of that knowledge will surely claim unique expertise in the field which cannot be shared by others.

The emergence of abstract principles in evaluation is clearly shown by the development of new terms that are used to define concepts that have grown up solely as a part of the evaluation endeavor. Consider, for example, outcome and process evaluation, the experimenting society, goal-free evaluation, goal attainment scaling, and summative evaluation, to name just a few. We do not mean to imply that these concepts are totally unique to evaluation, that they have no analogs in other fields, or that they are unrelated to concepts in other areas of study. We cite them only as examples of concepts which have taken on unique meanings within the context of program evaluation.

As we have already noted, there has been a rapid development of specialized training programs with their attendant aspects of adult socialization, recruitment standards, and control by members of the profession.

The concept of altruism, or at least the ideal of service to the greater community, is clearly evident in various writings in the field of evaluation. Campbell (1971) discusses the notion of using evaluation as a tool to promote constructive social policy. Rossi and Williams (1972, p. xiv) claim that their book is based on the premise that sound evaluation research is badly needed in order to improve social policy processes. Guttentag and Struening (1975, p. 3), in their introduction to volume two of the *Handbook of Evaluation Research*, emphasize that "evaluation must be useful."

These statements are just a few of the many that can be cited which sound the note of service to a particular constituency as a vital element in the evaluation endeavor. The value of evaluation for the continuation of optimal societal functioning is also clearly recognized by nonevaluators, as evidenced by the extremely large increase in funding for evaluation and by pressure from nonsocial science sectors for the performance of program evaluation.

The beginnings of specialized groups of evaluators set the stage for the institutionalization of the specialized interests of evaluators, further control over entry into the profession, and the like. Although formal codes of ethics and setting of standards for practice have not yet developed, the establishment of specialized organizations will certainly facilitate such events. Members of the evaluation profession have already begun to speculate on such development and to consider the implications of such events (Attkisson et al. 1978, chap. 16).

In sum, a comparison of events in the field of evaluation to the criteria for defining a profession make it quite clear that the process of professionalization will very likely befall evaluation, if in fact the process has not already started. Matching events in evaluation to the definition of a profession, however, does not allow one to understand the relationship between events that have taken place or to make predictions as to what is likely to occur in the future. Such understanding can only come from a study of theories of professionalization which postulate a process or a dynamic by which events can be understood and predicted. We will now turn to a brief review of such theories. Once they have been explained we will turn to a consideration of what they tell us about the future of evaluation.

THEORIES OF PROFESSIONALIZATION

The rich and diverse sociological literature on professions yields four theories which are particularly useful in understanding the development of evaluation.[2] Wilensky (1964) argues that professions pass through five phases on the road to professionalization. First, people begin to do, on a full-time basis, that which needs to be done. Second, training schools are developed in order to teach people how to perform the task(s) which must be carried out. Third, professional associations begin to form. Fourth, political agitation by members of the profession for the institution of licensure or other regulations concerning those who are allowed to practice the profession begins. Finally, codes of ethics begin to emerge. Wilensky cites the process of development of a large number of professions as support for his hypothesis. Although he admits that a relatively large number of exceptions to the sequence can be found, he argues that the exceptions are not large enough to negate the general principle.

Howard Becker (1970) claims that one must look at the characteristics of the symbol of a profession, and that the process of professionalization is governed by the attempts of an occupation to attain as much of the symbol as possible. (Becker uses ''symbol'' in its sociological sense, as an ideal conception about which there is general agreement among relevant members of a population.) According to this analysis the motivation to attain as much of the ''professional'' status as possible stems from two particularly desirable features of professionalization. The primary motivation is the autonomy of action that comes from being a profession. The notion is that judgment as to proper procedure must be left in the hands of the profession, and consequently only those who are members of a profession are qualified to judge the quality of work performed by fellow professionals. The second motivation for professionalization is the prestige that is perceived as being a part of the attainment of professional status.

Bucher and Strauss (1961) claim that professions are made up of various segments which form ''. . . loose amalgamations of segments pursuing different objectives in different manners and more or less delicately held together under a common name at particular periods in history'' (p. 326). They theorize that professions must be understood in terms of the conflicts that develop among the segments, and they specify the areas in which conflict will be found. They identify seven conflict areas. First, sense of mission: this is, in essence, the staking of a claim. A segment will attempt to show that a particular service cannot be provided adequately by those who are not specially devoted to a particular area of endeavor. Second, work activities: these are conflicts among segments concerning what Bucher and Strauss call ''the most characteristic professional act'' of a profession. The conflicts include different perceptions of what the profession should be doing, how it should be organized, and which tasks have precedence over others. Third, methodology and techniques: differences in this area are claimed to cut across specialties and often to reflect fundamental disagreement concerning the purpose of the profession. Fourth, clients: different segments are likely to have serious disagreements over the primary population that should be served by the profession. Fifth, colleagueship: Bucher and Strauss advance the idea of "circles of colleagueship," and claim that members of different segments of a profession may have very different patterns of associations with members of other professions. Sixth, interests and associations: different segments tend to have conflicting interests concerning issues such as footholds in institutions, recruitment, relations with the outside, the nature of contractual relations with other elements of society, and the like. Consequently professional associations must be understood in terms of the segments which control the association and the interests that are being served by the organization. Seventh, spurious unity and public relations: the notion is that professional associations tend to present a public relations image of unity of purpose and harmony within the profession. This public image is not fairly arrived at by consensus, but is, rather, an image which reflects the philosophy of the profession's most powerful segment.

The final theory of professional dynamics which we will consider was proposed by William J. Goode (1969). According to Goode the development of professions must be understood as part of the general competition in society for prestige, for power, and for income. These are the motivating forces behind the coalescing of particular specialties or areas of endeavor into professions. Goode attempts to determine which conditions will result in the development of a profession, given the existence of the motivations which he identifies. Goode's analysis begins with a review of the basic characteristics of a profession and quickly moves on to an attempt to differentiate the core, or generating, traits of a profession from those which are predictable outcomes of core characteristics. According to his analysis there are two generating characteristics: first, a "basic body of abstract knowledge," and second "the ideal of service" (p. 277). Goode attempts to discern the subdimensions of each of these categories, to establish each subdimension as a continuum, and to show how these two basic categories combine to generate all the other aspects of a profession.

THE PROFESSIONALIZATION OF EVALUATION

If we assume that these models of professional development have any validity, we can quite safely assume that evaluation will develop along professional lines. This we can deduce from the motivations and the initial conditions that must be present for the development of a profession.

Wilensky's (1964) first phase has certainly arrived, as an ever-growing number of people are devoting their full-time professional efforts to the practice of evaluation.

Clearly there is a good deal of prestige, power and income involved in the evaluation enterprise. As far as income is concerned, one need only consider the amount of evaluation work that has of late been funded, mandated and required by legislation. Coupled with the general shrinking job market and funding for sociology and psychology, the economic incentives to become an evaluation specialist are obvious. The elements of prestige and power are a bit more difficult to discern, given the traditional second place of applied work in the value system of many social scientists and in the reward structure of the social sciences. It is quite likely, however, that the lower status of applied social science within the scientific community may be changing. The ferment of the 1960s has certainly placed an increased value on the study of "relevant" problems. Although "relevant does not necessarily mean "applied," there is a kinship between the two concepts. It is also likely that the prestige of applied social science, i.e., evaluation, is on the rise in the eyes of many in the nonscientific community. The ability to provide accountability and the ability to demonstrate the effectiveness of programs are certainly becoming increasingly valued by many government officials and by the general public. Evaluation is also rapidly developing a specialized knowledge base and a service ideal. Thus Goode's criteria for the development of a profession are clearly met.

The motivations that Becker (1970) presents for the attainment of as much of the symbol of profession as possible are also present. The rise of prestige for those who can perform evaluation has already been demonstrated. Further, the program evaluator's desire for the greatest possible amount of autonomy in his or her work is easy to understand. The nature of evaluation is such that evaluators must work closely with program staff, with program administrators, and with policy makers. It is also quite likely that evaluators will have to deal with the needs of the general populace, either in the form of the climate of political opinion or in the form of citizen advisory and/or governing boards. There is no question that this is as it should be, as evaluators do perform a service which must be tailored to the needs of an intelligent, perceptive and thinking clientele who have a clear sense of their own needs and of what they want in the way of evaluation services.[3] It is also true, however, that there are many details of the evaluation process which are within the unique domain of the evaluator's expertise, and that evaluators often have considerable difficulty in asserting their authority in such matters (Morell 1977b; Twain 1975). Thus the cause of evaluation will be legitimately strengthened if evaluators are able to claim an authority which insulates them from undue interference in their work. Given the nature of evaluation services it is extremely likely that evaluators will have to fight for control over their work, and it is absolutely true that there are many areas in which they should have control.

Still another suggestion that evaluation will professionalize can be derived from the prestige mobility patterns which are characteristic of fields which have become professions. According to Goode (1969), four such patterns are evident. As Goode (p. 272) puts it:

In the mobility of occupations, the following patterns of upward movement are more likely than is the high ascent sometimes observed in individual mobility: (a) a semi-profession arises from a non-occupation, e.g., social work from individual philanthropy or "doing good to the poor"; (b) a semi-profession claims to have a special "package" of high level skills, e.g., the city planner; (c) a profession specializes in a task that another had considered partial, e.g., psychiatry; (d) a professional specialty is built on new instruments and techniques, e.g., cyrogenics or laser engineering.

It is easy to pick out the case of evaluation from among these patterns, as many books make it clear that evaluation involves a collection of skills from a very large variety of other fields. As examples, consider the positions taken in the following:

Franklin and Thrasher (1976, p. 31):

> The position taken in this volume is a reasonably broad one and includes within the boundaries of evaluation the process of securing valid, reliable, and applicable information about programs, structures, processes, outcomes and impacts, to permit managers to make decisions for program improvement and fulfill their responsibilities for public accountability.

Later on, the authors list twelve fields of study which are not in and of themselves evaluation, but which ". . . do help to highlight the proper scope and domain of program evaluation." The fields listed are: policy research, applied research, decision-oriented research, social audits, action research, operations research, discipline-related research, basic research, "front line" evaluation, utilization review, continuous monitoring, and quality control.

In Tripodi, Fellin, and Epstein's (1971) chapter on the techniques of evaluation, these authors list the following approaches as being legitimate aspects of the evaluation endeavor: accountability audit, administrative audit, time and motion studies, experiments, surveys, case studies, cost accounting, cost-benefit analysis, cost-outcome analysis, and operations research.

Coursey (1977) presents seven basic models of program evaluation, many of which exist in various different forms. The models listed are: the outcome model, the goal attainment model, systems analysis, cost analytic models, descriptive and quality assurance models, planning and management methodologies, and the legal model.

In sum, there are six strong indications that evaluation will develop along professional lines. First, evaluation is rapidly becoming a full-time activity for a growing number of people. (Or at least a growing number of people are beginning to view themselves as full-time evaluators.) Second, evaluators have a legitimate need for autonomy in their work. That autonomy is threatened from innumerable sources, and must be actively protected. Third, there is a rapidly growing specialized knowledge base in evaluation. Fourth, an increasing amount of power, prestige and income is beginning to accrue to evaluators. Fifth, evaluation has a strong ethic of providing service to the greater community. Finally, evaluators draw on specialized combinations of skills in order to do their work. Although each particular skill is employed in a variety of other fields, the importance of the combination is unique to evaluation. Theories of professionalization make it clear that these events all portend the professionalization of evaluation.

With such a prospect in mind we will now turn to a consideration of developments that can reasonably be expected to occur, and to an analysis of the implications of those developments for the performance of needed evaluation work.

PREDICTIONS FROM MODELS OF PROFESSIONALIZATION

The Nature of the Beast

Wilensky's "development stage" analysis (1964, p. 144) clearly indicates that we are in for a serious debate on the nature of just what it is that evaluators should be doing. We are beginning to see the rise of professional associations in the field, and one of the first undertakings of such associations is to ". . . engage in much soul searching on whether the occupation is a profession, what the professional tasks are, how to raise the quality of recruits, and so on."

The Bucher and Strauss (1961) analysis of conflicts among the segments of a profession yield similar predictions. Three of the areas of conflict which they include in their model have a direct bearing on developing definitions of the profession. In their discussion of work activities they argue that various segments of a profession will develop different concepts of ". . . what kinds of work the profession should be doing, how work should be organized, and which tasks have precedence" (p. 327). Later, (p. 328) they claim that ". . . members of a profession not only weigh auxiliary activities differently but have different conceptions of what constitutes the core—the most characteristic professional act—of their professional lives." These conflicts among professionals also spill over into Bucher and Strauss's categories of "methodology and techniques," and "clients." The problem of appropriate methods cannot be separated from concerns over which questions should be studied. Similarly, the question of who one's clients should be is intimately related to one's conception of what the profession should really be doing.

Although the existence of a profession is not a necessary precondition for the existence of such disagreements, sociological theorists make it clear that as evaluation proceeds along the path of professionalization, these disagreements are likely to become considerably more heated, numerous and serious. The desirability of control over professional associations, scarce resources, the "public face" of the field, and recruitment make such a conclusion inevitable.

We believe that although these problems cannot be avoided they can be ameliorated. It is extremely likely that disagreements among evaluators will be couched in terms of philosophical differences concerning what evaluators should be doing, and that the sociological dynamics brought out by the present analysis will go unrecognized as separate (although not necessarily independent) factors which fuel discord. A failure to recognize the existence of multiple sources of discord implies a failure to recognize solutions that are selectively effective for only some sources of disagreement. Further, philosophical differences and socio-logical forces may well potentiate one another, and it is difficult to deal with such interactions if only some of the interacting elements are recognized.

Development of a Knowledge Base

We can make several predictions beyond the obvious fact that the evaluation profession will expend considerable effort in developing and laying claim to a specialized knowledge base. First, the principles that define the knowledge will not be so broad as to seem obvious, simple, or intuitively easy to understand. If the principles are of this nature it will be difficult to convince the general population that one really needs a specialist to perform the necessary work. Wilensky (1964) points out that this is a problem in the social sciences, a field whose vocabulary seems intuitively obvious to the general populace. This seem-ing simplicity is cited as one of the reasons why various professions in the social sciences and in administration have had difficulty in establishing themselves. (In the language of Bucher and Strauss (1961), one would say that such professions have trouble convincing people that they have a "unique mission.") We can also be sure that the knowledge base will not be narrow and explicit to the point of seeming cookbook like in ease of application. Wilensky's analysis makes it clear that under such conditions the knowledge base becomes vulnerable to critical examination and to takeover by those who do not possess high levels of special skills.

Although these sociological factors do not determine the true level of abstrac-tion that is most appropriate for the evaluation knowledge base, they do tempt evaluators to search in particular directions. They will certainly influence the way in which evaluators present their expertise to the public, and the risk of believing one's own propaganda must always be considered.

A second prediction is that the profession will expend considerable effort in trying to convince the public that its knowledge base is important for the general good. As Becker (1970, p. 94) puts it during a discussion of the characteristics of a profession:

> . . . this knowledge is considered to be necessary for the continuing functioning of the society. What the members of the profession know and can do is tremendously important, but no one else knows or can do these things.

Goode (1969, p. 281) makes essentially the same argument:

> On both the prestige and the economic markets, the aspiring profession must be able to offer its control over a more substantial body of codified, applicable knowledge than that controlled by other occupations.

Whatever the motivation for professionalization—autonomy, prestige, power or income—a profession must convince its customers that it possesses unique and important knowledge. Having such knowledge is one thing—making people believe it is another. There can be little doubt that as evaluation develops into a profession, and as it develops a structure which is charged with looking after its interests, efforts at selling the concept of a specialized knowledge base will grow.

The problems that might arise due to efforts at selling the idea of a specialized knowledge base are closely related to the issue of control over who should perform program evaluation. Consequently we will defer discussion of these problems until the matter of control over work is presented.

Control over Who Performs Evaluation

As the profession of program evaluation develops we are likely to see greater and greater specification of who is allowed to perform specific types of evaluation tasks. The primary boundary will be those who are specifically trained as evaluators versus those who are not. Wilensky (1964) argues that two consequences of the development of professional organizations are conflict between the "home guard" who learned their profession without specialized training and new members of the profession whose credibility stems from graduation from a specialized training program. The fact that evaluation has already developed specialized training programs, that many are doing evaluation who have not graduated from such programs, and that we are on the brink of developing highly structured professional organizations, does not augur well for the avoidance of this type of conflict.

A second aspect of the problem is competition with other professions for program evaluation work. Wilensky argues that such competition is a natural outgrowth of the development of professional associations. Becker (1970) believes that if autonomy and prestige are to accrue to a profession, then entry into the profession must be strictly controlled by the profession. Goode (1969) argues that competition between professions for power, prestige and income is (over the short term, at least) a zero-sum game. Advantages to one profession necessarily mean losses to some other profession. These insights give us excellent reason to expect the profession of evaluation to develop a strong sense of the exclusive ability of trained evaluators to do program evaluation work. We can also expect ever-increasing attempts to convince the general public of this proposition, and to impose exclusive jurisdiction in the performance of program evaluation tasks.[4]

A third aspect of control over who does the work concerns differentiations within the profession as to which tasks should be performed by people with particular qualifications. According to the segmentation model of Bucher and Strauss one should expect groups within a profession to differentiate on the basis of different missions which only their subgroup is capable of performing. Wilensky believes that as particular core tasks of a profession are identified and/or defined, a pecking order develops in which some tasks are delegated to people of varying status and education within the profession.

Thus we see that any profession contains within itself a strong tendency to appropriate particular tasks to itself, to exclude outsiders from the performance of those tasks, and to develop an internal differentiation of tasks. This tendency is not tangential to the process of professionalization, but is an integral element of the process by which an occupation, specialty, or field of inquiry becomes a profession. The process is based on competition for scarce resources and on the need of a profession to convince the public that it alone can provide needed services.

One can already find signs that these phenomena are occurring. The state of New York for example, has recently set up a special civil service track for program evaluators in mental health. The track defines a variety of levels of evaluation positions, sets out the tasks and salary for each, and defines the educational requirements that are needed for each position. Implicit in this process is the internal differentiation notion advanced by Wilensky (1964). Although there was no input into this process by a formal association of the evaluation profession, there can be little doubt that once such associations develop they will not allow such a track to be set up without their input and suggestions. Is a doctoral level social scientist without special training in evaluation more qualified as an evaluator than a person with a masters degree in program evaluation? What are the relative merits of a doctorate in evaluation as opposed to a master's degree in the same field? There is no doubt that one of the first tasks of the emerging evaluation profession will be an attempt to develop a solution to these problems, and to see to it that those who hire evaluators know and observe that recommended solution.

A consideration of problems that derive from attempts to develop a specialized knowledge base along with attempts to control who does program evaluation work points out the likelihood of serious problems for the cause of program evaluation. There is an inherent exclusivity in the process of laying claim to specialized knowledge or setting standard qualifications for the performance of a task. The rub is that we cannot guarantee that these standards reflect reality, or that those who approach the concept of "program evaluation" from what might be considered "different" backgrounds are in fact not doing a better type of evaluation than orthodox members of the profession.

Are we really ready to exclude from consideration any evaluator who philosophically rejects the experimental model of evaluation; or who does not believe that the primary purpose of evaluation is to aid high level policy makers; or who is a believer in the use of Bayesian statistics; or who accepts the goal-free model of evaluation as the only legitimate one, or whose roots are in a field not usually associated with evaluation? One might answer that evaluation is of course an eclectic enterprise and that all points of view are welcome. But how long would such goodwill hold up under the strain of honest and deep-seated philosophical differences which are overlaid by power struggles for control of associations and training programs, or the acquisition of evaluation contracts and seats on advisory panels?

One might be able to certify a person's competence in the performance of factor analysis or survey research, but it is far more difficult to decide which basic approaches to the concept of program evaluation should be given serious consideration. One could claim that the best answers to such questions are most likely to come from those who devote full time to serious consideration of such matters, and on the basis of probability alone this is very likely true. But it still may not be desirable for a solution to such questions to be imposed on the public. Also, there may be many competent social scientists who do not wish to do program evaluation full time or to make it their primary area of professional interest, but who may on occasion engage in such efforts. Is it advisable to exclude such people from evaluation work as a result of their lack of some type of certification?

We believe that the possibility of such exclusion is not quite as remote as it may at first seem. There is, after all, an ever-growing amount of money, power and prestige in the field of program evaluation. These are always fertile conditions for the development of exclusion processes. Civil service requirements for evaluators have in at least one case already been established. The Community Mental Health Act of 1975 mandates that at least two percent of all state funds go toward evaluation (Public Law 94-63, sec. 206). How many steps is this away from mandating the skills and educational requirements of those who are put in charge of all that money, and where will the lobbying come from to input into such regulations?

We are not sure how to avoid unnecessary exclusion or regulation, but we do feel compelled to warn of the likelihood of its occurrence. Forewarned is, we hope, forearmed.

Training Programs

A final prediction concerns the development of training programs and problems related to the curricula of those programs. One of the foundations of a profession is a body of abstract knowledge and principles which can be applied to specific cases in order to solve real problems. Presumably the curriculum of a training program is set up to impart that knowledge and to give neophytes practice in its application. It is extremely likely however, that there will be very poor correspondence between what is taught and what is actually needed. As Goode (1969, p. 282) points out:

> . . . most professionals do not use much of their abstract knowledge and perhaps for most problems do not really apply principles to concrete cases, but instead apply concrete recipes to concrete cases.

If that is the case, why is professional education so consumed with abstract principles and with knowledge that is seldom used? According to Goode it is because the public insists that professionals be prepared to deal with a crisis, i.e., with nontypical cases when they do develop.[5] An important implication of this analysis is that the curriculum which is developed in the classroom will be highly discrepant from the actual work carried out by the professional.

The same theme is echoed by Becker (1970) in his discussion of how the real life of a professional differs from the symbol of professional action. He states (p. 103):

> Professional education tends to build curricula and programs in ways suggested by the symbol and so fails to prepare its students for the world they will have to work in.

One must also consider a third element concerning the development of curricula. Any classroom learning of necessity involves the construction of artificial models of reality. It cannot be otherwise, and models by their very nature are simplifications of the real world (Kaplan 1964, chap. 7). Thus any training school is doomed to provide its students with inadequate preparation for the practice of their profession. There can be no doubt that a recognition of this problem is the motivation for the numerous "practicum" and internship-type experiences that are built into professional education. These experiences certainly ameliorate the problem, but they cannot eliminate it. It is almost impossible to predict the exact type of work that a person will carry out once he or she leaves graduate school. Thus training programs must rely on teaching abstract principles that can be applied in a variety of situations. Also it must couple that training with practice designed to build up generalized learning sets in the students. The direct relevance of professional education to the actual practice of the profession, however, will always leave much to be desired.

There is no doubt that as the field of program evaluation grows it will continually confront the problem of the irrelevance of its professional training. We are fortunate in being at the beginning of professional education in evaluation, and thus able to deal with the problem before particular models of education become too entrenched. We believe that because evaluation training is still in its infancy the profession is in a particularly good position to keep the symbol from straying too far from the reality, and to implement training programs that meet the needs of students, the profession and society at large.

SPECIAL PROBLEMS AS A FUNCTION OF TECHNOLOGICAL AND TYPE-VALIDITY-USEFULNESS PERSPECTIVES

If the advice in this book is followed, the professionalization of evaluation is likely to accelerate. The special body of evaluation knowledge is likely to become more and more distant from its intellectual and historical roots in other fields. The viewpoint of evaluators on social research is likely to diverge from the traditional perspectives of other fields. As evaluation develops perspectives which are different from other areas of social research, competition among the various fields is likely to grow. Intellectual differences may become more heated. A greater need will be felt by evaluators to socialize neophytes to believe in the new paradigm. Competition with other fields and points of view may also increase evaluators' feelings for a need for autonomy. Finally, if the ideas in this book increase the public's esteem for evaluation, there is likely to be a considerable amount of power, prestige and money which the new profession may wish to guard and nurture. In short, the development of a powerful and useful evaluation paradigm is likely to accelerate or enhance those aspects of the field which will lead to professionalization. In many ways this is a serious problem because, as we have seen, the professionalization of evaluation may lead to an exclusivity and a control over work which may not be useful for society at large.

The development of a profession is a sociological process which has at least as much to do with power, influence, and access to resources as it does with providing a service to society or advancing the cause of understanding. Quite frankly, we are not at all sure that it would be a good thing to concentrate that kind of power in a relatively small group of people or in one profession, especially in the case of an amorphous field such as evaluation, where it is by no means clear how evaluators can best help to solve social problems.

As a solution, we propose that evaluators consciously stay away from those professional activities which are most likely to lead to rigorous control over the work which is done, or which will further the exclusivity of a small group of people. As an example, consider the issue of training, which is a major concern in any profession. It would be a disaster for evaluation groups to dispense official approvals for particular training programs. If such approvals became generally recognized and accepted by employers, many people would be excluded from evaluation work because their professional backgrounds did not fit the perspective of the small segment of people who were instrumental in organizing and implementing the approval apparatus. It is not likely that an objective, definitive statement could be made on what constitutes an appropriate evaluation background. If definitive statements cannot be made, rigorously enforced training standards can only be artificial and unjustifiably exclusive. In this regard, it might be worthwhile to note that empirical evidence suggests that professional licensing does not protect consumers against incompetents (see Gross 1978).

In lieu of approvals, evaluators might settle for recommended curricula, courses of study, or guidelines for training; but this option still does not solve the problem. Once recommendations are made, training programs may be tempted to mold themselves after those guidelines in order to improve their credibility and woo students. Also, it is a relatively short step from recommendations to approvals, and by setting guidelines we may make it easier for future generations to set up an approval apparatus.

As a substitute for these activities, evaluators might concern themselves with training issues which are of great importance, but which are not likely to lead to a hegemony or to a control over evaluation by a relatively small group.

Five examples of safe and useful training activities come to mind. First, directories of training opportunities could be compiled which would be of considerable use to students, employers, and faculty members. Second, many people might wish to see the results of a survey designed to determine what evaluation skills are actually required in various types of positions. Third, publicizing different models of evaluation training would be very useful for potential students and for those who run evaluation programs. Fourth, more than other professions, evaluators are often faced with the difficult problem of explaining complex technical issues to lay persons, and it might be useful to investigate and publicize efficient methods of accomplishing this task. Finally, many practicing evaluators are "professional retreads," whose original field was not evaluation. Training such people presents a different problem from training the completely inexperienced, and efficient methods of retraining should be a major concern to evaluation experts.

All of the above suggestions have an important aspect in common. All are much needed projects which would enhance the training of evaluators, but which would not increase the evaluation profession's control over who is allowed to do evaluation, or the type of evaluation work which is carried out.

A second example of important but innocuous professional activities can be found in the realm of ethics. Ethics are a matter which should be of major concern to each individual evaluator and to the profession as a whole. But how should that interest be manifest? One of the most obvious possibilities is the establishment of a code of ethics. Unfortunately such a project might have some very negative consequences in terms of undue control over evaluation activity. There is bound to be legitimate disagreement about what is and is not ethical, and codes of ethics tend to ensconce the opinion of the relatively small group of people which had the energy, prestige and position to develop the code. Further, most people do not refer to codes of ethics in their everyday work, and professions tend to invoke infractions of such codes only in the rare instance when it is necessary to censure particularly errant and troublesome members of the profession.

As a substitute for investing time and effort in developing a code of ethics, one might mount educational programs for evaluators and their employers on the subject of ethics in evaluation. Although there is no guarantee that these programs would be more useful than a code of ethics in increasing ethical evaluation, such a possibility is not unreasonable. In any case, the value of codes of ethics in ensuring ethical behavior has certainly not been demonstrated, and such codes can be used unfairly to control who does evaluation, and how. Thus evaluators have a choice between two activities. Both deal with the important issue of ethics, but one activity is likely to increase the profession's control over the practice of evaluation, and one is not. Whenever such a choice is present, we recommend the activity which will not increase control by evaluators over evaluation. The tendency to develop such control is an inherent aspect of the process of professionalization, and we do not believe that such tendencies are beneficial. As evaluation becomes more useful to society the trend to professionalization is likely to intensify, and so too must our efforts against the negative consequences of that trend.

CONCLUSION

There is ample evidence for the assertion that the importance of program evaluation is rapidly increasing, and that the events which are causing that rise are taking place both within the social sciences and within the sociopolitical arena. It remains for us to attempt to understand the interplay of these forces and to fit them into a model which will allow us to predict the future course of program evaluation. The present chapter is based on the assumption that theories of professionalization, as developed by sociologists, provide the conceptual tools that will lead to the sought-after understanding. Although one cannot prove that evaluation is truly a profession, theories of professionalization are extremely useful for the task at hand.

Classic descriptions of the characteristics of a profession were offered in order to demonstrate that the field of evaluation is in all likelihood perched on the verge of professionalization. Four theories concerned with the dynamics of professionalization were then advanced and these theories were used to understand recent events in program evaluation, to determine the probable future course of the field, and to identify likely problems that should be guarded against. These problems involve increasingly heated debates concerning the true purpose of evaluation, the development of an excessive sense of exclusivity concerning who is qualified to do evaluation, and the development of evaluation training programs with inappropriate curricula.

We feel that these problems are not merely by-products of progress in program evaluation, but are unavoidable consequences of the process by which evaluation will become an independent profession. Further, the suggestions in this book concerning the organization of evaluation and the use of technological models are likely to accelerate the process of professionalization, together with its attendant negative aspects.

The problems are discussed not so they may be eliminated but so that we will recognize them for what they are, and will be better able to reduce the intensity of difficulties when they arise.

NOTES

¹This chapter is an elaboration of Morell and Flaherty 1978.

The authors would like to thank Joel Gerstl, Sherri Sheinfeld and Jeffrey Travers for their critical reviews of early drafts of the original paper. Thanks also go to Marcia Guttentag for the support and encouragement of the ideas developed there.

[2]No attempt will be made here to evaluate the relative merit of their four theories. Each has elements which can help us explain the development of evaluation, and that is sufficient for our present purpose.

[3]Stating the problem in this manner quite obviously gives the evaluator's clientele a great deal of credit and the benefit of more than several doubts, but perhaps this is as it should be. Evaluators are not omniscient. Evaluation is in large measure a service function, and people very often do know what they want and need.

[4]We doubt that these efforts will ever get as far as the legislation of licensure for evaluators, but most writers on the subject of professions agree that this is an end toward which most professions strive.

[5]Goode (1969) also points out that where parts of a professional's knowledge do become routinized, ancillary occupations develop and workers in these fields are employed by the professional. As examples, consider the physician's assistant, the dental hygienist, and the paralegal.

8

Evaluation in an Innovating Society

CURRENT TRENDS AND FUTURE PROMISE

Evaluation can be made into something different from management science, policy science, or traditional forms of applied social research. If evaluation is construed as merely a new twist to these already developed fields, its full potential will be overlooked, and an opportunity will be missed to develop a particularly useful and relevant form of social research. Evaluation as we know it today contains the seeds of an important new perspective on solving social problems, and that perspective will be lost if too much energy is put into using evaluation as a minor variation on already well-established themes. Outcome evaluation can be made into something different from its historical/intellectual antecedents, and efforts must be put specifically into that objective.

Arguments presented in this book indicate several important notions which bear on the directions evaluation must take if it is to realize its full potential. First, many social service settings provide important contexts which cannot be artificially duplicated, and which are vital arenas for relevant and important social research. Second, although the use of service agency settings for research purposes may produce some inconvenience for the agency, methods do exist to minimize the inconvenience. Third, even though inconvenience cannot be eliminated, researchers do have a legitimate right to demand cooperation from service agencies. Fourth, outcome research can take on a large variety of forms. Because of the numerous methods which exist to do outcome evaluation, *valid* research can be performed in a very wide variety of "messy" field settings. Fifth, some evaluation research does necessitate specially constructed settings, and all concerned parties must appreciate the need for constructing such settings. Sixth, social research can lead to *powerful* guides to successful practical action if evaluation is modeled on a technological paradigm. Such modeling will involve a shift in our choice of variables, a change in our choice of theories, and an appreciation of the distinction between field testing research and development research. Finally, evaluation studies can be fine tuned to meet the needs of its audiences.

These facts lead to the conclusion that relevant and powerful evaluation research can be carried out. The essence of this research is its capacity to yield information which is valid and generalizable to more than the immediate research setting, which will yield causal information about program effects, which will be useful in a practical sense, and which will serve as a guide to improving solutions to social problems. A management model of evaluation is not sufficient for the development of such research because of the management model's emphasis on immediate utility for program administrators. Those administrators are often preoccupied with specific problems of immediate relevance to their agency's functioning or survival, and their needs for information do not focus on long-range policy issues. Social experimentation, research, and policy study perspectives may also be incapable of leading to valid and powerful solutions to social problems. The difficulty with these approaches is the scientific models on which they are based.

If evaluation is developed appropriately it can be made into an approach which will have greater potential than its predecessors to yield substantive solutions to substantive problems. The evaluation I have in mind will: be generalizable to a reasonable number of different settings; take place partially within existing service agencies and partially in specially constructed settings; emphasize the search for causal relations between program actions and program outcomes; place a heavy emphasis on validity; be built on the technological model; and be fine tuned to the constraints of its setting and the needs of its audiences.

The Importance of Generalizability

Evaluation must yield results which are generalizable to settings other than the immediate context of the research. This is a crucial element of evaluation, and stands in sharp contrast to arguments which claim that the primary objective of evaluation is immediate usefulness in specific settings. Generalizability is important because the drive for immediate use of evaluation is likely, in the long run, to lead to a great deal of work which will have very little value.

The need for generalizability in evaluation can be justified on several grounds. First, the process of information utilization for practical decision making is governed by a dynamic of its own, and extensive research makes it clear that the utilization dynamic does not allow for immediate usefulness. The translation of research into practice is slow, convoluted, and diffuse.[1] Clear-cut cases of quick utilization are rare exceptions. Organizations will not function smoothly if too many changes are introduced into their standard operating procedures. Funding priorities often dictate policy, and research results are slow to be felt at the funding policy level. Professionals are socialized into particular philosophies of treatment procedures, and will not be quick to change those beliefs in the face of contradictory information.

A second line of reasoning which argues for an emphasis on generalizability in evaluation derives from the problems involved in drawing inference from data. The emphasis on *replicability* in research stems from a strong feeling that results from any single study, no matter how well designed, might be idiosyncratic, or in error. Given the inherent uncertainty of any single investigation, and given the added difficulties of conducting valid research in evaluation contexts, it does not seem wise for evaluators to advocate the immediate incorporation of their work into the practical decision-making process. On the other hand, the priorities of society may change by the time reasonably trustworthy conclusions can be drawn from a variety of evaluation studies. Hence a need for generalizability—for working on problems that have some enduring saliency, and which will not evaporate with each whim of our collective decision making.

A third reason to avoid attempts at immediate usefulness of evaluation comes from the nature of the political decision-making process. In a short but cogent analysis, Brandl (1978) points out that politicians are not primarily interested in the *outcomes* of social programs. Rather, politicians are interested in the number and diversity of interests and constituencies which advocate a particular position. If enough people advocate a particular course of action, that is good enough to make a decision. The actual value of that course of action, or its effect on the problem for which it was instituted, is of secondary importance. If there is any truth to this analysis, it is small wonder that information on the effectiveness of programs is not quickly integrated into political decision making. By the time such information is available, politicians are being pressed by other constituencies on other matters. What, then, must the evaluator do in order to be relevant and useful? The answer is that attempts must be made to influence not only politicians, but *also* the constituencies which lobby politicians. That is a much slower process than feeding information to a small body of decision makers. It involves the process of bringing about a change in the thinking of large numbers of people—of convincing those people that particular programs may bring about a desired result.

It is not enough to convince decision makers that a particular type of compensatory education will help disadvantaged children. One must also convince those who lobby decision makers to institute compensatory education programs. Valid data on the incidence of child abuse did not bring about child abuse programs. Those programs were brought about by the actions of citizen's groups who believed that such programs were needed. Social research might have hastened the advent of anti-child-abuse programs, but that hastening would have taken place only if concerned groups knew of and believed in that research. Given the need to influence a diversity of people and groups, it is certainly not likely that the results of any single evaluation will be immediately useful. The most appropriate time for evaluation seems to be *before* a new program is set up, rather than after it has been implemented. This implies a considerable amount of foresight, patience, and planning on the part of evaluators. It also implies that attempts to influence politicians by providing information on the effectiveness of existing programs are likely to fail. Hence the need for a longer-term perspective, and for an emphasis on generalizability which must inevitably accompany that extended perspective.

Finally, it is instructive to look at some of the problems of information utilization which are faced in the business world. It seems reasonable to expect that where the profit motive is operating in a direct way, useful innovation will be seized upon whenever it can be made to pay. Not so. Even in that world, innovation and the incorporation of useful information is frustratingly slow. A recent analysis of innovation in American industry contained the following points (*Economist* 1978, p. 86):

> Many top executives, when they are not coping with government regulations, are too busy bothering about the balance sheet for the quarter after next to spend much of their daily work on the product after next.

Later, the article continues:

> Picking holes is another easy part of innovation: new ideas can nearly always be criticised on economic or technical grounds, or both. The real hurdles are finding the guts to back some of these inventions, the managerial skill to turn them into marketable products and the money to pay for them.

These arguments sound depressingly similar to numerous analyses of the innovation problems in social service.

Thus, the problem of slow innovation on the basis of new information is pervasive and difficult. It is simply not reasonable to expect immediate integration of evaluation information into decision making. For all the aforementioned reasons, any more new information is simply not likely to have immediate impact. If information generated by evaluators really is applicable only to a constrained time and place, the evaluator's findings may be valueless by the time they filter through the utilization process.

There is no point in evaluators' engaging in "quick draw" contests to see whose evaluations are used first, as such attempts are likely to lead to quick and dirty studies of crisis problems. Crises do arise, and evaluators should try to help, but the real substance and contribution of evaluation lies in its ability to suggest solutions to recurrent problems. Crises pass, problems remain. True relevance cannot be measured only by the speed of utilization. Rather, true relevance must be measured by the extent to which research suggests practical solutions to problems which are important and of general public concern. Crisis-based evaluation cannot do this. Generalizable evaluation can.

Evaluators must focus their efforts on increasing the flow of rational planning information into the decision-making process: the more, the sooner, the better, This objective is, however, far different from attempting to generate immediately useful information. In fact, the two goals are antithetical, as one leads to poor methodology, inadequate background work, and studies which cannot be trusted to add valid information to the store of knowledge which eventually will work its way into practical use.

Social problems are cyclic. To be more precise, there is a political process through which particular issues become defined as crucial social problems, fade from priority attention, and after a period of time, reassert themselves under a somewhat different guise. Further, programs and agencies are in a constant state of flux, as are the services which they deliver and the populations which receive those services. For both of these reasons planners must have knowledge of *essential program elements* which can be trusted to have an effect when invoked each time a problem becomes important. That requirement necessitates evaluation results which are generalizable. Without such generalizability, evaluation will be of only short range minimal utility.

Evaluation Settings

Evaluation must take place, at least in part, within ongoing service delivery agencies. Field testing of new approaches cannot take place in artificial settings because the essence of the field test is an attempt to see if a program will work as designed without the special attention, special funding and enthusiastic sponsorship which exists during the development of new treatments. Further, as Boruch and Gomez (1977) point out, treatments are not usually implemented as they were designed, and meaningful evaluation must take this problem into account.

Agency settings are also important because they often provide the only practical context in which particular populations can be obtained, skilled personnel found, or particular types of services implemented. The study of some social problems may demand settings which cannot be artificially duplicated, and if research is to be meaningful, some cooperation from service delivery organizations is needed. Since there is an imperative for research to be valid, evaluators have a legitimate reason to ask for changes in an agency's standard operating procedure to accomodate the requirements of sound research design.

Some evaluation activity must also take place in settings constructed specially for the purpose of testing a particular treatment. In a sense, these settings will be laboratories devoted to social technological research. Some research on social problems may require a concentration of resources or a set of procedures which are clearly and legitimately beyond the scope of existing service delivery agencies. In such cases special settings must be constructed for the express purpose of developing and assessing specific new approaches to well-defined problems. (The concept of the "lab school" comes to mind in this regard.)

Emphasis on Outcome and Causal Links

Evaluation must have a strong emphasis on outcome and on causal links between program actions and program effects, both positive and negative, both planned and unanticipated. Causal data can give planners a sense of what is most likely to happen as a result of their actions, and that type of knowledge forms the substance of rational planning. Although true experiments may often be the ideal design for such research, they are by no means the only alternatives. Depending on the setting and the problem, other approaches may be available, and even preferable. Causal modeling has been attempted through the use of observational data (Cooley 1978). Sociological and anthropological methodologies have been used in evaluation (Britan 1978; Patton 1978). The jury model of knowledge gathering has been used (Levine et al. 1978). Quasi-experimental designs are plentiful (Cook and Campbell 1976).

The crucial issue is not the methodology employed, but whether the goal of causal inference guides evaluation work from beginning to end. Evaluators must make many choices concerning levels of analysis, research design, theories, hypotheses, and data analysis. All of these choices are influenced by the basic intent of a study, and all must be chosen with the aim of causal inference in mind. In the long run, working on causal inference will allow evaluation to be relevant, as planners will begin to regard evaluation as a powerful aid in the solution of recurrent problems. This process can be facilitated if evaluators pay attention to principles of research utilization, but there is no point in speeding up that process unless evaluation information is truly of value, and the most valuable information is that which deals with causal inference.

The Importance of Validity

If we attempt to see our findings implemented, if we are pretentious enough to believe that our work can make a difference, then we must strive to generate the highest possible quality of data. The validity issue is in a way more serious in evaluation than in science, as scientific studies are not intended to have a direct influence on the expenditure of public funds or the choice of solutions to social problems. By the time scientific results filter into the political decision-making world they have probably gone through considerable debate, testing, and refining within the scientific community. Evaluators, on the other hand, make special attempts to hurry the utilization process, and as a result, findings may not be subject to the scrutiny which they deserve. It is a serious problem if we convince people to take our advice, and we have told them wrong. We have a responsibility to minimize that possibility, and that necessitates considerable efforts at increasing the validity of our findings.

Technological Models in Evaluation

Technological models have many desirable characteristics which make for relevant and applicable research. First, technological problems and solutions are shaped by the same factors which forge the problem/solution context of administrators, politicians, policy makers and concerned citizens.

Second, technological theory is developed specifically as a guide to practical action, and not as a model of truth or reality. Technological investigations are aimed specifically at clarifying the relationship among factors which make a difference in the world of everyday action, and which can be (at least to some degree) manipulated or controlled through available means.

Third, one of the goals of technological work is to help decision makers work better with *all* the inputs which go into decision making—theory, experience, intuition, judgment, and experimentally obtained information.[2]

Finally, technological research involves a clear distinction between development research and field test research. This distinction helps determine appropriate settings for the study of different types of problems, helps set the proper context for methodological critiques of evaluation, clarifies the reasons for attempting a given piece of research, and increases the likelihood that useful information will emerge from evaluation activity.

In sum, evaluation built on the technological model will be responsive to the needs of practical decision makers, concentrate efforts on developing useful guides to action, sharpen the decison-making ability of decision makers, and generate research which is powerful for its intended purpose.

Making Evaluation Appropriate to Settings and Audiences

Outcome evaluation is a multifaceted concept which touches on issues related to research design, research quality, and information utility. Any of these factors may make an evaluation plan inappropriate, and all must be considered if the value of an evaluation plan is to be maximized. Changing any one aspect of an evaluation is likely to have serious implications for other aspects, and trade-offs must be made among the three dimensions of evaluation. Consider, for example, the choice of particular variables because of the need to be relevant to a particular audience. It may be that the most relevant variables are also the most difficult to measure. In such a case, choosing the most relevant variables will necessitate the lowering of an evaluation's validity. The issue is not learning to avoid such compromises, as they are an inescapable element of the evaluation business. It is necessary, however, for evaluators to develop a fine sense of how decisions concerning each aspect of evaluation affect the others. Trade-offs among type, validity and usefulness are a fact of evaluation life, and those decisions must be made in a careful and calculated manner. Priorities must be set, relationships among factors must be understood, and a clear sense of minimal acceptable levels for each dimension must be developed. Only then can really worthwhile evaluation plans be developed, and only then can evaluation be made truly appropriate for its settings and its audiences.

CONSEQUENCES AND RESPONSIBILITIES

If the vision is fulfilled, if a powerful evaluation technology is developed, evaluators will have to bear responsibility for the consequences of that development. Apple (1974) has identified four serious problems which may arise as consequences of evaluation activity. First, the process of conducting evaluation may serve to turn people's attention away from the real problems which need to be solved, or to use a phrase favored by confidence men and sociologists, evaluation might be used to "cool the mark out." Substantive improvement to a social institution might well involve fundamental changes in organizational structure, in the locus of power, and in other difficult-to-change characteristics. According to Apple's (1974) analysis, certain types of linguistic metaphors can be used by those who hold power to turn people's attention *away* from the need for this type of fundamental change. As examples, he cites terms such as "accountability" and "cost-benefit analysis," both of which make it seem that by tinkering with the present system, all will be made well. As Apple (1974, pp. 13-14) puts it:

> Like abstractions such as democracy and justice, they are reified by and become identified with existing institutions. The terminology becomes what Edelman has called "socially pathetic" language that tends to encourage attachment to existing institutional structures that may actually "deny (individuals) values that they prize."

The second problem presented by Apple (1974, p. 14) involves the role of the experts who in their

> . . . failure to see that by committing themselves to the study of officially defined goals and procedures using official categories they may also be giving the rhetorical prestige of science to extant bureaucratic regularities.

Third, Apple argues that evaluators may base their work on existing clinical assumptions about the root causes of problems, and in so doing, support a treatment or a social philosophy that may be incorrect, inappropriate, or ineffective. As an example, he cites the case of evaluators who base their work on the assumption that underachievement in school is the fault of the student or the student's social group. Such an assumption leads evaluators away from studying the role of the school system in underachievement, and it may well be that the school system is a major cause of the problem. Such misdirected activity may inhibit the search for meaningful solutions to problems, or institutionalize social philosophies and social structures which should be changed.

Finally, Apple (1974) argues that evaluation may serve to increase control over people rather than as a method to increase society's responsiveness to human needs. Two factors combine to cause this problem. First, our scientific approach in general strives for control and certainty over events. To the extent that this value pervades the human sciences, we attempt to carefully control situations in order to increase the certainty of our results. Second, the need for certainty also pervades decision making within political institutions and, as a result, politics becomes a way to manipulate people rather than a process designed to respond to human needs. To the extent that science, i.e., evaluation, and politics become integrated, the recognition of individuality may be subjugated to the needs of certainty and control.

In additon to these four consequences of evaluation, Berk and Rossi (1977) note additional problems. First, they argue that evaluation is inherently a conservative activity because programs which do not exist do not get evaluated, and of the programs which are evaluated, one can only assess the range of action which is actually taken by those programs. This too, may inhibit the search for truly effective solutions to social programs, or to institutionalize particular approaches to the solution of social problems. Second, Berk and Rossi (1977) claim that our methodologies are far better at measuring individual than organizational factors. Since there is always a desire to use the best tools available, we are systematically led away from an entire class of analysis and exploration which might prove the key to developing effective programs.

A final negative consequence of evaluation is its possible dehumanizing influence. In an analysis of the social consequences of social research, Kelman (1968, pp. 47-48) has made the following point about the effects of social research on man:

> . . . social research deprives him of his wholeness and his unique individuality. We are interested in him as part of a group, to whose mean score he contributes. We try to wash out the random error generated by his idiosyncracies. . . . I do not deplore this, because the task of the social scientist, unlike that of the novelist, is not to capture the richness of an individual's existence but to develop general propositions, and his orientation to man is completely consistent with this task. Nevertheless, by taking this orientation, for perfectly valid intellectual reasons, are we not contributing to those forces in our society that tend to transform man into a depersonalized object?

It is important to note that all of the negative consequences just mentioned need not arise through malicious intent. On the contrary, they are likely to arise out of the best of intentions and in a quite subtle manner. As conscientious evaluators we want our work to be as valid as possible, hence our reliance on the best available methods. Our interest in experimental control over situations, careful dissection of issues into their component parts and a reliance on aggregate data, are a natural consequence of our wish to be accurate. We certainly wish to be relevant and answerable to our audiences, hence our sensitivity to their social ideologies and to the specifics of the programs which they have instituted. Thus problems arise from the nature of our work and from the natural human motivations which guide us all.

All of these problems may have consequences for evaluation activity, and all will become more serious as evaluation becomes an important and powerful element in social service planning. If evaluation gains a reputation for having value and credibility, people will listen to evaluators' advice, and the more that happens, the greater the harm wrong advice will do. As evaluators learn to act according to the principles of research utilization, their work will be more quickly assimilated into political and planning processes, often without enough time for the critical review and discussion that any research should have. Another problem is that the more evaluation becomes a powerful and respected tool, the greater the needs of vested interests to exert influence over the course and conduct of evaluation activity.

The entire thrust of this book has been to develop a plan for making evaluation activity more generally respected, more powerful in suggesting solutions to problems, better targeted toward measuring the value of programs, and more central to the needs of decision makers. To the extent that the proposed plan is successful, the threat of negative consequences of evaluation activity will increase. As a matter of personal and social responsibility, evaluators cannot ignore these issues. If we try to develop a powerful evaluation, and if we actually try to make others recognize that power, we must assume at least partial responsibility for the misuse of our works. Methods do exist for avoiding the abuse of evaluation, and evaluators must incorporate these methods into their professional lives.

The undesirable consequences of evaluation can be lessened if evaluators organize their activity in appropriate ways, and if their personal conduct conforms to certain principles. Windle and Neigher (1978), in a general discussion of ethical issues in evaluation, cite three aspects of personal conduct which should guide evaluators. First, evaluators must be humble. As Windle and Neigher (1978, p. 105) put it:

> The evaluator who creates unrealistically high expectations for evaluation utility increases the possibilities of compromising ethical integrity in order to deliver on past promises. The principle of humility can also be phrased as having respect for the ability of others, including lay persons, to make appropriate judgments if presented with information.

A second principle of personal conduct cited by Windle and Neigher (1978) is that evaluators should strive as much as possible to clarify their role in any given evaluation situation prior to the commencement of the evaluation work. Numerous competing demands beset the evaluator in any complex evaluation setting, and evaluators, program personnel and funders must understand the scope and the tasks of an evaluation. Without such understanding, competing demands and ill-defined expectations are bound to confuse the true implications of an evaluation activity, raise people's apprehension, and make it more difficult for the evaluator to present accurate, specific information.

Windle and Neigher's (1978) third piece of advice is for evaluators to strive to understand and be aware of the ethical aspects of their work. Ethical implications of evaluation activity cannot be overlooked, and ignorance of those issues can only make matters worse.

A healthy respect for the weaknesses in our work is bound to increase our readiness to caution others about the worth of our actions. Hence the importance of humility. A clear sense of whom we are working for will help us understand how all parties will perceive the consequences of our actions. Hence the need to clarify tasks and roles. Finally, ethical concerns about our work will help us understand the value base from which we are working, and the implications of those values for the people and institutions with whom we interact.

In addition to these three elements of personal conduct, there are several methods of organizing evaluation in order to reduce the biases and ethical problems which are a function of evaluation activity. One solution has been proposed by Michael Scriven (1976), in an analysis of the roots of bias in evaluation. Scriven's thesis is that the people with whom evaluators work and the sources which fund evaluation activity impose an inevitable bias on what evaluators do, what they look for, what they find, and the interpretation of their data. Scriven feels that since this source of bias cannot be eliminated, the only solution is to have multiple sources of evaluation, each responsible to a different constituency. If the findings of these various evaluation teams agree, one can have some faith in the results and recommendations of the evaluators. In cases of disagreement, there is the possibility of finding the truth through attempts to resolve the differences.

A similar proposal has been made by Cook (1974) in his advocacy of secondary evaluation. Cook's argument is that the data from primary evaluations should be available to be re-analyzed by other evaluators who may have different perspectives, less time pressure than the original evaluation team, or specialized data analysis skills.

In line with the notion of multiple perspectives on evaluation, we should not forget Scriven's (1974) notion of goal-free evaluation, or the current trend in community mental health to include citizen review boards in evaluation activities (Windle and Woy 1977).

The thrust of all of these plans is to guard against misleading evaluation by means of multiple perspectives on the same problem. By so doing, all interested parties may serve as a check on the special interests of each other.

A second structural check on ethical problems in evaluation may come from building up codes of ethics which are developed specifically with the political nature of evaluation in mind. Windle and Neigher (1978) cite the examples of psychological testing and erotic contact between therapists and clients. In both of these areas, specific empirical studies were carried out in an attempt to identify relevant issues of ethical guidelines. Windle and Neigher (1978, p. 106) also argue that "Program evaluators might consider the types of court precedents they would like to see established, and the cases which could be used to set these precedents."

Finally, evaluators may guard against the misuse of their work by attempting to retain control or influence over the use of evaluation information. One method of accomplishing this goal is by developing a respected advisory capacity. Campbell (1971) has suggested the development of an "advisory legislature" to be made up of social scientists who advise legislators as to the consequences of proposed actions. The role would be strictly advisory, as Campbell feels that social decisions are a political process, and should not be controlled by the social science establishment. Still, by developing such an advisory capacity, evaluators would be able to stay in touch with the consequences of their actions, and hopefully, to provide decision makers with a sense of the appropriate use of evaluation.

A second method of retaining control over evaluation activity has been proposed by Ostrander, Goldstein, and Hull (1978), who believe that in order to aid the evaluation implementation and utilization process, evaluators should try to gain power, in the political sense of the term. Presumably, that same power could be used to guard against the misuse of evaluation by others.

It is by no means clear whether the world will be better off with evaluators as advisors or as a power center, but both of these suggestions are based on the notion that evaluators simply do their work, communicate their results, and leave well enough alone. Both suggestions are based on the idea that an evaluator's work and responsibility must include some form of involvement in the political decision-making process, and both have the potential to reduce the inappropriate use of evaluation by society at large.

Whatever form the political involvement of evaluators takes, that involvement must include a sensitivity to those aspects of evaluation studies which are most important for making decisions about programs. Evaluators must be ready, willing, and able to identify such information and to emphasize its importance to decision makers.[3] (The evaluator's audience certainly has a right to ignore this type of advice, but that right does not obviate the evaluator's responsibility to provide it.)

As we have seen, evaluation has the potential to entrench ineffective solutions to serious problems, dehumanize individuals, support social philosophies which may be inappropriate or incorrect, and inhibit the search for innovative solutions to social problems. On the other hand, multifaceted valid data on causal links between program actions and program effects can be an invaluable aid in judging program effectiveness, improving existing programs, and suggesting new solutions which may have a good chance of success. There are methods of increasing the power of evaluation without increasing the negative consequences of evaluation activity, but this objective can be met only if evaluators work *actively* for the constructive use of their products and labors. Merely turning out valid or relevant information is not enough, as the more relevant the data, the greater its political sensitivity; and the more valid the data, the more power it has to do damage. Further, the evaluator's responsibility is collective, as no single evaluator can foresee how the public will combine information from different sources, when an evaluation will be "discovered" by one or another constituency, or the impact that any type of evaluation activity will have on the reputation of evaluators and evaluation.

Finally, evaluators must always be guided by what Kelman (1968) terms "radical thinking." According to Kelman (p. 49-50), radical thinking has two aspects. First:

> . . . it views any particular social arrangement or policy as one of many possible ones and helps us escape the trap of thinking that what is must therefore be. It throws into question the assumptions on which current arrangements and policies are based, and tests out alternative assumptions.

Second:

> It tries to get away from abstractions, from thinking about institutions as if they had a life of their own apart from the men who have created them and who are served by them. In analyzing social arrangements and policies, it asks what they mean to concrete human beings. In seeking solutions to pressing social problems, it asks what institutions and what courses of action are most likely to meet the needs and enhance the dignity and self-fulfillment of individuals.

I believe that if we are guided by radical thinking, if we share the responsibility for the consequences for each others actions, and if we organize our work appropriately, evaluation can be made into a positive force in the search for powerful solutions to pressing social problems.

INNOVATION AND EVALUATION

Evaluation can be developed into a relevant and powerful method of guiding the course of social innovations. It can best do so by developing into a technology which is truly relevant to the needs of society and of decision makers, one which provides valid data on salient issues, and which recognizes that although immediate utilization is unlikely, a body of generalizable information is needed to help solve problems which are bound to continually recur. As evaluation is developed into such a tool, the potential for its abuse and misuse will increase. As a matter of social responsibility, evaluators must be continually ready to counteract that negative potential.

As a technique of social research, evaluation can become more relevant than its predecessors to the needs of society. This book has been an attempt to lay out a blueprint for that development.

NOTES

[1]There is an immense literature on the topic of research utilization. The following works are recommended for those who wish to explore this area in more detail:
Davis and Salasin (1975); Havlock (1970); National Institute of Mental Health (1973, vols. 1, 2); Patton 1978).
[2]This list of decision-making inputs comes from Wiesner (1970) where it was presented in an essay titled "The Need for Social Engineering."
[3]I would like to thank Steve Pellegrini for pointing out that helping to make judgments is not the same as providing information on program effects. Each can be done without the other, but it is the evaluator's responsibility to do both.

BIBLIOGRAPHY

Ackoff, R. L.; Gupta, S. K.; and Minas, S. 1962. *Scientific method: Optimizing applied research decisions*. New York: Wiley.

Adams, S. 1975. *Evaluative research in corrections: A practical guide*. Washington, D.C.: U.S. Department of Justice, Law Enforcement Assistance Administration.

Agassi, J. 1966. The confusion between science and technology. *Technology and Culture*. 7:348-366.

―――. 1968. The logic of technological development. *Proceedings of the XIV international congress of philosophy*, Vienna, pp. 383-388.

Allen, D. 1976. Evaluation—An ethical perspective. In *Trends in mental health evaluation*, ed. E. W. Markson and D. Allen, pp. 131-140. Lexington, MA: Lexington Books.

Apple, M. W. 1974. The process and ideology of valuing in educational settings. In *Educational evaluation: Analysis and responsibility*, ed. M. W. Apple, M. J. Subkoviak, and J. R. Lufler, Berkeley, CA: McCutchan.

Argyris, C. 1975. Dangers in applying results from experimental social psychology. *American Psychologist* 30:469-485.

Aronson, S. H., and Sherwood, C. C. 1967. Researcher versus practitioner: Problems in social action research. *Social Work* 12: 89-96. Also in *Evaluating action programs: Readings in social action research*, ed. C. H. Weiss. Boston: Allyn & Bacon, 1972.

Astin, A., and Panos, R. 1969. *An analysis of the effectiveness of different (mailed questionnaire) follow-up techniques*, Appendix D. Washington, DC: Vocational and Educational Development of College Students.

Attkisson, C. C.; Hargreaves, W. A.; Horowitz, M. J.; and Sorensen, J. E. 1978. *Evaluation of human service programs*. New York: Academic Press.

Backstrom, C., and Hursh, G. 1963. *Survey research*. Evanston, IL: Northwestern University Press.

Baekeland, F., and Lundwall, L. 1975. Dropping out of treatment: A critical review. *Psychological Bulletin* 82: 738-783.

Baumrin, R. H. 1970. The immorality of irrelevance: The social role of science. In *Psychology and the problems of society*, ed. F. F. Korten, S. W. Cook, and J. J. Lacey, pp. 73-83. Washington, DC: American Psychological Association.

Becker, H. S. 1970. The nature of a profession. In *Sociological work*, ed. Howard S. Becker, pp. 87-103. Chicago: Aldine.

Beit-Halahmi, B. 1974. Salvation and its vicissitudes: Clinical psychology and political values. *American Psychologist* 29: 124-129.

Bem, D., and Allen, A. 1974. On predicting some of the people some of the time: The search for cross situational consistencies in behavior. *Psychological Review* 81: 506-520.

Bennis, W. G.; Benne, K. D.; Chin, R.; and Corey, K. E., eds. 1976. *The planning of change*. New York: Holt, Rinehart and Winston.

Benveniste, G. 1972. *The politics of expertise*. San Francisco, CA: Boyd and Fraser/ Glendessary.

Bergen, B. J. 1969. Professional communities and the evaluation of demonstration projects in community mental health. In *Program evaluation in the health fields*, ed. H. C. Schulberg, A. Sheldon, and F. Baker, pp. 121-135. New York: Behavioral Publications.

Berk, R. A., and Rossi, P. H. 1977. Doing good or doing worse: Evaluation research politically reexamined. In *Evaluation studies review annual*, Vol. 2, ed. M. Guttentag and S. Saar, pp. 77-90, Beverly Hills, CA: Sage Publications.

Bloom, B. C. 1972. Mental health program evaluation. In *Handbook of community mental health*, ed. S. E. Golann and C. Eisdorfer, pp. 819-839. New York: Appleton-Century-Crofts.

Bond, G. L., and Tinker, M. A. 1973. *Reading difficulties—their diagnosis and correction*, 3rd ed. New York: Appleton-Century-Crofts.

Boruch, R. F. 1974. Bibliography: Illustrative randomized field experiments for program planning and evaluation. *Evaluation* 2: 83-87.

Boruch, R. F., and Gomez, H. 1977. Sensitivity, bias, and theory in impact evaluations. *Professional Psychology* 8 (November): 411-434.

Brandl, J. E. 1978. Evaluation and politics. *Evaluation*, Special Issue: 6-7.

Britan, G. M. 1978. Experimental and contextual models of program evaluation. *Evaluation and Program Planning* 1: 229-234.

Brody, E., and Brody, N. 1976. *Intelligence: Nature, determinants and consequences*. New York: Academic Press.

Bronfenbrenner, V. 1975. Is early intervention effective? In *Handbook of evaluation*, Vol. 2, ed. M. Guttentag and E.L. Struening, pp. 519-603. Beverly Hills, CA: Sage Publications.

Brown, R. 1963. *Explanation in social science*. Chicago: Aldine, 1963.

Bruner, J. 1957. Going beyond the information given. In *Contemporary approaches to cognition*, ed. J. S. Bruner, et al., pp. 41-69. Cambridge, MA: Harvard University Press, 1957.

Bucher, R., and Strauss, A. 1961. Professions in process. *American Journal of Sociology* 66: 325-334.

Bunge, M. 1963. *The myth of simplicity: Problems of scientific philosophy*. Englewood Cliffs, NJ: Prentice Hall.

———. 1966. Technology as applied science. *Technology and Culture* 7: 329-347.

———. 1967. Action. *Scientific research: II. The search for truth*. New York: Springer-Verlag.

Calesnick, B. 1971. Intimate study of drug action IV: Applied pharmacology, animal and human. In *Drill's pharmacology in medicine*, ed. J. R. DiPalma, pp. 70-83, 4th ed. New York: McGraw-Hill.

Callahan, R. *Education and the cult of efficiency*. Chicago: Univ. of Chicago Press, 1962.

Campbell, D. T. 1971. Methods for the experimenting society.

———. 1974. *Qualitative knowing in action research*. New Orleans: Kurt Lewin Memorial Address, Society for the Psychological Study of Social Issues, Meeting with the American Psychological Association, September 1, 1974.

Campbell, D. T., and Erlebacher, A. 1970. How regression artifacts in quasi-experimental evaluation can mistakenly make compensatory education look harmful. In

Disadvantaged child vol. 3: Compensatory education, a national debate, ed. J. Hellmath, pp. 184-210. New York: Brunner Mazel, 1970.

Campbell, D. T., and Fiske, D. W. 1959. Convergent and discriminant validation by the multitrait-multimethod matrix. *Psychological Bulletin* 56: 81-105.

Campbell, D. T., and Stanley, J. C. 1966. *Experimental and quasi-experimental designs for research*. Chicago: Rand McNally.

Caro, F. G. 1971. Evaluation research—An overview. In *Readings in evaluation research*, ed. F. G. Caro, pp. 1-34. New York: Russell Sage Foundation.

Cherns, A. 1971. Social research and its diffusion. In *Readings in evaluation research*, ed. F. G. Caro, pp. 63-72. New York: Russell Sage Foundation.

Chin, R. 1976. The utility of system models and developmental models for practitioners. In *The planning of change*, W. G. Bennis, K. D. Benne, R. Chin, and K. E. Corey, 3rd ed., pp. 90-102. New York: Holt, Rinehart and Winston.

Chronical Guidance Publications. 1977. *Chronicle guide to external and continuing education*. Moravia, NY: Chronicle Guidance Publications.

Clum, G. A. 1975. Intrapsychic variables and the patient's environment as factors in prognosis. *Psychological Bulletin* 82: 413-431.

Cohen, J. 1969. *Statistical power analysis for the behavioral sciences*. New York: Academic Press.

Cook, T. D. 1974. The potential and limitations of secondary evaluations. In *Educational evaluation: Analysis and responsibility*, ed. M. W. Apple, M. J. Subkoviak and J. R. Lufler, pp. 155-222. Berkeley, CA: McCutchan.

Cook, T. D., and Campbell, D. T. 1976. Design and conduct of quasi-experiments and true experiments in field settings. In *Handbook of industrial and organizational psychology*, ed. M. Dunnette, pp. 223-324. Chicago: Rand McNally.

Cook, T. D., and Reichardt, C. 1976. Statistical analysis of non-equivalent control group designs: A guide to some current literature. *Evaluation* 3: 136-138.

Cooley, W. W. 1978. Explanatory observational studies. *Educational Researcher* 7: 9-15.

Copeland, R. W. 1970. *How children learn mathematics: Teaching implications of Piaget's research*. New York: Macmillan.

Coursey, R. D., ed. 1977. *Program evaluation for mental health: Methods, strategies, participants*. New York: Grune and Stratton.

Crano, W. D., and Brewer, M. B. 1973. *Principles of research in social psychology*. New York: McGraw Hill.

Crider, D. M.; Willits, F. K.; and Bealer, R. C. 1971. Tracking respondents in longitudinal surveys. *Public Opinion Quarterly* 35: 613-620.

Cronbach, L. J. 1975. Beyond the two disciplines of scientific psychology. *American Psychologist* 30: 116-127.

Davis, H. R. 1973. Four ways to goal attainment. *Evaluation* 1: 43-48, 95.

Davis, H. R., and Salasin, S. E. 1975. The utilization of evaluation. In *Handbook of evaluation*, vol. 1, ed. E. L. Struening and M. Guttentag, pp. 621-666. Beverly Hills, CA: Sage Publications.

De Leon, G.; Skodol, A.; and Rosenthal, M. 1973. Phoenix House: Changes in psychopathological signs of resident drug addicts. *Archives of General Psychiatry* 28: 131-135.

De Sola Price, D. J. 1965. Is technology historically independent of science? A study in statistical historiography. *Technology and Culture* 6: 553-567.

Eaton, J. W. 1969. Symbolic and substantive evaluative research. In *Program evaluation in the health fields*, ed. H. C. Schulberg, P. S. Sheldon, and F. Baker, pp. 506-524. New York: Behavioral Publications.

Eckland, B. K. 1965. Effects of prodding to increase mailback returns. *Journal of Applied Psychology* 49: 165-169.

Edwards, A. L. 1974. *Statistical analysis*, 4th ed. New York: Holt, Rinehart and Winston, 1974.

Edwards, W.; Guttentag, M.; and Snapper, K. 1975. A decision-theoretic approach to evaluation research. In *Handbook of evaluation research*, vol. 1, ed. E. L. Struening and M. Guttentag, pp. 139-181. Beverly Hills, CA: Sage Publications.

Etzioni, A. 1969. Two approaches to organizational analysis: A critique and a suggestion. In *Program evaluation in the health fields*, ed. H. C. Schulberg, A. Sheldon and F. Baker. New York: Behavioral Publications.

Fairweather, G. W. 1967. *Methods for experimental social innovation*. New York: Wiley.

Fairweather, G. W.; Sanders, D. H.; and Tornatzky, L. G. 1974. *Creating change in mental health organizations*. New York: Pergamon Press.

Feibleman, J. K. 1961. Pure science, applied science and technology: An attempt at definitions. *Technology and Culture* 2: 305-317. Also in *Philosophy and technology*, ed. C. Mitcham and R. Mackey. New York: Free Press, 1972.

Finch, J. K. 1961. Engineering and science. An historical review and appraisal. *Technology and Culture* 2: 318-332.

Flaherty, E. W., and Morell, J. A. 1978. Evaluation: Manifestations of a new field. *Evaluation and Program Planning* 1: 1-9.

Flanagan, J. C. 1954. The critical incident technique. *Psychological Bulletin* 51: 327-358.

Forcese, D., and Richer, S. 1973. *Social research methods*. Englewood Cliffs, NJ: Prentice Hall.

Franklin, J. L., and Thrasher, J. H. 1976. *An introduction to program evaluation*. New York: Wiley.

Freeley, A. J. 1976. *Argumentation and debate: Rational decision making*. 4th ed. Belmont, CA: Wadsworth.

Fringe, J. 1952. Research and the service agency. *Social Casework* 33: 343-348.

Gaebelein, J.; Soderquist, D.; and Powers, W. 1976. A note on variance explained in the mixed analysis of variance model. *Psychological Bulletin* 83: 1110-1112.

Gergen, K. J. 1973. Social psychology as history. *Journal of Personality and Social Psychology* 26: 309-320.

Gilbert, N., and Specht, H. 1977. *Planning for social welfare: Issues, models and tasks*. Englewood Cliffs, NJ: Prentice Hall.

Goffman, E. 1961. *Asylums*. Chicago: Aldine.

Goldberg, L. 1973. Student personality characters and optimal college learning conditions: An extensive search for trait—by treatment interaction effects. *Instructional Science:* 153-210.

Goode, W. J. 1969. The theoretical limits of professionalization. In *The semi-professions and their organization*, ed. A. Etzioni, pp. 266-313. New York: Free Press.

Goodwin, L., and Tu, J. 1975. The social psychological basis for public acceptance of the social security system: The role for social research in public policy formation. *American Psychologist* 30: 875-883.

Gross, S. J. 1978. The myth of professional licensing. *American Psychologist* 33: 1009-1017.

Gruender, D. C. 1971. On distinguishing science and technology. *Technology and Culture* 12: 456-463.

Guttentag, M., and Struening, E. L., eds. 1975. *Handbook of evaluation research*, vol. 2. Beverly Hills, CA: Sage Publications.

Guttman, E. 1963. Effects of short-term psychiatric treatment on boys in two California court authority institutions. *Research Report No. 36*. Sacramento: California Youth Authority.

Harré, R. 1970. *The principles of scientific thinking*. Chicago: Univ. of Chicago Press.

Harré, R., and Secord, P. F. 1973. *The explanation of social behavior*. Totowa, NJ: Littlefield, Adams.

Hatry, H.; Winnie, R.; and Fisk, D. 1973. *Practical program evaluation for state and local government officials*. Washington, DC: Urban Institute.

Havlock, R. G. 1970. *A guide to innovation in education*. Ann Arbor: Center for Research on the Utilization of Scientific Knowledge, Institute for Social Research, University of Michigan.

Hogan, R.; DeSoto, C. B.; and Solano, C. 1977. Traits, tests and personality research. *American Psychologist* 32: 255-264.

Holt, W. L., and Marchionne, A. M. 1967. Personality evaluation of correctional institution inmates awaiting plastic surgery and a control group of inmates. *International Journal of Neuropsychiatry* 3: 337-342.

Hyman, H. H. 1955. *Survey design and analysis*. Glencoe, IL: Free Press.

———. 1972. *Secondary analysis of sample surveys: Principles and potentialities*. New York: Wiley.

Hyman, H. H.; Wright, C. R.; and Reed, J. S. 1975. *The enduring effects of education*. Chicago: Univ. of Chicago Press.

Isaac, S., and Michael, W. 1974. *Handbook in research and evaluation for education and the behavioral sciences*. San Diego: Robert R. Knapp.

Jarvie, I. C. 1972. Technology and the structure of knowledge. In *Philosophy and technology*, ed. C. Mitcham and R. Mackey, pp. 54-61. New York: Free Press.

Jensen, A. R. 1973. *Educability and group differences*. New York: Harper and Row.

Kaplan, A. 1964. *The conduct of inquiry: Methodology for behavioral sciences*. Scranton, PA: Chandler.

Kay, F. D., Jr. 1978. Applications of social area analysis to program planning and evaluation. *Evaluation and Program Planning* 1: 51-64.

Kelman, H. C. 1968. *A time to speak: On human values and social research*. San Francisco: Jossey-Bass.

———. 1974. Attitudes are alive and well and gainfully employed in the sphere of action. *American Psychologist* 29: 310-324.

Keppel, G. 1973. *Design and analysis: A researcher's Handbook*. Englewood Cliffs, N.J.: Prentice Hall.

Kissin, B., and Su, W. 1970. Social and psychological factors in the treatment of chronic alcoholism. *Journal of Psychiatric Research* 8: 13-27.

Kozol, J. 1967. *Death at an early age*. Boston: Houghton Mifflin.

Kuhn, T. S. 1971. *The structure of scientific revolutions*, 2nd ed. Chicago: Univ. of Chicago Press.

Lakatos, I. 1972. Falsification and the methodology of scientific research programmes, pp. 91-196. In I. Lakatos and A. Musgrave, eds., *Criticism and the growth of knowledge*. London: Cambridge University Press.

Langenauer, B., and Bowden, C. 1971. A follow-up study of narcotic addicts in the NARA program. *American Journal of Psychiatry* 128: 41-46.

Lehmann, S. 1975. Psychology, ecology and community: A setting for evaluative research. In *Handbook of evaluation research*, vol. 1, ed. E. L. Struening and M. Guttentag, pp. 485-496. Beverly Hills: Sage Publications.

Lettieri, D. 1975. *Predicting adolescent drug abuse: A review of issues, methods and correlates*. Washington, DC: National Institute of Drug Abuse.

Levine, D.; Levin, D. B.; Sloan, I. H.; and Chappel, J. N. 1972. Personality correlates of success in a methadone maintenance program. *American Journal of Psychiatry* 129: 456-460.

Levine, M. 1974. Scientific method and the adversary model: Some preliminary thoughts. *American Psychologist* 29: 661-677.

Levine, M.; Brown, E.; Fitzgerald, C.; Goplerud, E.; Gordon, M. E.; Jayne-Lazarus, C.; Rosenberg, N.; and Slater, J. 1978. Adapting the jury trial for program evaluation: A report of an experience. *Evaluation and Program Planning* 1: 177-186.

Lippitt, R.; Watson, J.; and Westley, B. 1958. *The dynamics of planned change*. New York: Harcourt, Brace and World.

Lipsey, M. W. 1974. Research and relevance: A survey of graduate students and faculty in psychology. *American Psychologist* 29: 541-553.

Liska, A. E. 1975. *The consistency controversy*. Cambridge, MA: Schenkman.

Lofland, J. 1971. *Analyzing social settings: A guide to qualitative observation and analysis*. Belmont, CA: Wadsworth.

Lorenzen, B. L., and Braskamp, L. A. 1978. Comparative influences of political, cost/benefit, and statistical evaluation information on administrative decision making. *Evaluation and Program Planning*, 1: 235-238.

Macht, L. 1976. Mental health programs, past, present, and future: Bases for evaluation. In *Trends in mental health evaluation*, ed. E. Markson and D. Allen, pp. 3-11. Lexington, MA: Lexington Books.

Mann, J. 1965. Technical and social difficulties in the conduct of evaluative research. In *Changing human behavior*, ed. J. Mann, pp. 177-189. New York: Scribners. Also in *Readings in evaluation research*, ed. F. G. Caro. New York: Russell Sage Foundation, 1971.

Marcus, A. C. et al. 1972. *An analytical review of longitudinal and related studies as they apply to the educational process*, vol. 3. Washington, DC: National Center for Educational Statistics (DHEW/OE).

McNemar, Q. 1969. *Psychological statistics*, 4th ed. New York: Wiley.

Meltzoff, J., and Kornreich, M. 1970. *Research in psychotherapy*. New York: Atherton Press.

Miller, G. A. 1969. Psychology as a means of promoting human welfare. *American Psychologist* 24: 1063-1075.

Mischel, W. 1973. Toward a cognitive social learning reconceptualization of personality. *Psychological Review* 80: 252-283.

Mischel, W. 1977. On the future of personality measurement. *American Psychologist* 32: 246-254.

Moles, O. C. The honest broker project: Social science and the Congress. *Journal of Social Issues* 29: 203-211.

Morell, J. A. 1977*a*. Evaluating outcome in correctional drug abuse rehabilitation programs. In *Evaluative research in correctional drug abuse treatment: A guide for professionals in criminal justice and the behavioral sciences*, ed. J. J. Platt, T. Labate, and R. Wicks, pp. 79-104. Lexington, MA: Lexington Books.

———. 1977*b*. The conflict between research and mental health services. *Administration in Mental Health* 4: 52-58.

———. In press *a*. Issues in the psychological consultant's interaction with paraprofessionals. In *The psychological consultant*, ed. J. J. Platt and R. J. Wicks, New York: Grune and Stratton.

———. In press *b*. Follow-up research as an evaluation strategy. In *Vocational Education Program Evaluation*, ed. T. Abramson and C. K. Tittle. Beverly Hills, CA: Sage Publications.

Morell, J. A., and Flaherty, E. W. 1978. The development of evaluation as a profession: Current status and some predictions. *Evaluation and Program Planning* 1: 11-17.

Moscovi, S. 1972. Society and theory in social psychology. In *The context of social psychology*, ed. J. Israel and H. Tajpel. New York: Academic Press.

National Association of Social Workers. 1977. 22: no. 2, p. 8.

National Institute of Mental Health. 1973. *Planning for creative change in mental health services: A distillation of principles on research utilization*, vol. 1. Washington, DC: Government Printing Office.

National Institute of Mental Health. 1973. *Planning for creative change in mental health services: A distillation of principles on research utilization (bibliography with annotations)*, vol. 2. Washington, DC: Government Printing Office.

National Task Force on the Continuing Education Unit. 1974. *The continuing education unit: Criteria and guidelines*. Washington, DC: National University Extension Association.

Newman, F. L.; Burwell, B. A.; and Underhill, W. R. 1978. Program analysis using the client-oriented cost outcome system. *Evaluation and Program Planning* 1: 19-30.

Ostrander, S. A.; Goldstein, P.; and Hull, D. 1978. Toward overcoming problems in evaluation research: A beginning perspective on power. *Evaluation and Program Planning* 1: 187-194.

Palmer, F. 1972. Minimal intervention at age two and three, and subsequent intellective changes. In *Preschool in action*, ed. R. Parker, pp. 437-464. Boston: Allyn & Bacon. 1972.

Parlett, H., and Hamilton, D. 1976. Evaluation as illumination: A new approach to the study of innovatory programs. In *Evaluation studies review annual*, ed. G. V. Glass, pp. 140-157. Beverly Hills, CA: Sage Publications.

Patton, M. Q. 1978. *Utilization focused evaluation*. Beverly Hills, CA: Sage Publications.

Platt, J., and Labate, C. 1976. *Heroin addiction: Theory, research and treatment*. New York: Wiley.

Platt, J. J., and Spivack, G. 1973. Studies in problem solving thinking of psychiatric patients: Patient-control differences and factorial structure of problem solving thinking. *Proceedings of the American Psychological Association*, 1973, vol. 8, 461-464. 81st annual meeting, American Psychological Association, Montreal, Canada, Aug. 27-31, 1973.

Popper, K. R. 1965. *Conjectures and refutations: The growth of scientific knowledge.* New York: Harper and Row.

Reagles, K. W.; Wright, G. N.; and Butler, A. J. 1970. *A scale for rehabilitation gain for clients of an expanded vocational rehabilitation program.* Monograph no. 13. University of Wisconsin (Madison) Regional Rehabilitation Research Institute.

————. 1972. Toward a new criterion of vocational rehabilitation success. *Rehabilitation Counseling Bulletin* (June) 15, no. 4, pp. 233-241.

Ricks, F. A. 1976. Training program evaluators. *Professional Psychology,* vol. 7, 339-343.

Riecken, H. 1972. Memorandum on program evaluation. In *Evaluating action programs: Readings in social action research,* ed. C. H. Weiss, pp. 85-104. Boston: Allyn & Bacon.

Riecken, H., and Boruch, R. F., eds. 1974. *Social experimentation: A method for planning and evaluating social interventions.* New York: Academic Press.

Rodman, H., and Kolodny, R. 1964. Organizational strains in the researcher-practitioner relationship. *Human Organizations* 23: 171-182. Also in F. Caro, ed. *Readings in evaluation research.* New York: Russell Sage Foundation.

Rosen, H. 1977. *Pathway to Piaget: A guide for clinicians, educators and developmentalists.* Cherry Hill, NJ: Postgraduate International.

Rossi, P. H. 1972. Boobytraps and pitfalls in the evaluation of social action programs. In *Evaluating action programs: Readings in social action research,* ed. C. H. Weiss, pp. 224-235. Boston: Allyn & Bacon.

Rossi, P., and Williams, W. 1972. *Evaluating social programs: Theory, practice, and politics.* New York: Seminar Press.

Scriven, M. 1972. *Evaluating action programs: Readings in social action research,* ed. C. H. Weiss, pp. 123-136. Boston: Allyn & Bacon. Also in *Perspectives on curriculum evaluation,* ed. R. W. Tyler, R. M. Gagné and M. Scriven. Chicago: Rand McNally, 1967.

————. 1974. Exploring goal free evaluation: An interview with Michael Scriven. *Evaluation* 2: 9-16.

————. 1976. Evaluation bias and its control. In *Evaluation studies review annual,* vol. 1, ed. G. Glass, pp. 119-139. Beverly Hills, CA: Sage Publications.

Sewell, W. H., and Hauser, R. M. 1975. *Education, occupation and earnings.* New York: Academic Press.

Sheinfeld, S. N., and Morell, J. A. 1977. *Research skills are not enough: A model for the successful implementation of evaluation.* Paper presented to the Third Annual Conference of the Evaluation Network. September 25-27, 1977, St. Louis, MO.

————. 1978. Research skills are not enough for the evaluator. *C.E.D.R. Quarterly* 11: 11-14.

Sherwood, M. 1969. Scientific explanation: Some preliminary observations. In *The logic of explanation in Psychoanalysis,* ed. M. Sherwood, pp. 7-36. New York: Academic Press.

Skolimowski, H. 1966. The structure of thinking in technology. *Technology and Culture* 7: 371-383. Also in *Philosophy and technology,* ed. C. Mitcham and R. Mackey. New York: Free Press, 1972.

Sporn, P. 1964. *Foundations of engineering.* Elmsford, NY: Pergamon Press.

Stephan, F., and McCarthy, P. 1958. *Sampling opinions: An analysis of survey procedure.* New York: Wiley.

Struening, E. 1975. Social area analysis as a method of evaluation. In *Handbook of evaluation research*, Vol. 1), ed. E. L. Struening and M. Guttentag, pp. 519-536. Beverly Hills, CA: Sage Publications.

Suchman, E. A. 1967. *Evaluative research: Principles and practice in public service and social action programs.* New York: Russell Sage Foundation.

———. 1969. Evaluating educational programs. *Urban Review* 3: 15-17. Also in *Readings in evaluation research*, ed. F. G. Caro. New York: Russell Sage Foundation.

Tajfel, H. 1972. Experiments in a vacuum. In *The context of social psychology*, ed. J. Israel and H. Tajfel, pp. 69-119. New York: Academic Press.

Tripodi, T.; Fellin, P.; and Epstein, E. 1971. *Social program evaluation. Guidelines for health, education and welfare administrators.* Itasca, IL: F. E. Peacock.

Truax, C., and Carkhuff, R. 1967. *Toward effective counseling and psychotherapy.* Chicago: Aldine.

Twain, D. 1975. Developing and implementing a research strategy. In *Handbook of evaluation research*, vol. 1, ed. E. L. Struening and M. Guttentag, pp. 27-52. Beverly Hills, CA: Sage Publications.

Walentynowicz, B. 1968. On methodology of engineering design. *Proceedings of the XIV international congress of philosophy.* Vienna, September 2-9, 1968, pp. 586-590.

Warheit, G.; Bell, R.; and Schwab, J. 1974. *Planning for change: Needs assessment approaches.* Washington, D.C.: National Institute of Mental Health.

Webb, E.; Campbell, D. T.; Schwarts, R.; and Sechrest, L. 1966. *Unobstrusive measures: Nonreactive research in the social sciences.* New York: Rand McNally.

Weiss, C. H. 1970. The politicization of evaluation research. In *Evaluating action programs: Readings in social action research*, ed. C. H. Weiss, pp. 327-338. Boston: Allyn & Bacon. 1972. Also in *Journal of Social Issues* 26: (1970) 57-68.

———. 1973. Where politics and evaluation research meet. *Evaluation* 1: 37-45.

———. 1975. Evaluation research in the political context. In *Handbook of evaluation research*, vol. 1, ed. E. L. Struening and M. Guttentag, pp. 13-26. Beverly Hills, CA: Sage Publications.

Wiesner, J. 1970. The need for social engineering. In *Psychology and the problems of society*, F. Korten, S. Cook, and J. Lacey, pp. 85-94. Washington, D.C.: American Psychological Association.

Wildavsky, A. 1972. The self evaluating organization. *Public Administration Review* 32: 509-520. Also in *Evaluation studies review annual*, vol. 3, ed. T. D. Cook et al. Beverly Hills, CA: Sage Publications, 1978.

Wilensky, H. L. 1964. The professionalization of everyone. *American Journal of Sociology* 70: 137-158.

Windle, C. and Neigher, W. 1978. Ethical problems in evaluation: Advice for trapped administrators. *Evaluation and Program Planning* 1: 97-108.

Windle, C., and Woy, R. J. 1977. Federal guidelines for CMHC evaluation, part 2: Guidelines for program evaluation in CMHCs. *Evaluation* 4: 30-34.

Zusman, J., and Bissonette, R. 1973. The case against evaluation (with some suggestions for improvement). *International Journal of Mental Health* 2: 111-125.

NAME INDEX

SUBJECT INDEX

ABOUT THE AUTHOR

Jonathan A. Morell is an Associate Professor in the Department of Mental Health Sciences of the Hahnemann Medical College, where he is Associate Director of the Evaluation Training Program. Dr. Morell's chief interests lie in the methodology of applied social research, and in the relationships which exist among social science, the political process, and practical decision making. In addition, he has a lively interest in issues relating to training and ethics in evaluation. He is co-Editor-in-Chief (with Eugenie W. Flaherty) of *Evaluation and Program Planning,* and has written extensively on the program evaluation process. His writings include evaluation methodology articles in areas such as drug abuse and education, and a sociological analysis of the development of evaluation as a profession. Recently, Dr. Morell's time has been spent designing research on complex organizations, and in a cross-disciplinary exploration of the concept of "relevance" as it relates to applied social research. Dr. Morell's professional activities include chairmanship of the Evaluation Research Society's Training Committee, and active participation in the Society's Ethics Committee. In addition, he has served on several conference organizing committees for the Pennsylvania Evaluation Network. Dr. Morell was trained as a social psychologist at Northwestern University, where he received his Ph.D. in 1974. Prior to coming to Hahnemann, he held a Research Associate position in the Department of Psychiatry at the University of Chicago. He has been at Hahnemann since 1975.

Pergamon General Psychology Series

Editors: Arnold P. Goldstein, Syracuse University
Leonard Krasner, SUNY, Stony Brook